UPSTREAM

UPSTREAM

SEARCHING

FOR

WILD SALMON,

FROM

RIVER TO

TABLE

LANGDON COOK

BALLANTINE BOOKS

NEW YORK

Copyright © 2017 by Langdon Cook
Map copyright © 2017 by Mapping Specialists, Ltd.
Illustration copyright © 2017 by Frank Boyden

Published in the United States by Ballantine Books,
an imprint of Random House, a division of
Penguin Random House LLC, New York.

BALLANTINE and the HOUSE colophon are registered
trademarks of Penguin Random House LLC.

LIBRARY OF CONGRESS CATALOGING-IN-PUBLICATION DATA
NAMES: Cook, Langdon, author
TITLE: Upstream : searching for wild salmon, from river to table /
Langdon Cook.
DESCRIPTION: First edition. | New York : Ballantine Books, [2017] |
Includes bibliographical references.
IDENTIFIERS: LCCN 2017012853 | ISBN 9781101882887 (hardback) |
ISBN 9781101882900 (ebook)
SUBJECTS: LCSH: Salmon—Pacific Coast (U.S.) | Salmon fishing—
Pacific Coast (U.S.) | Salmon fisheries—Pacific Coast (U.S.) |
Salmon stock management. | Nutrition. | BISAC: NATURE /
Animals / Fish. | SOCIAL SCIENCE / Agriculture & Food.
CLASSIFICATION: LCC SH167.S17 C68 2017 | DDC 639.2/7560979—dc23
LC record available at lccn.loc.gov/2017012853

Printed in the United States of America on acid-free paper

randomhousebooks.com

98765432

Title page image from © istock

Book design by Barbara M. Bachman

For the Boydens, Frank and Bradley,
who opened the gates to the river—

And for my parents, Lyn and Langdon,
who encouraged me to walk through

Great Brown Bear is walking with us,

Salmon swimming upstream with us,

as we stroll a city street.

—GARY SNYDER, FROM *The Practice of the Wild*

CONTENTS

MAP   *xiii*

CHAPTER 1:   **Coming Out of the Woodwork
              on Copper River Day**   *3*

CHAPTER 2:   **Thirteen Seconds**   *17*

CHAPTER 3:   **The Case of the Missing Adipose Fin**   *36*

CHAPTER 4:   **Bridge of the Gods**   *55*

CHAPTER 5:   **Of Zombies and Strongholds**   *68*

CHAPTER 6:   **Last Run of the *Midnight Express***   *91*

CHAPTER 7:   **A Tenebrous Future**   *120*

CHAPTER 8:   **The Reef Netter's Off-Season**   *146*

CHAPTER 9:   **The Ballad of Lonesome Larry**   *169*

CHAPTER 10: **Attack of the Killer Blob**   *191*

CHAPTER 11: **Cocktail Hour on the Kispiox**   *218*

CHAPTER 12: **Make Way for the Floodplain Fatties**   *242*

CHAPTER 13: **Herding the Pinks**   *264*

CHAPTER 14: **Rhythm of the River**   *284*

ACKNOWLEDGMENTS   *307*

WHEN A TROUT IS A SALMON:
A NOTE ON TAXONOMY   *311*

SELECTED BIBLIOGRAPHY   *313*

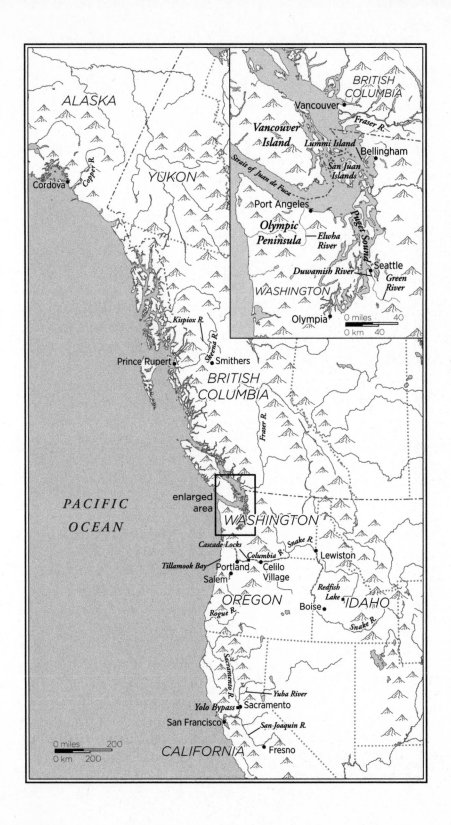

ALASKA

Copper R.

Cordova

YUKON

Kispiox R.

Prince Rupert

Skeena R.

Smithers

BRITISH
COLUMBIA

Fraser R.

PACIFIC
OCEAN

enlarged
area

WASHINGTON

Snake R.

Cascade Locks

Columbia R.

Lewiston

Tillamook Bay

Portland

Celilo
Village

Salem

OREGON

*Redfish
Lake*

IDAHO

Rogue R.

Boise

Snake R.

Sacramento R.

Yuba River

Yolo Bypass

Sacramento

San Francisco

San Joaquin R.

0 miles   200

0 km   200

CALIFORNIA

Fresno

BRITISH
COLUMBIA

Vancouver

*Vancouver
Island*

Lummi Island

Bellingham

*San Juan
Islands*

Strait of Juan de Fuca

Port Angeles

Puget Sound

Olympic
Peninsula

*Elwha
River*

Seattle

*Green
River*

Duwamish River

WASHINGTON

Olympia

0 miles   40

0 km   40

UPSTREAM

COMING OUT OF THE WOODWORK
ON COPPER RIVER DAY

THE SKIES DARKENED ALL AT ONCE, AS IF A CURTAIN SUDDENLY dropped, and rain engulfed the city. Across Puget Sound to the west, the Olympic Mountains disappeared into pillows of low clouds that filled the horizon. A ferry bound for Bainbridge Island plowed steadily into the squall, cutting through slants of gray, its blue beacon flashing through the pall. At Pike Place Market—the collection of produce, meat, and seafood stalls overlooking Seattle's downtown waterfront— throngs of people escaping the weather gathered around comforting displays of food. King and sockeye salmon, their scales burnished with a silver sheen, lay on beds of ice like mounds of treasure. A whole king of twenty or more pounds was selling for $38 per pound. Cleaned and filleted, the same fish was $60 a pound. It was mid-May, and the first Copper River salmon of the year had just arrived from Alaska that week. Trying to stay dry like everyone else, I wandered the stalls, admiring both the catch and the crowds that pressed in on all sides to take a measure of these handsome fish.

A young bearded musician with tattooed arms and a guitar case squatted down on his haunches to study a fifteen-pounder more closely at eye level. One of the fishmongers, a burly man who patrolled the front of his shop in bright-orange deck pants, hurried over and put his hands on his hips, drumming up a little theater for curious bystanders fingering their wallets, and asked the guy what his problem was—hadn't he ever been introduced to the king before? The young man admitted to being from out of town and quickly added that he was playing a gig that night across the street at the Showbox, as if this disqualified his tourist status. "Color me impressed," the fishmonger said loudly, looking around for another mark. The crowd tittered nervously. He turned his gaze on an elderly couple from Kansas. They didn't hesitate, pointing to a smaller—and cheaper, at $20 per pound—Copper River sockeye, to be filleted and packaged for shipment home. The fishmonger barked a few words and tossed the six-pound fish to his colleague behind the counter, who made a backhanded circus catch before brandishing a large fillet knife that gleamed in his hand.

Flying salmon is a ritualistic practice at Pike Place Market, one that attracts mobs of onlookers as well as the negative attention of PETA. When the couple had left with their boxed sockeye, I asked the fishmonger if many people were ponying up for the more expensive kings. In the past it was my custom to get a whole fish each spring during the Copper River frenzy and fillet it myself, filling the freezer at home, but in recent years the price tag for kings had escalated to a level more in line with luxury goods, and I found myself reduced to the status of window shopper. This year was the highest price anyone had ever seen. The fishmonger beckoned me to follow him around back, where a thirty-eight-pounder lay submerged in a tub of slush ice, its shiny skin slightly flushed with a faint pink, a ring of deep-red meat visible at the collar, where the head had been removed. He hefted it up by the tail. "This one is already spoken for. The lady buys five thousand dollars' worth of Copper River every year. She always wants the biggest fish." Whipping out his calculator, he claimed his client could afford it—she was one of the first thirty employees at Microsoft, he said. The single fish came to $1,443.62. I asked if she would get a break on price as a regular customer. The fishmonger shook his head. "It's Copper River. Nobody gets a break."

The commotion generated by Copper River salmon amuses many

locals, mystifies those not accustomed to the importance placed on salmon culture in the Pacific Northwest, and downright pisses off a few, who consider it all a marketing ploy. Alaska exports millions of pounds of salmon around the world each year—why get so excited about one particular river and its fish? And what about the salmon that can be caught right here in Puget Sound?

Well, for one thing, the sound is no longer the fishery it once was, local iconography aside. Most of the boats docked at Fisherman's Terminal in Seattle make the long trip up to Alaska to fish. The rivers of Puget Sound wind through timber farms, golf courses, and housing developments with names like Cedar Grove and Crystal Waters—apt descriptions of what they've replaced. The Copper River, by contrast, embodies the attributes many customers have come to expect from wild salmon. The river rises out of the untrammeled Wrangell Mountains and races through some of the most breathtaking territory anywhere in the world before reaching the Gulf of Alaska. Wrangell–St. Elias National Park, a sweeping jumble of high volcanic peaks, protects the headwaters, while the lower reaches flow through the temperate rainforests and open tundralike expanses of Chugach National Forest. At nearly three hundred miles long, with a watershed draining twenty-four thousand square miles, the Copper is the tenth-largest river in the United States and is known for its broad delta, an important rearing ground for waterfowl and shorebirds. Full of bears, eagles, and salmon, this vast watershed is worthy of the finest nature documentaries, and just knowing that a place like this still exists makes people happy. There was a time, not that long ago, when much of the West Coast of North America was as wild and bountiful as the Copper River region is today.

I pushed my way through the crowds to another stall. A blue banner from Seafood Watch, the environmental-watchdog organization run by the Monterey Bay Aquarium, vouched for its 100% SUSTAINABLE SEAFOOD. Handwritten signs festooned the displays of others. "We sell only wild salmon caught by wild fishermen!" boasted one. "First of the season Copper River king salmon," promised another.

The king is the most celebrated species of Pacific salmon and has been for longer than anyone can remember. Native Americans called it *tyee*, which means "headman" in Chinook Indian jargon, the common language of trade and commerce among Northwest tribes in the 1800s. Today the king is also called chinook in honor of those same people, who lived along the lower Columbia River and depended on it. For a multitude of reasons, from high fat content to great size and countenance, the species enjoys a mythopoeic position atop the salmon totem pole, and, befitting a headman, it dwarfs other salmon, with occasional reports of giants in excess of eighty pounds. But the king is also the least common of all Pacific salmon, and it is declining in number throughout its range along the West Coast, from Nome, Alaska, to Ventura, California, the result of human impacts known and probably unknown—another reason for its value relative to other species.

My own interest in salmon, however, began on the opposite coast. Though I live in Seattle now, the taste of salmon is one I used to identify with my New England childhood. Every year on the Fourth of July, my grandparents served a baked Atlantic salmon at their cottage on Cape Cod, along with fried potatoes, steamed green peas, and a tureen of egg cream sauce. In our family, salmon was viewed as a regional delicacy and something reserved for special occasions. My grandmother bought the salmon at Wimpy's, a local fish market with an attached bar, where she might have had a few belts before navigating a giant wood-paneled Chrysler station wagon back home. Years later I would realize that the fish riding shotgun beside her, wrapped in brown butcher paper, was not actually local, as we all assumed (the Cape being a place with a long history of commercial fishing). In fact, it was almost certainly a farmed Atlantic salmon from overseas—a distinction my family didn't know enough to make at the time. Back then we didn't give food-sourcing much thought.

While it's nice to think of a crusty New Englander hauling in his catch somewhere off the coast of Massachusetts, our Independence Day salmon likely began its life in a sanitized egg tray before being hatched in an indoor rearing facility and eventually transferred to a net pen anchored in a Scandinavian fjord, where it was fed a diet of fish meal laced with chemical colorants to give its gray flesh the expected pinkish hue. By the time I was old enough to buy and cook my own salmon, such farms, pioneered in Norway, were being replicated in Scotland, Ireland, Canada, Chile, Australia, New Zealand, and on both coasts of the United States, without much thought given to what they had replaced. The Connecticut River, not far from my childhood home and once a productive Atlantic salmon breeding ground, hasn't seen a viable wild population in decades, possibly not since the American Revolution. An ambitious plan to restore runs to the Connecticut was finally abandoned in 2012 after forty-five years of effort and countless dollars. Other than a stream or two in Maine, New England is no longer home to wild Atlantic salmon in any sort of meaningful way, and very few people alive today have ever even tasted one. As the wild fish were traded in for the farmed variety on both sides of the Atlantic, the will to safeguard wild populations eroded, and now wild Atlantic salmon are mostly a memory across Northern Europe and the East Coast of North America, a memory that may soon wink out altogether.

IF MY FIRST TASTE of salmon came at a young age, it wasn't until I was an adult that I actually saw a live one in the wild, in southwestern Oregon's Rogue River Canyon. I was in my early twenties, a born New Englander recently relocated to the Pacific Northwest, new to salmon country. That year I took a leave of absence from my schooling to caretake a secluded homestead in the coastal mountains, a couple of hours from civilization via rough forest roads. The owners of the homestead, two brothers, unlocked a pair of heavy steel gates, the sort that typically close off a logging road, to let me in. These gates might as well have opened up a new continent, a new dimension even. I entered the domain of bears, cougars, and salmon. The Rogue River is one of the few large watercourses left in the contiguous United States that isn't dogged by a road or highway for most of its length. In July, as the roadless canyon heated up, reaching triple-digit temperatures, the air heavy and nearly viscid, I swam daily in the Rogue to cool off. The trail to the river, built by a German-born mule skinner in the mid-1800s, dropped eight hundred feet in less than a mile through a fragrant grove of old-growth Douglas fir and Pacific madrone. My summer swims coincided with the upstream spawning migration of king salmon, which stack up by the hundreds at creek mouths along the river course to rest and drink in the cold, highly oxygenated water that tumbles down from fir-clad mountains. Where a rushing tributary called Kelsey Creek marries its flow to the Rogue, I jumped off twenty-foot cliffs into the river's refreshing embrace and paddled among the salmon that lingered around the creek mouth. Exhausted and lethargic from their journey, they didn't spook at my alien presence in the pool. Thirty-pounders finned right past me to reach the cool outflow, some of them brushing against my bare legs, their rippling sides exposing equal measures of strength and vulnerability.

The Rogue River is where I first began to see the long-standing bond between people and salmon. The owners of the wilderness homestead gave me flies tied by their late father, a heart surgeon, and the gesture made me feel as though I belonged to a heritage that stretched back to a time before words could make sense of it. Every summer as boys they had come to this remote canyon, and it was here that they had learned to fish, hunt, and travel through the backcountry. One became a high school biology teacher, the other an artist who models nature's elegant forms into his work. I was now a part of that tradition. In the fall, I walked the river trail every day in late afternoon as the sun slipped behind canyon walls, packing along my fly rod. The first time a fish rose off the bottom to take my feathered ruse, I was too surprised to set the hook. A swirl of quicksilver and it was gone. Lucky for me, the fish hooked itself in its ardor and I was attached to my first steelhead, the most prized game fish in the Northwest, a seagoing trout in the same family as Pacific salmon. The line between us went taut. It was a tether, both a connection to the past and a lead to the future. I've been chasing salmon ever since.

Not long after returning to the city, I attended a Tulalip Indian sweat lodge ceremony. My girlfriend, Martha (who would become my wife), taught English at a college in Everett, Washington, near the reservation; one of her students invited us. The sweat lodge was a foxhole in the earth covered with tarps. A rickety wooden ladder led into the hole. We climbed down to join a dozen others seated around a fire pit filled with hot rocks. Someone outside threw a blanket over the entrance, and everything went dark. Martha gripped my hand. An elder slowly beat a small skin drum and explained that we would go around the circle, giving thanks. He sprinkled water over the rocks; steam hissed in the darkness. Already, sweat was rolling down my cheeks. We each gave thanks in turn.

Many of the Indians (as they preferred to call themselves) thanked grandparents or distant relatives who had raised them or otherwise gotten them to school, kept them out of trouble. I thought about the abject poverty I had seen as we drove through the reservation earlier that morning. Next the elder asked us to offer a prayer and a hope for the future. He threw more handfuls of water on the rocks. I could hear moaning all around me as the temperature rose and the claustrophobia mounted in this damp, dark hole in the ground. I squeezed Martha's hand tighter. Some of the sweat lodgers had brought wet towels inside with them, and now they wrapped their heads in the towels. We hadn't known any better, and I worried I might pass out from the heat. At the same time I didn't want to bring any dishonor upon Martha or myself. I can't recall exactly what sort of prayer for the future I offered. I do remember feeling embarrassed by it. It was trite and inconsequential in comparison to those of my fellow sweat lodgers, who spoke of traditions that went back centuries or even millennia and were now in jeopardy of falling to pieces.

At last the elder banged on his drum and said we were finished. Each of us hurried up the ladder and collapsed on the lawn within a few feet of the lodge, gulping at the cool air like fish out of water. Afterward, feeling surprisingly buoyant and refreshed, Martha and I went to a salmon picnic at the tribal community center, a drab double-wide parked in a cul-de-sac. The salmon, grilled outside and served without special adornment, was as good as any I had ever tasted, and I was reminded of being a child at my grandparents' home and eating with the adults, how that first taste of salmon was one I associated with having a place at the table. "Do you usually eat this well after a sweat?" I asked the cook, a heavyset man with a ponytail, wearing a Hawaiian shirt and earrings. "We are not rich," he replied, "but we always have salmon."

FISH ARE MYSTERIOUS BY NATURE. They remain apart, in an underwater world we can only visit. Perhaps this is why we seek them out. They are tantalizing and seemingly unknowable, and more than any other fish, the salmon occupies a singular, mythic place in human cultures around the globe. Two salmon bedeck the Glasgow coat of arms. Loki, the trickster of Norse mythology, transforms himself into a salmon to elude capture. In Native American art, the salmon is a symbol of abundance and renewal.

Salmon move between river and ocean, leaving the freshwater nurseries of their natal streams to migrate far-flung distances across the Atlantic or Pacific before returning miraculously to their home rivers as adults. Whether sipping insects from the surface of clear mountain pools as minnow-sized fry or chasing down baitfish in the salt as adults, salmon are built for speed and endurance. Their broad, powerful tails propel them with sudden bursts of acceleration; torpedo-shaped bodies withstand long journeys through both fresh and salt water.

Salmon and their kin have been vaulting through our imaginations since the dawn of time (the name comes from the Latin *salmo*, "to leap"). More recently they've been turning up frozen in time in the fossil record, revealing their evolutionary path. The first salmonlike fish, *Eosalmo driftwoodensis,* lived about fifty million years ago, soon after the first primates appeared, and was discovered in Driftwood Creek, British Columbia, in 1977. So began the Salmonidae family, which includes a number of species with confusing common names that defy taxonomic sorting, including trout, salmon, and char. At some point, with continental drift and the uprising of the Pacific Rim, the lineage split between Atlantic and Pacific basins, perhaps as far back as twenty million years ago. The genus *Salmo* includes Atlantic salmon and brown trout, while the genus *Oncorhynchus,* which means "hooknose" in Greek, includes the Pacific salmon such as king, coho, sockeye, chum, and pink, as well as two other species, which we call rainbow and cutthroat trout; all of them will develop, to a lesser or greater degree, a curved or hook-shaped jaw at reproductive maturity.

Salmon evolved during a period of geologic tumult. To survive in an age of intermittent glaciation, earthquakes, and volcanic eruptions, they devised migratory ways and a hankering for the wide-open ocean. The term is *anadromy:* Both the Pacific and Atlantic salmon are anadromous, which means they spawn and rear in fresh water but mature in salt water. A life spent largely at sea protects the fish from the upheavals on land, and when it comes time to spawn, if their natal river is unexpectedly iced over by glaciers or flooded with a torrent of volcanic debris, they might search for nearby streams or freshets that will suffice. In this way, they abandon or recolonize habitat as it disappears or emerges with the times. The other noteworthy detail in the Pacific salmon's life cycle is that the fish dies after spawning. Pacific salmon-bearing streams, if they're productive, are often spectacles of death and decay, which in turn promote an abundance of life, from the many small invertebrates that feed on spawned-out carcasses to other fish, birds, and mammals that join the feast. Even the great old-growth forests of the Pacific Northwest have literally taken root on the backs of decomposing salmon. In this sense, the salmon's life cycle is an object study of the virtuous circle.

It's also fair to say that salmon represent more subjective values we hold most dear in ourselves: strength, beauty, resilience. A willingness to fight upstream. They nourish both body and spirit. At Pike Place Market, overlooking Elliott Bay—the scene of a flourishing salmon culture through the ages—I thought about the ties between salmon, people, and place as I ducked into one fish stall after another and watched a surge of customers mesmerized by these charismatic fish. In the American tradition of starting a new life through mobility, I had crossed the continent and made a home for myself in the Northwest. Even though I was a recent arrival, I understood that great runs of salmon had shaped this landscape as much as the glaciers and volcanoes and waves of new immigrants. Now that Martha and I were raising a family in salmon country, I wanted to see what sort of future our children would inherit. Would they feel a connection to the region's most indelible natural resource? Would wild runs of salmon, diminished as they were, still continue to shape the character of the place and its inhabitants?

There are people throughout salmon country who have devoted their lives to these fish in one way or another: commercial fishermen, tribal fishermen, scientists, activists, anglers, merchants, chefs, and so on. Many of them see the health of wild salmon runs as indicators of our own health as a society. I resolved to search them out. Like the salmon, they struggle against a prevailing current.

WHILE I EXPLORED THE MARKET, Brian Hayes sat in his cubicle on the first floor of a featureless office building in a suburb north of Seattle, waiting. A fitful wind rustled the new foliage of big-leaf maples outside as yet another rain shower rolled in off Puget Sound, dousing the streets and causing traffic jams up and down I-5. But Hayes, a Pacific Seafood Company sales representative based in Mukilteo, Washington, didn't notice the weather. He sat in his cubicle waiting for fish. Two in particular.

Hayes didn't have time to contemplate the mysteries of fish or the idyllic spawning grounds of Copper River salmon right now. He had sold all of what he called his "Day One kings," and he needed more. Every year restaurants from coast to coast jockey to list Copper River salmon on their menus. As the first major salmon run of the year—and one that's been promoted with a savvy marketing machine for more than two decades—the wild kings and sockeye caught by the fishing fleet based in Cordova, Alaska, make for an annual event. Earlier that week, the inaugural Alaska Airlines shipment had arrived in Seattle to much fanfare, with 24,100 pounds of fish. After touchdown, the pilot emerged with a bloodstained forty-eight-pound ceremonial king and carried it down the gangplank to a waiting trio of chefs, who served up grilled hunks of bright-red salmon to reporters and local dignitaries such as the sure-footed field-goal kicker for the Seattle Seahawks. Clients like Canlis, Salty's, Ray's Boathouse, and the restaurant atop the Space Needle absolutely *needed* to have the first Copper River salmon of the year. And that was just Seattle. In New York, the Grand Central Oyster Bar was serving a six-ounce pan-seared fillet of Copper River sockeye with an artichoke-garlic beurre blanc, competitively priced at $29.95. Who knew where they were getting it, maybe from another one of Pacific Seafood's sixteen distribution centers, or perhaps from Ocean Beauty, one of their main competitors.

In the first week of the Copper River fishery, Hayes fielded a lot of calls from would-be customers who had never bought an ounce of fish from Pacific Seafood before. Soon, maybe a week or two from now, when the market was flooded with Alaskan salmon, these same customers would stop calling. Hayes's boss, Stephen Kelly, had the final word on who got fish and who didn't. "It all comes down to loyalty," Kelly likes to say. He calls it "Coming out of the woodwork on Copper River day," because so many restaurants and supermarkets come knocking for the first time. "You either make friends or you make enemies on Copper River day. You can make people extremely happy or you can piss them off. There's always collateral damage."

Openings for the fishery—those days when the fishermen are allowed to fish—would continue up in Cordova on Mondays and Thursdays throughout May and June, subject to the blessings of the state biologists, who busy themselves analyzing sonar graphs that show salmon escapement upstream—*escapement* being the weirdly appropriate term for salmon that *escape* the nets and make it to their spawning grounds. If the run looks healthy, openings can be bumped up to twenty-four-hour and even thirty-six-hour shifts. The air-freight would go on daily for another couple of weeks, until there was enough salmon in the pipeline to incentivize trucking them down from Anchorage instead, at which point eighteen-wheelers loaded with thirty-two thousand pounds of fish would make the twenty-four-hundred-mile haul to Seattle in fifty-two-hour marathon drives. The majority of these salmon would be smaller sockeye, the main target of the fishery. Estimates by Alaska Fish and Game put the Copper River harvest at 1.6 million sockeye and 22,000 kings, this catch differential partially explaining the price disparity. The larger, fattier kings are considered by most consumers to be the finest of all the Pacific salmon. The biologists who manage the run take extra care to ensure that enough of these big kings make it to the spawning grounds, which is why the fishery is kept outside the inner waters of the Copper River Delta, in mostly deeper water, where the bottom-hugging kings can avoid the nets. Not so the sockeye, which school higher in the water column, where the gillnetters lie in wait. Every now and then a king makes a mistake and lands in the net. These are the fish everyone wants.

Now it was "Day Two," as Hayes called it. The second opening had taken place the day before, another twelve-hour stint of fishing. The two kings he needed for a longtime client had been caught in a gill net, a long stretch of nylon mesh that hangs like a curtain in the water and snares salmon by a gill or fin as they try to pass. After delivery to a dockside processing plant in Cordova, the salmon were cleaned and relieved of their heads before being airfreighted to Seattle–Tacoma International Airport. He was expecting two hundred eighty pounds of Copper River kings in total, about sixteen fish give or take, all of them spoken for days ago. The kings had arrived that morning at Sea–Tac, where they were loaded by a driver and delivered to the Pacific Seafood distribution center in Mukilteo, an hour north of the airport in light traffic. The wholesale price hadn't dropped a nickel.

These highly anticipated salmon would fetch $26 per pound by the time they sold to supermarket chains and restaurants all over the country, flying out the door regardless of price. In the minds of many, Memorial Day weekend—right around the corner—signaled both the kickoff of the outdoor grilling season and the first fresh salmon of the year.

All morning Hayes had been in contact with the transport guys. As a sales rep, Hayes had his book filled with eighty restaurant clients, a few of whom were very on edge now that it was Copper River time. His office looked like a boiler room in a penny-stock outfit—everyone wearing headsets, taking orders on the phone, calling customers, brokering deals. He worked with a dozen or so other salesmen on his side of the room; all of them repped restaurants. On the other side sat just two reps, who handled all the retail clients between them. After a late lunch, Hayes put down his headset and went to find his fish. He grabbed a smock off the rack outside the break room, where a digital clock announced that 377 days had elapsed since the last workplace accident. The smock, bleach-white and knee-length, was an XXL. At six-four, with the build of a quarterback, Hayes looked younger than his forty-one years and was still competitive in a game of touch with his two teenage sons. He pulled a hairnet over his head, then stepped into a tray of antibacterial water.

Hayes knew the routine. He had been at Pacific Seafood for seven years, and though his office smelled like a shrimp cocktail, he had long since stopped noticing. He walked through rubber curtains into a chilly, high-ceilinged warehouse. The temperature was thirty-four degrees—downright balmy in comparison to the freezer storage at the far end, with its windy zero degrees and a breakaway door in case of emergency. Forklift drivers maneuvered their vehicles, building up and taking down towers of pallets, their warning lights flashing yellow and backup alarms ringing out in the cavernous building. Hayes wove his way deliberately through the obstacle course of pallets into an aisle that would be familiar to any Costco customer. Boxed products with company logos sat stacked on metal shelving that reached twelve feet in the air. The aisle opened into another yawning room, where mostly Latino employees filleted and skinned salmon. The woman with the scimitar-shaped knife that might have been a machete in an equatorial country was a world-champion skinner with her name on a trophy; she undressed a fillet in seconds, with a single fluid motion. Another employee worked a specialized machine that pulled pin bones from the fillets, an otherwise tiresome, time-consuming chore that many chefs approached with a pair of pliers. The floor was littered with thin white bones and pink liquid. A mist of bacteria-killing ozone water filled the air.

Finding the boxes he was looking for, Hayes cut them open and started sorting through nearly three hundred pounds of fresh H&G salmon (headed and gutted), some of which were still in rigor and stiff as a board. He was after two in particular for a regular client. The day before, Kevin Davis, the chef-owner of Blueacre Seafood in Seattle, had complained about one of the fish he had received, calling it "thin in the belly." Hayes hadn't picked that fish, but he wanted to keep his client happy. He found two almost identically bright twenty-four-pound kings and heaved them into a box, iced it, strapped it, invoiced it, and carried the box to his own car, a white '98 Buick Regal, which waited at the loading dock. He put the thousand-dollar box in his trunk. Normally the company used typical delivery vans and drivers, but not during the first couple of weeks of Copper River season. The clock was ticking. Hayes took a quick look around him. The sun had come out and a faint mist rose from rain-washed streets. Rush hour was just starting. He jumped into the driver's seat and took off with his single delivery. He knew the route by heart. It was exactly twenty-two miles to Blueacre Seafood.

CHAPTER 2

THIRTEEN SECONDS

After a few hours at the market, I continued up Pike Street and jogged north on 7th Avenue to the corner of Olive Way. The sun felt good. A group of twenty-somethings shouldering messenger bags sat outside amid the puddles at a table littered with empty cans of Rainier, their bikes stacked nearby. It wasn't quite 5:00 P.M., and the long mahogany bar inside was nearly full with happy-hour drinkers. With seating for 260, Blueacre Seafood can accommodate many customers with different agendas. A few couples eating early dinners or late lunches sat at scattered tables in the main dining room. Larger groups of businessmen—and they were all men today, with their ties off and top buttons undone—occupied banquet tables in an airy, glass-ceilinged room facing Olive Way. A hostess brought me into the kitchen, where Kevin Davis was briefing his waitstaff.

Davis was not the stereotypical rotund chef, maybe because he spent time in the outdoors and went fishing whenever he could finagle a day off, which wasn't often enough. He had the sort of open face and wide, unsuspecting eyes that people naturally trusted, an asset in a business with such high employee turnover. This briefing was a daily feature. Davis didn't care for drama. There would be no surprises. Dungeness crab was limited, he told the staff. "I don't know what's

going on with the crab fishery. Anyone wanna go catch some crabs?"
Instead he had soft-shelled blue crabs from Maryland, a seasonal and
short-lived special that would be given a Cajun treatment. A new
server asked why the menu specified sea scallops as "dry pack." The
chef explained how scallops shipped wet lost much of their flavor to
leaching. The finned offerings looked good for the evening. They had
plenty of the staples from Alaska—halibut and rockfish—and now,
fortunately, wild salmon. Davis looked over his clipboard. A large
group had called ahead and preordered a set menu. They wanted the
albacore tuna, lightly seared. He rubbed his forehead and put the clipboard away. Why would anyone order tuna when the most desirable
fish in the country had just landed in Seattle?

The pre-dinner staff meeting adjourned, and Davis made a beeline
for the cooler, where a special delivery had just arrived, thanks to his
personal fish picker at Pacific Seafood, Brian Hayes. Davis had a half
hour or so to prepare the night's allotment of Copper River king
salmon before the rush started. Blueacre Seafood is strategically located downtown, across the street from the convention center. Business people from out of town came into the restaurant after meetings,
and they expected salmon. This was Seattle, after all. Didn't you order
salmon in Seattle? Never mind that the commercial-fishing fleet had
been shrinking for decades or the fact that most of the salmon came
from Alaska anyway. In Seattle you ate salmon. But even as recently as
the 1990s, the salmon might have been a rock-solid log caught months
earlier and needing a good thaw, with maybe a little freezer burn, the
meat dry and mealy, requiring restaurants to cook it into submission
and cover it with a mango salsa or some other indignity.

Kevin Davis owns three restaurants downtown. Years ago, when
he was starting out, he would have waited a few weeks, until prices
had come down, to put Copper River salmon on the menu. These
days, as a chef who specializes in seafood, he can't afford not to serve
the name-brand fish from the get-go. Tourists expect it. Along with
bluefin tuna, it's the most in-demand fish on the planet. But unlike
bluefin, the salmon sold under the Copper River name are carefully

managed to be sustainable, and many of the environmental costs of doing business, unlike those of so many other products, are built into the price. Customers are not discouraged. "Everyone has Copper River salmon these days," Davis told me with amazement. "It used to be that you saw them only in Seattle or New York." Now an aspirational restaurant in Peoria might have the fish as a special of the day. It's in this competitive climate that an experienced chef can really prove his mettle. Davis has worked in Australia, Napa, New Orleans, and the south of France—all places where fresh seafood is on the menu. He's been around fish all his life. But cooking the fish expertly is just half the battle. The other half is choosing wisely. Davis knows fish. He's an angler and a pescatarian. He personally orders fish for his restaurants every day of the week. This sometimes means navigating a cutthroat business in which someone is always getting screwed.

Blueacre has a sizable cooler with a sink and filleting table. It's big enough for one person to work comfortably in, with a jacket on. Like the Pacific Seafood warehouse, it's kept at thirty-four degrees. A line cook shouldered past to grab a tin of halibut cheeks. "Those were like three bucks a pound when I first started," Davis said. "No one wanted them. Now they're fourteen dollars." With food awareness come price jumps. Similarly, every year it's harder to get the choicest salmon. The previous night they only had a single Copper River king and some sockeye, burning through thirty and forty orders of each respectively before 8:30 P.M., leaving nothing for lunch today. A king of about eighteen pounds, caught on a baited hook by a troller out at sea, its head still on to distinguish it from a net-caught fish, lay on a lower rack, awaiting the smoker. It was from the Washington Coast, also bright silver, with sea lice (a pea-sized type of parasite that looks like a miniature horseshoe crab) still attached near the tail and indicative of its freshness. "A lot of people who fish for salmon, the old school, this is what they want. They call them feeder kings," Davis said, looking it over. "They're at the apex of their life cycle, still eating." These are just the sorts of distinctions aficionados like to debate—the subtle differences in flavor between different runs of salmon, how and at what stage of their life cycle they're caught. Most everyone agrees, though, that once a salmon's silver scales have turned dark with its spawning colors, the meat will be off. All the salmon's vitality shifts to the reproductive task ahead and the flesh goes soft. "Old boot" is how some describe such a fish.

The best piece of salmon Davis ever ate came from the Yukon River, where some king salmon swim two thousand miles to their spawning grounds. With such epic journeys against the current, they need heavy stores of fat. When Davis put it on the grill, the fillet burst into flames. He laughed at the memory. "It was like trying to grill a pound of butter!" But the salmon that changed his life was a Columbia River spring king. This was years ago, when he was a fledgling restaurant owner in Seattle. Up until then he'd never fully appreciated what a fresh thick cut of salmon could do in the kitchen. Comparing it to prime aged steak was an insult, he said, to the salmon.

Davis lifted the first of his two handpicked twenty-four-pound Copper River kings out of its box and onto a large cutting board. Except for black spots dotting its back, the fish was metallic silver, every scale intact. He placed a metal sheet tray lined with wax paper next to it. I watched him carefully as he filleted the fish. It had been a while since I'd handled one of this size. Mostly I eat salmon that I catch myself, and if I buy salmon at the market it's usually by the piece. The exception is Copper River sockeye, which I'll buy as whole fish once the price drops, a few weeks into the run. I fillet the sockeye, cut them into grilling or roasting portions, and vacuum-seal them for the freezer. But those fish rarely exceed eight pounds. Filleting a twenty-four-pound king that costs more than $20 a pound wholesale is another skill altogether. On the one hand, you have more fish to work with, so it's easier; on the other, you need the right assortment and sizes of knives, and in the case of a Copper River salmon, the fish is so expensive you don't want to make a mistake that mars the presentation or detracts from the bottom line.

Davis ran his hand over the king, approving of its taut muscle. "As a chef, my job is to not get stuck with a crappy piece of fish. My job is to get the best piece of fish they have." To that end he works every day with Brian Hayes at Pacific Seafood. Davis tells him what he wants and the salesman picks it himself. Occasionally they haggle over the price, but this rarely happens now, because Davis and Hayes have reached a détente of sorts: The salesman respects that Davis knows what makes a good piece of fish and he also recognizes what Davis likes, the little quirks of taste that define his aesthetic. A deep belly, for instance. They work together and rarely have to argue over the price. It wasn't always like this. Davis had to tutor Hayes in the early years, especially after his favorite picker was fired. "The guy was a fish maniac," he said of the previous picker. "He loved good fish. I could always count on him finding me the best stuff. He got fired ten years ago for getting in a fight at work. The guy got in a fistfight over a piece of fish!"

After years of working together, Davis's directions to Hayes are simple and clear: "Put on your jacket and pick some fish." They speak every day, seven days a week. "His wife doesn't like me," he added with an uncomfortable chuckle. "Every Saturday morning he's on the phone with me. He could be at a soccer game with his kids." Davis has two menus at Blueacre, lunch and dinner, and these menus change daily based on whatever is fresh and in season. This means being in constant contact with his fish picker. Dealing with a large wholesaler like Pacific Seafood is not for everyone. "If you have a forty-seat res-taurant, they won't give you the time of day." Davis is buying thou-sands of pounds, not hundreds, every year. He buys only fish from U.S. waters, which makes his purchases tougher and more expensive. Though foreign-caught fish might be less regulated and cheaper, they come with environmental costs on the back end, costs that will have to be paid eventually, by someone. Davis believes in the importance of safeguarding the resource.

At this point, he has his buying operation down to a science. Be-sides, he doesn't need the aggravation. "I'm almost fifty. Yesterday, after dropping my boys at school, I was at the restaurant by eight-thirty and on my feet until ten at night." Haggling over fish was not part of his day, and he was glad for that. Still, he wants the best. "What I'm talking about is the difference between 'whoa, this is good' and 'this is the best piece of fish in my life.'" Even so, the fish-buying end of his operation doesn't always go according to plan. Yesterday his regular picker, Brian Hayes, was unavailable. Davis received a box of small kings, unremarkable fish of about seven pounds apiece. "I call those jacks," he said, referring to the precocious males that will try to spawn with adult females. A seven-pound fish is not the Platonic ideal of a Copper River king, nor does it boast the thick, fatty fillets Davis prefers to serve. Even worse, his order also contained a colored-up king with a seal bite taken out of it. "I was not happy," he said. The fish was dark, as if ready to spawn. Though Davis didn't fully understand the science, he thought the dark color might indicate a fish that would soon spawn in the lower river. He was after big, bright, sterling fish with every scale intact, salmon that had many miles of fast, turbulent river to navigate before they reached spawning grounds well upstream of the mouth. These are the fish with the highest fat content. A dark fish with a thin belly—and a seal bite, no less!—was not what he wanted to foist off on his customers.

"Did you see the fish from the plane?" he asked me, referring to the forty-eight-pound ceremonial king that had kicked off the season a few days earlier. All the local TV news stations had covered its emergence from the Alaska Airlines cockpit. "I would have rejected that fish. It was colored up." Davis wasn't sure what was going on, because so much of the Copper River fishery was cloaked in mystery, but he thought something was amiss. There were rumors of low river flows and salmon milling around in the salt waiting for something to happen. A reliable source said the gillnetters were working out in the middle of the Gulf of Alaska rather than at the river mouth. If this were true, it would mean they were pulling up any salmon that happened to swim by, as opposed to targeting the early-running fat-laden fish with the most mileage to cover that got waylaid as they tried to enter the river in May. I told him about the large king I'd seen at Pike

Place Market, the one with a slight blush. "Bullshit," he said. "If they say that fish eats as well as a chrome-bright fish, they're lying."

Davis pulled out a surprisingly small fillet knife—nine inches—and sharpened it up. Laying the fish on its side, he used his first cut to remove the right collar, one of those parts considered cut-rate in the past and now rightfully recognized as a delicacy because of its rich flavor. He counted on having a knowledgeable customer request a collar at some point during the night's service, so it was the first piece to go on the tray. Next he ran his knife barely skin deep along the backbone, from adipose fin to neck, in order to get the fillet to lay down flat before cutting. After a quick slice to free the meat from the tail, he was ready to remove the entire fillet from the fish's right side, a process that required three lateral cuts from neck to tail as he worked progressively through the flesh. "That's what you want, right there," he said, running his hand across the belly. "Feel how thick that is." The fillet, weighing about nine pounds, got put aside on the tray, and next, without flipping the fish, Davis deftly removed the backbone and tail with his knife. He held them up in the light, showing how little meat was left on the bone. These got tossed in the trash. Davis doesn't make stock from his salmon leftovers, finding it too overpowering. Some of the scraps he saves for smoking, but mostly he tries to fillet his fish as cleanly as possible. "This is a big restaurant," he said. There's a limit to how much time he can spend on any one task.

Next he cut off the left collar and placed it beside the right one. Now he had two glistening fillets. He trimmed up the dorsal sides, then, switching to a longer knife, he made a series of shallow cuts to remove the rib bones from each. For the tedious chore of pulling the pin bones, he used a simple pair of hardware-store pliers, after which he switched to a large skinning knife—"Careful so I don't eviscerate you," he warned me—to separate the meat from its scaly coat. The skin peeled away easily, coiling into a long, thin strip. It was going into the garbage.

Of all the salmon's parts, the skin might be the one that Jon Rowley, my dinner companion that night, would request. Rowley had been working with salmon most of his life, first as a fisherman and later as a restaurant consultant. These days he was working as an adviser for a variety of artisan food producers, from shellfish farmers to organic-fruit orchardists. His palate was respected from coast to coast. The first time I shared a meal of salmon with him was at a beach barbecue on Samish Island in northern Puget Sound. He walked around in dismay, picking discarded salmon skins off paper plates scattered atop the picnic tables. "Do you eat the skins?" he asked me, folding one up, popping it in his mouth like an oversize gumdrop, and admiring its flavor. "Sometimes," I evaded. "You can tell a good salmon from its skin," he said soberly.

"A lot of my customers don't know what to do with salmon skins," Davis replied. "My restaurant is more geared to making people happy than educating them. Jon is a teacher. I'm in the business of making people happy."

The salmon was ready for apportioning. Returning to the nine-inch fillet knife, Davis removed the lower couple of inches of tail meat and then divided the fillet lengthwise and trimmed the bloodline, a thin, dark band of blood-rich meat that's too fishy for many diners. Using his free hand as a caliper, he worked from back to front, carving off single servings, each of which got weighed to ensure a standard seven- to eight-ounce size. When he reached the thickest portions in the middle, he put one aside. "This is yours." It was a beautiful piece of fish, perhaps three inches thick, deep red, the flesh marbled with white lines of fat. "That's the piece of fish of a lifetime. You'll remember that forever." By the end he had thirty-two servings. Now it was time to repeat the process all over again with the second fish. You never see a fishmonger fillet a large fish this way at the market, where customers are waiting in line to get their orders. At my own local market, the well-regarded Mutual Fish in south Seattle, they wield enormous knives that look more like saw blades, and a fillet is removed in a single rapid cut. Though quick, this method leaves meat on the backbone even when performed expertly. Davis's approach is designed to limit wastage. He needs to get the most out of his fillets. When I met him he had a family of five depending on his restaurant income, with a fourth child on the way.

KEVIN DAVIS INVITED ME into his kitchen because, like me, he's an angler, and because he has an emotional attachment to salmon that is something nearly akin to love. I know the feeling. Ever since those months spent in the Rogue River wilderness of southwestern Oregon, I have been drawn to the wild as a source of rejuvenation and sustenance. I learned to fish for salmon and steelhead there— discovered the charms of many other foods produced only by nature, from huckleberries to miner's lettuce to chanterelle mushrooms. Though I returned to the city after a year, the natural world continues to be my escape hatch, the place I go to think, to exercise my limbs, to get over disappointments and let my imagination wander. Learning how to find and prepare wild foods—salmon, in particular—has become a regular part of my life. In many ways salmon are the last great wild food. American bison, along with the cultures they supported, are basically finished, their days of roaming the continent over. The once-ubiquitous passenger pigeon: gone, driven to extinction by market hunters. Elsewhere around the world, the wild foods that formerly nurtured humanity have disappeared or are forgotten. Salmon remain. Catching, killing, and eating one is a reminder of our most basic connection to the natural world. People have been doing this in North America for thousands of years, in Asia for even longer. Yet salmon are becoming more abstracted by the day—as icons of a faded past or talking points on an environmental wish list. They're dissolving into fable as we wring our hands and file our white papers—Exhibit A of a society that doesn't understand the first thing about what sustains it.

One afternoon, many years ago, I was hanging around a tackle shop, hoping to extract any information I could from the owner about sea-run cutthroat trout. Another customer in the store overheard our conversation. "You're too late!" he said. "Should have been here in the eighties." In some ways, he was right. Sea-run cutts had been badly depleted up and down the West Coast. In Puget Sound it was illegal to kill one. This was a species known to settlers as the harvest trout, because it returned from the salt to its natal rivers to spawn during the harvest months and also because it was a favorite for the frying pan. Until it was nearly wiped out. Now there's just a catch-and-release sport fishery so the population can rebuild. One of the shop employees, over in the corner tying flies, jumped in. "The eighties?" he scoffed. "Try the seventies." At which the owner, behind the cash register, adjusted his ratty old ball cap and twisted his white-bearded face into something that looked like a cross between a grin and a frown. "Children, children," he chided us. "They say you weren't really there if you can remember the sixties, but I'll tell you what, the fishing was even better than the sex and the drugs."

Scientists would recognize this exchange as a form of something known as the Shifting Baseline Syndrome. Each generation has its own concept of abundance. Without concrete data on historical fish populations, fisheries managers rely on a hypothetical baseline. In the absence of institutional memory, this baseline tends to shift from one generation to the next, based on each generation's perception of abundance. In a growing population, with increasingly more pressure on the resource, the trend is ever downward, until the resource is managed nearly to extinction.

Even as a toddler, my son loved to fish. At the age of three he hooked (and lost) his first steelhead. At six he learned how to clean a brook trout and panfry it himself with a little butter. Will wild salmon still be on the menu when he becomes an adult?

AT 6:00 P.M. I GOT A MESSAGE from Jon Rowley. He was stuck in traffic. "I don't want him in the kitchen," Davis said, carving out the last servings from his second Copper River king. He told me Rowley had a way of pulling him aside when he was at his busiest, making suggestions or asking pointed questions. "I love the guy, I really do," he added, "but sometimes he gets under my skin. It's like the Japanese and apples. They don't want any apple—they want the perfect apple. He'll be telling me something, saying I should do this and do that, and I'll find myself getting annoyed. Then later I'll think about it and realize, *The fucker is right!*" I knew just what Davis was talking about.

One time Rowley came over to my house for a party. Clad in his signature khakis and white sneakers, he shuffled outside to my back patio, where most of the food had already been devoured, and found a cold piece of salmon on a platter. After taking a bite he turned to me jovially. "You might want to lower the heat," he said. Then he went back out to his Volkswagen van and returned with a produce box full of peaches from one of his clients. The assembled knew enough to put down their beers and dive in before the box was empty. Twenty different friends of mine spent the rest of the night telling me how they had just eaten the single best peach of their life. Rowley was the same way about salmon. Many would say he was the one who put the Copper River on the map.

Kevin Davis got back to work, and the maître d' led me to a booth near the kitchen. It was a quarter after six and Rowley was still MIA. I looked over tonight's fare. A dozen varieties of West Coast oysters topped the menu. Every starter was a type of shellfish, except for the pickled herring. Under main courses I found the salmon, without any special typography or bold font to stand out. It was grilled and served with port-soaked cherries, smoked almonds, cracked rosemary, and brown butter—$45 for sockeye and $56 for king. A brief note below the description was the only tip-off for anyone wondering how a piece of salmon might approach filet mignon status: "This is the most sought-after fish on the planet." I went ahead and ordered an appetizer.

Rowley appeared just as the server delivered a plate of Stellar Bay oysters, a large, tumbled variety from Deep Bay on Vancouver Island's east coast. Dressed as usual, Rowley was slightly disheveled, his button-down shirt partially untucked and his waxen bangs looking wind-tossed. "I couldn't find a parking space," he said. He ordered us each a glass of white wine to go with the oysters, waving away the mignonette and imploring me in his soft voice, barely audible over the hubbub of the restaurant, to "just chew the oyster and use the wine as an accompaniment." I could see how Davis might get irked by our friend. Rowley was on another level. I simply couldn't taste the things that he could.

Rowley looked over the night's fare and spotted his selection. He closed the menu. "Did I ever tell you my story about making a gill net in college? I was living in a girls' dorm. Well, not really, but almost." This was in Portland, Oregon, he said, in the sixties. He'd been hanging around the dorm because his own room was off campus. In fact, it was just a tent, stashed in a thicket of blackberry brambles down in a ravine. "I didn't have any money," he explained of his seriously off-campus housing. Eventually some administrators caught wind of their student's situation and remedied it, but not before Rowley spent a few weeks in the girls' dorm, where he passed the time showing some of his classmates how to construct a gill net with nylon and other household objects. He tied a bunch of mason jars to it for floats, and one moonlit night during a party on the banks of the Sandy River, he deployed the net. Minutes later there was "a great commotion." Two or three big kings migrating upstream had gotten caught and were thrashing around. "It was crazy," he told me. "The net was moving all over the place and there was this wild party going on under the stars." Eventually he and some others managed to haul the net in, along with the catch. "That was a good meal," Rowley said with typical understatement.

After a second appetizer of soft-shelled crabs—flash-fried in a creole meunière with small cubes of Andouille sausage, a nod to Kevin Davis's days in the Crescent City—we turned our attention to the main event. Servers passed by at a steady clip with plates of king and sockeye. For Rowley, a wild salmon dinner is just another way of marking time. After college, he continued to chase the fish as a troller and gillnetter, mostly around southeast Alaska; then in 1979 he sold his boat and "worked from the beach," as he put it, trying to improve what he considered to be the lack of a serious seafood culture on the West Coast compared to other maritime locales where he had spent time—France, for instance, a place where even people of modest means understood what a good piece of fish should look like and how to prepare it.

On the most basic level, Rowley explained, the fish deserve respect. "It's important that they have every scale," he said, "because that's what makes them luminous." Fish lose scales when they've been dropped on deck, stepped on, or otherwise mishandled. "Not only are they beautiful—and it creates a perception of value with the customer—it also tells how the fish have been taken care of, how they've been handled." Handling is in fact paramount. The key is to bleed and ice the fish immediately. "Salmon blood is kind of sticky. It's not like bleeding cod, when you just sever an artery and all the blood runs out. With salmon you need low-pressure water running through the system. One of the things we figured out was a way to get all the blood out. It results in a cleaner-tasting fish. There's iron in blood that gives fish an off-taste. The longer it's in the freezer, the stronger it tastes. I was working with Julia Child at the time. We got Copper River fish in front of her. She said on her show that if we could all eat fish like this, we'd be well-off." He said it again. "Well-off." For Rowley, eating good-quality ingredients is the definition of being well-off.

Over the years Rowley had tasted salmon from watersheds up and down the Alaskan coast, had gone so far as to have their fat content tested in a lab. He knew the early-running Copper River kings were some of the fattiest anywhere. Most of these fish ended up at the canneries, and to Rowley this was a crime. "Back then I was very outspoken about quality. I made a lot of friends and a lot of enemies." One of his friends was a chef named Wayne Ludvigsen, an early proponent of Copper River salmon. Ludvigsen loved the Copper River kings so much, Rowley explained with an impish smile, that his girlfriend left him. "How come you never touch me like that?" she said, catching him in the act of massaging a sumptuous fillet in the kitchen. Rowley approached Ludvigsen and suggested they try to put the Copper River on the map. "I had all this experience behind me, with the fishing and fishermen, and especially with the markets—how to excite people."

There had never been any fresh fish from the Copper River. It was all going into cans, and a certain amount was frozen and sent to Japan. Rowley talked to some of the fishermen in Cordova. "The farsighted ones were trying to figure out how to change their fishery. They have an airport and the fishing grounds are right there, but they were getting very poor prices." Still, he met resistance. So he took a different tack and approached a few restaurants in Seattle—McCormick's Fish House, Ray's Boathouse, Rosellini's, stalwarts like that. The thing was, in order to get the salmon down from Alaska back then, it had to be frozen. "We did a tasting at Ray's Boathouse because they wouldn't serve frozen fish. I said, 'Are you willing to do a blind tasting?'" The restaurant supplied its usual fresh salmon, and Rowley brought some frozen Copper River fish from Cordova. "We used fillets of the same size and thickness and had Wayne cook them up. It was no contest." As a result of that tasting, Ray's Boathouse started serving frozen Copper River salmon in the middle of winter.

Now the problem became one of scale. In order to put Copper River salmon on restaurant menus all over town, the fishery needed to change. The boats weren't outfitted correctly. Rowley continued to pester the fishermen. "You have to bleed the fish and get it into ice before it goes into rigor mortis," he told them. A few fishermen decided to risk the change, installing ice holds on their boats and taking the extra time to bleed the catch. The first Copper River fish landed in the fresh market the following year. It was 1983. Rowley picked up four hundred pounds at Sea–Tac in the initial shipment, four boxes, all kings. "It was the first fresh Copper River salmon in Seattle. I bring a box into the kitchen, take the lid off the box . . ." He folded his arms and looked at me. Hand-delivering this one strain of salmon—the audacity of it all. At Ray's Boathouse, Chef Wayne Ludvigsen cooked some up, tasted it, and said he needed to serve some to the staff right away. "They put it on the menu. I was there when the waiters started coming back saying, 'My customers said that was the best salmon they'd ever had.'" Rowley's next customer was Spago.

Fish eaters like Jon Rowley and Kevin Davis have strong opinions about salmon and how to cook it. I know a troller out of Port Townsend, Washington, with forty-two fishing seasons notched in his hull, who has conducted methodical experiments on each species of Pacific salmon to determine the optimum time for eating. He believes a king should stay on ice for a minimum of three days between the time it's caught and eaten; five to seven days is better, he told me. "A large king cooked the day after catch is the absolute worst," he explained, calling it "tough, rubbery, with an acrid taste." But five days later? Then it's tender and sweet. He figures four days is best for silvers and sockeye, though pinks are soft enough to eat the same day they're caught. Rigor mortis—the state of stiffening up that a fish, like the rest of us, goes into after dying—plays a pivotal role. Rowley stood up from his seat to show me the difference between a fish that's in rigor and one that isn't. He waved his arms up and down like a big goofy bird flapping its wings. Other diners watched him uneasily. The bird routine simulated a fish in rigor, how its flesh tightens up and then releases all at once, herky-jerky, becoming flabby and tasteless. Then he held his arms at his sides and lifted them ever so slightly, more like an orchestra's conductor on a slow burn. That represented a fish that has passed through the rigor phase properly iced and cared for, how it opens slowly and gracefully, like a good bottle of wine.

The server returned and Rowley ordered a Willamette Valley Pinot Noir. He wanted the Illahe but settled for the Broadley. After the server decanted it, he took a taste and said it was fine, waiting until we were alone before telling me it was a bit jammy for his taste. At last the star of the show appeared. Cherries and almonds spilled over the grilled salmon, and thin medallions of roasted potato poked out from underneath. A few fried basil leaves perched on top. I took my fork to it. A piece flaked off in a single smooth stroke. Though pink on the inside, the salmon was cooked through, I was pleased to see; the trend of undercooking salmon so that its interior is sushi-grade was still alive in some quarters, but thankfully not here. The fillet was crisp on the outside and extra flavorful with some sort of rub. No sooner had I taken a bite than Rowley pronounced it slightly oversalted. He wasn't convinced by the fruit and nuts either. That was okay. I had expected as much from him. To me, this was just about the best piece of salmon I had ever eaten, though admittedly I was a dilettante next to my white-haired dinner companion.

While Rowley was still consulting for a few handpicked purveyors, such as Taylor Shellfish and Frog Hollow Farm, he wasn't needed up in Cordova anymore. The Copper River Marketing Association had taken his initial work and built the most famous brand of wild salmon in the world. He was glad for them. Meanwhile, to get a piece of salmon just the way he likes it, he usually cooks it himself. Much of what he had learned over the years about salmon cookery had come from eating with Native Americans. "The Lummis have a whole different way of cooking salmon," he said, wiping his mouth with a napkin and pushing his plate away. "They have a long cedar stick and they cut the salmon in chunks. It's just like a giant shish kebab, a javelin with chunks of salmon on it." The fish are then slow-roasted beside the fire. This was one of the critical pieces of information Rowley had learned from tribes up and down the coast. Though they had different methods—some filleted the fish and impaled the fillets on sticks that surrounded the fire, while others cut the fish into pieces like the Lummis, and others wrapped the fish in ferns and buried it in coals—the important thing was to cook it slowly at a low temperature so that the fat didn't burn up all at once. This was the way to get that silky smooth texture and juicy interior. One of the constants he had discovered from eating with various tribes was the heat of the fire and the proximity of the fish to that heat. He figured this out during a eureka moment one night at a tribal salmon bake by simply positioning his open hand next to the flames, as if it were a piece of salmon.

Rowley took a long sip of ice water and replaced his glass carefully on the table. "Thirteen seconds," he said finally, waiting for me to grasp the significance of the digits. He could keep his hand next to the fire for thirteen seconds before pulling it away from the heat. He paused to let the magic number sink in. "It took me two years to figure out how they do it. I tried to replicate the result in my home kitchen. That thirteen seconds turns out to be about two hundred twenty degrees." This was just the sort of revelation that I expected from Rowley—that I would expect from anyone who had spent a lifetime hanging around the crossroads of nature and food.

CHEF DAVIS REAPPEARED FROM his busy kitchen, his face shiny with sweat. He was getting ready to go home for the night so he could see his kids before bedtime. For a second I worried that Rowley would offer him some unsolicited cooking tips. Instead, he made a gesture of tipping his cap. "Wonderful fish," he said. Davis looked over at me, saw my cleaned plate, and we shook hands. He wanted to know when we might go fishing together. At the end of the day he isn't just a food guy. He's a fisherman. One of his other restaurants is called Steelhead Diner, after all. He invited me to join him on the Klickitat, a Columbia River tributary, to which he hoped to sneak off on a slow day in October, or maybe the famed Dean River in British Columbia next year, to spey-fish for wild spring kings.

Davis is also active in fish politics. He even went to Washington, D.C., on behalf of salmon, to voice his opinion on the proposed Pebble Mine, a gold mine that would be excavated by a multinational in the headwaters of Bristol Bay, Alaska, home to the world's largest run of sockeye salmon. The chef was vehemently opposed to the mine, as was a large coalition of Native Americans, environmentalists, and everyday citizens who valued the last of America's wild places. A gold mine—the largest on the planet, no less, with a tailings dam the size of Grand Coulee, built in a seismically active area—had no place in that vision. Davis dressed up in a coat and tie for the occasion. Like the rest of the delegation from Trout Unlimited, the nation's oldest trout-and-salmon-conservation organization, he expected to be handed off to various aides. He was ready for that. The others in his group decided he would be their spokesperson when and if the time came.

And when the time did come, it turned out that Maria Cantwell, junior senator of Washington State, would meet with them in person. Davis's mouth filled with sawdust. His hands got clammy. "I was nervous," he told me, even though Cantwell had eaten in his restaurants on numerous occasions. He'd met her before, but this was different. "I didn't understand the process until that moment, and suddenly I realized how lucky we were." This was during the lead-up to Obamacare. The halls of Congress bustled with activity unrelated to anything having to do with fish or the environment. Cantwell's office seemed hot. "When it came time to talk, I couldn't get the words out. I'm not a public speaker—I'm a cook!" But he finally blurted out his feelings about gold mines, wild fish, and the renewable resources of Alaska, and though Davis worried afterward that he'd botched it, Cantwell would soon announce her opposition to the mine, a move that infuriated the elected officials in neighboring Alaska. "She really stepped up and put her neck out," Davis marveled. "Other states don't take kindly to that." At the same time, the chef and restaurant owner learned something about the political process. "You as a citizen of the United States have a right to request an audience and be heard." Davis is proud that his voice—and the voices of so many others—has, so far, kept the mine at bay.

That night, when I got home after dinner, my kids were asleep and I found my wife, Martha, reading a newspaper in the kitchen. I told her the Copper River salmon were running, that it was a madhouse at the fish markets and restaurants, that everyone wanted a piece of the action while it lasted. She looked at me, taking this in, and then said, "You know, they found a new planet. It's forty light-years away. The planet is made of graphite and liquid diamonds." Pencils and diamonds. I thought about this development for a moment. Every day you can open the paper and read something astonishing about nature, about the universe. I caught myself wondering: How long will it take before we try to mine a diamond planet? Lately there has been a lot of talk about colonizing space, talk that depresses me no end. Our planet, the only one known to have life on it, is nothing short of a miracle. People like Kevin Davis and Jon Rowley understand this. You can't watch a river boiling with salmon on the spawn—millions of years of evolution distilled into a moment—without being reminded of how miraculous *this* planet, Earth, really is.

CHAPTER 3

THE CASE OF THE
MISSING ADIPOSE FIN

COPPER RIVER SALMON COMMAND TODAY'S NAME-RECOGNITION game, but for hundreds of years, probably longer, the most revered salmon in North America lived nowhere near Alaska. Instead, they returned to the West Coast's largest river, more than a thousand miles to the southeast. With Kevin Davis's evaluation of Columbia River spring kings on my mind ("the piece of fish that changed my life"), I went down to the Big River, as it's known to Native Americans, where it borders the states of Oregon and Washington, following a route that would have been familiar to indigenous fishermen and traders long ago—before a grid of modern highways and interstates criss-crossed the map, their red and blue lines dulling the imagination.

The drive took me east over Snoqualmie Pass to the far side of the Cascade Mountains, lush forests giving way to sagebrush-dotted pla-teaus, the fresh yellow blooms of balsamroot announcing the season. With a high desert wind at my back, I skirted the Yakama Nation and the volcanic cone of Mount Adams before dropping over the lip of the Columbia River Gorge, where I met a man in a dark cove, pacing rest-lessly beside his half-beached jet boat. My watch said 5:20 A.M.; I was five minutes late. "Time's a-wasting," he said truculently, dispensing with any introductions or greetings.

John, my fishing guide for the day, ushered me aboard his boat before pushing us off the beach. From ankle-deep water, he jumped onto the bow and took the helm. We motored slowly out of the cove into inky darkness. It was disconcerting not being able to see. I checked the time again and looked in the direction of where the sun should be rising. Headlights on the hillside; the sound of a distant train. I poured myself a mug of coffee from my thermos and tried to relax. The beginning of any fishing trip is a confusion of heightened senses and emotions. There's hope, of course, and also, maybe, a touch of worry. Would I get lucky? Would I go home with the fish that everyone in the know talked about? The best way to sample any cut of fish, after all, is to catch it yourself.

The worthiness of salmon and trout as fishing quarry dates back to Roman times. *A Treatyse of Fysshynge wyth an Angle,* attributed to a fly-fishing nun named Dame Juliana Berners, was printed in 1496 and contains the sage reminder that an angler suffers no annoyances unless he brings them upon himself. How many times have I needed to remember this bit of wisdom! *The Compleat Angler* by Izaak Walton, first published in England in 1653, is still popular today for its advice and whimsical stories. Since medieval times, the literature of fishing has been a regular feature of the English-language bookshelf. Though many sport anglers on today's crowded rivers have adopted a catch-and-release ethic to sustain these workhorse fisheries, throughout history the red-fleshed salmon in particular has been venerated around the temperate world as food, as a gift from the sea, sometimes returning to spawning grounds in eye-popping numbers and enabling entire societies to prosper. From California to Alaska, Native Americans on the West Coast survived largely on salmon. This plenitude allowed the tribes to develop "gift economies," in which a family's wealth was measured not by accumulation but by what it could afford to give away, and the reliable food source that swam upriver each year gave them plenty of time to do other things, like tell stories and make art.

These days, many anglers in salmon country don't think kindly toward the Native American fishery. They see the Indians as competitors for a dwindling resource and decry the nets that catch endangered runs of wild fish. Tensions run high on a place like the Olympic Peninsula, in far northwestern Washington State, a four-hour drive and ferry ride from my home in Seattle. The peninsula was once thought to be sheltered from the forces of civilization that have decimated salmon populations elsewhere, but its famous fish runs are in steady decline. Many blame the Indian nets, none more so than hook-and-line anglers hoping to put a fat salmon in the freezer. The Columbia River Gorge is another place where cultures clash over salmon.

John wore a heavy parka over polyvinyl bibs and rubber boots. The gorge was forecast to warm up to eighty degrees today—the hottest day of spring so far—but at this hour it was cold on the water. He also wore a pair of thin black gloves that fit his hands snugly, like a surgeon's. These, he explained, while cutting up strips of cured herring by the light of his headlamp, were for masking any human scent as he tied on lures and baits. He handed me a rod with instructions to let out seventy feet of line so we could pull plugs—a type of deep-bodied lure—through the placid waters of Drano Lake.

In keeping with a name that suggests a clogged bathtub, Drano isn't really a natural lake. It's more of a bay, a man-made impoundment with a narrow outlet to the main river channel. Fill from the Bonneville Dam project created it, and it's fed by the icy flow of the Little White Salmon River, which comes plunging out of the mountains to the north. Anadromous fish nose into Drano during their migration up the Columbia, just like those Rogue River kings with which I'd first taken a swim, seeking its cooler temperatures as a place to rest and refuel. Up and down the Columbia River Gorge, fish and fishermen congregate at such places, as they have for thousands of years.

The gorge itself is a hundred-mile cleft in the Cascade Mountains. West of the Cascade Crest, the gorge slices through a damp region of evergreens; eastward, in the rain shadow of the mountain range, which runs north to south, it rends desolate badlands that receive as little as six inches of annual precipitation. Nowadays the crossover

from wet to dry takes mere minutes on I-84. It's stunning in its sud-
denness. Toward the end of the last Ice Age, about fifteen thousand
years ago, colossal floods from ancient Lake Missoula carved the Columbia's path to the sea as volcanic mountains rose and showered the
area with debris. Exposed ramparts of columnar basalt tower above
either bank, revealing this alternating sequence of deep scouring and
uplift. Even from a car, which always strikes me as a banal way to con-
front any of our natural splendors, the sheer destructive power that
formed this landscape is hard to miss. Imagining a wall of water, unleashed from a glacial lake nearly the size of Lake Huron and crashing
through this desert terrain, gives me shivers. It was a massive reset
button that was pushed every fifty years on average for about two
thousand years. And each time the floods subsided, salmon, resilience
etched into their DNA, reemerged from their refugia in various nooks
and crannies throughout the watershed to repopulate the river.

To put the whole Columbia Basin in perspective, picture a region
slightly larger than France that drains parts of seven western states and
one Canadian province: a conglomeration of high glacial peaks, dense
conifer forests, fragrant sagebrush plateaus, and arid canyons, all of
this rugged topography incised by a capillarylike network of creeks,
streams, and white water rivers that sends sixty-five trillion gallons of
snowmelt to the Pacific each year. Before Euro-American settlement,
it was the greatest salmon nursery on the planet and the locus of king
salmon abundance in particular. Recent estimates suggest that as many
as thirty million salmon returned annually to spawn (this is twice the
outdated number that used to get bandied around), many of them the
early-running spring kings that travel hundreds of miles upriver
through cataracts and rapids to spawn in high-mountain tributaries.
For thousands of years these were the fish that organized entire cultures of humanity. Long before the kings of the Copper River impressed us, there were the Columbia River spring kings. John preferred
to call them spring chinook, or springers.

The term *spring chinook* is misleading. It's a reminder of our need to
name and categorize. The first Columbia River chinook of the year

are counted as early as February at Bonneville Dam's fish ladder, 146 miles from the river mouth, and they will continue to arrive at the ladder each subsequent month through the rest of the year, spawning from late summer through fall. We refer to these fish as spring chinook, summer chinook, and fall chinook, based on the approximate season of their entrance into the river. While there are distinct genetic differences, observable in the DNA, there is no clear dividing line in the run timing; rather, there is a continuum that reflects the diverse life histories of the fish. Generally speaking, the name spring chinook corresponds to the early-running kings that usually travel farther and hold longer on their spawning grounds than fish that arrive later in the year. Because salmon don't actively feed once they enter fresh water, they rely on their fat reserves to survive sometimes for months on end before spawning. This is what had impressed Kevin Davis. Springers are noteworthy for having large stores of fat and for maintaining their silver-plated complexions, evolutionary adaptations that help them in the river leading up to the spawn. Unlike fall salmon of the lower river, which often turn dark and soft as soon as they enter fresh water, the springers stay shiny and firm. They have long journeys ahead and can't shift all their energy into reproduction quite yet. Many of the Columbia's fish are destined for headwater tributaries hundreds of miles from the salt, earning them another nickname: upriver brights. And because of their wonderfully rich, fatty meat, these were historically the most desirable salmon to Native American tribes living along the Columbia River, who caught and traded huge volumes of the fish, spreading their reputation far and wide.

My lure was a boldly colored fraud in green and orange called a Mag Lip, carefully wrapped with a strip of herring that John had cured the day before, using a recipe he'd refined over the years. "It drives the fish crazy," he said, his mood starting to lighten. I clicked the release on my reel and started paying out line, ten feet, twenty feet, forty, sixty . . . until John told me to stop, at exactly seventy-two feet. Once the lure was in the water, he explained his impatience.

"This is when the bite started yesterday, and by six-thirty it was over. Done." His clients had gone two for five and didn't have another strike for the next eight hours, which is to say that in the space of an hour they managed five strikes, resulting in two fish landed. Measured in terms of an hour's fishing, this would be a solid burst of king salmon action; measured across the span of a full day, it was something of a disappointment—though, when it comes to springers, any fish in the boat can be considered a success. Some years the spring chinook fishery doesn't even open. Salmon runs in the Columbia are a fraction of what they once were, before the river was harnessed for power.

I admitted to John that I had never done this sort of fishing before and wasn't quite sure what to expect. Most of my salmon angling up to this point had been with a fly rod, for species smaller than chinook. I asked him if the take would be obvious. "Oh *gawd*!" he said, shaking his head. "There's no messing around with these fish. Just hold on tight and do what I say." He was optimistic. The day before, 5,500 fish were counted coming over Bonneville Dam's fish ladder, twenty miles to the west. Those fish would start arriving anytime this morning, and even here, more than 160 miles upstream from the river mouth, some of them would still be carrying sea lice. "They'll be here," John said, with the confidence of a missionary.

I wasn't so sure. The salmon move through the Big River as if made of water themselves, their migration hidden from sight. We stare at the roiling surface and see nothing. Only when they enter the man-made fish ladders at the dams do they suddenly appear to us, as if someone has thrown a light switch, making the imperceptible almost knowable. These ladders are a jarring sight. The fish enter a chute below the dam, because they're naturally drawn to current. Back and forth they swim through a hard-edged concrete channel that flows like a water slide, gaining elevation through a series of stair-stepping switchbacks, until they've summited and reached the reservoir on the other side. Many of the dams have a viewing chamber within their bowels, where the public can witness the effort. The salmon don't seem to see us as they pass. Their unblinking eyes betray no recognition. Unlike a curious leopard or gorilla at the zoo, they move through with their otherness intact.

While I pondered this otherness, John gestured toward a boat fifty yards away in the blue light of early dawn, which washed across the gorge like a window cleaner, everything just a little brighter and more visible now. Standing in the boat was a friend of his, another guide, holding a big net vertically aloft as if planting a flag, waiting for the moment of capture as his client sat hunched, rod doubled over. Such moments are as close as we can get to knowing these fish.

THIS WAS ACTUALLY MY SECOND TRIP to the Columbia River Gorge that spring. A few weeks earlier I had attended a First Salmon ceremony at Celilo Village, one of the most hallowed crossroads in indigenous America. Situated between the Chinookan-speaking people of the lower Columbia and the Sahaptin speakers of the Columbia Plateau east of the Cascades, Celilo has been referred to as the "Wall Street of Indian Country." Lewis and Clark landed there on October 22, 1805. Noting the many different tribal groups gathered to fish and trade, they called it "the great mart" of the West. My destination was the Celilo longhouse on the Oregon side of the Columbia, two hundred river miles from the mouth and overlooking the site of the former Celilo Falls. Called *Wy-am,* which means "the echo of water upon the rocks," the sound of these falls hasn't been heard since March 10, 1957, when the Dalles Dam closed its gates for the first time and flooded the most sacred of all fishing sites in North America.

Despite its distance from the coast, Celilo Falls was the epicenter of the salmon universe for thousands of years. A new longhouse stands near the site of the former village. At one end of the gymnasiumlike interior, a large painting depicts the falls as they once were: a horseshoe-shaped choke point in the river, where cascades of white water crashed over basalt formations into frothing cauldrons below. Historically, native tribes from up and down the river traveled to Celilo each spring to catch salmon in dip nets from wooden platforms built precariously over the falls. The fishing couldn't begin, however, until the salmon had been shown the proper respect. Variations of the First Salmon ceremony still take place throughout salmon country. They differ slightly from tribe to tribe, but the general outline is the same: The first salmon of the year is ritualistically shared among everyone in the community, and its skeleton is returned to the river and floated downstream. In this way, the ambassador from the salmon tribe can return to its underwater kin and tell of the respect it received from the human beings living upstream, so that more of its kind will ascend and nourish the Indian people. Once the First Salmon ceremony has been performed—with its associated rituals of drumming, dancing, fasting, and feasting, which might take place over the course of days—the fishing season can begin in earnest. Whether it was fully understood or not, the fishing closures built into such rites had the effect of allowing more salmon to reach their upstream spawning grounds, ensuring future runs for harvest. "Spiritual game management," it's been called.

During the powwow in the longhouse, which that day was open to the public, men and boys sat on one side and women and girls on the other. Most of the participants, a few hundred strong, were dressed casually in denim, though a few wore feathers, buckskin, and elaborate necklaces. Drummers stood beneath the painting of Celilo Falls while dancers paraded up the middle. Songs began with a drumbeat and gathered force. The lead dancer carried a bell, which he rang in time to the music, occasionally giving it a good shake for emphasis. The audience followed the rhythm, moving their hands back and forth as if ringing an invisible bell: the heart beating in time. There were songs and speeches and prayers, most of them unscripted, and the powwow went on like this for hours—as long as it took for everyone, especially the elders, to speak their minds, invoke memories from the past, and offer a prayer.

A man shuffled to the front, where a microphone awaited. His pig-tails had gone gray and hung down the front of his black vest. He was a Vietnam vet, he said. He'd been at war all his life, abroad and at home, and he imagined a day when his people took back their land and the salmon were plentiful. Another elder came forward and spoke of the dams. "Up and down the river they flooded our longhouses. We're strong people. We made it through the sickness. We're still strong." Then a very old man, older than the rest, with a beautifully beaded vest and moccasins, slowly made his way to the front. He stood before the crowd, as straight as he was able. "I'm at the end of my life," he said, leaning into the microphone, hands clasped behind his back. "I feel the water rising all around me."

Afterward, the elders waited inside; they would be served first, while the rest of us filed outside. It took the rest of the afternoon to feed everyone. Piles of spring chinook, their backs a lucid green with black spots, spilled out of burlap bags left on the ground, some of them showing net marks where they'd been caught. Tribal members gutted and filleted the big fish, and arranged them on sprawling home-made barbecues. They wrapped salmon heads in foil and tossed them on the grill. Off to one side, a few women tended to more traditional cooking methods, the salmon fillets staked out with sharpened sticks and left to roast by a fire. Skins of several freshly killed mule deer hung from a nearby chain-link fence, their ribs crackling on the grill. A woman sold fry bread for two dollars; another sold jewelry. I ate a big piece of fillet with a plastic fork while a man next to me used his fingers to carefully extract all the meat from a charred salmon head, its eyes cloudy white. He licked his fingers and looked up. "Good," I said, not quite sure how to fill the space between us. He nodded and went back to excavating salmon heads. Nearby, a boisterous table full of self-identified social-justice warriors from Portland dug into plate-fuls of salmon, their blond dreadlocks swinging and brightly colored kaftans glinting in the afternoon sun. The Indians ignored them. We all washed our food down with Dixie cups of fruit punch. There wasn't a drop of alcohol in sight.

———

SALMON HAS BEEN ON the menu in North America for a long time. At the height of the last Ice Age, forty-five thousand to thirteen thousand years ago, when water was locked up in glaciers and the world's sea levels were much lower than today, hunter-gatherers from Siberia made a slow migration across the Bering land bridge to an unpeopled continent. By the time they arrived on the other side centuries later and started infiltrating interior Alaska, they were a changed people, genetically speaking. Archaeologists now call these first Americans Paleo-Indians. With warming temperatures, the ice sheets retreated, opening pathways down the continent. Some of the Pleistocene foragers settled on the banks of the Columbia, where they eventually became known in indigenous America as the river people, or people of the salmon.

Fishing sites along the Columbia represent the longest continuous human habitation in the Americas, at least ten thousand years. But the river people didn't become full-time fishermen right away. Evidence suggests they continued to hunt land mammals as their primary food source until about four thousand years ago, when, for reasons that are not entirely clear, they shifted their efforts to salmon. Did new technology allow them to more fully exploit the fish runs? With the end of Ice Age floods, did the fish themselves increase in number enough to allow the shift? We just don't know. We do know that Native Americans from all over the greater Pacific Northwest and sometimes from as far away as the Great Plains would gather along the Columbia River at favored fishing sites like the Cascade Rapids and Celilo Falls when the salmon started running in the spring. They represented many tribes and language groups, and intermarriage created loose affiliations. Some lived in seasonal villages; others pitched temporary camps. They fished, socialized, bartered, picked berries, hunted, played games, and gambled. A man could catch enough salmon in a month to feed his family for the year. The women preserved the fish by drying it in the sun, smoking it, and pounding the jerklike meat with berries to make pemmican. Surplus was traded for other necessities or given away as a show of personal wealth to reinforce bonds within the community.

Before the first white settlers arrived, the region's economy was rooted in subsistence living and trade rather than profit. Lewis and Clark encountered scores of indigenous villages and camps as the Corps of Discovery floated down the Columbia in October 1805. The encampments were full of fishermen and drying fish, but despite this abundance, the Indians were loath to trade any of their harvest, preferring instead to give a dog to the hungry explorers. Though early written accounts of the river people depicted primitive communities living in an Edenlike setting of inexhaustible bounty, modern historians paint a different picture. Evidence shows that many tribes had developed sophisticated fishing cultures using a variety of tools and techniques, from spears and weirs to dip nets and gill nets, and through a process of trial and error over the course of centuries had learned to exploit salmon runs to the fullest extent possible without depleting the resource. Before postcontact disease, war, and dispossession eliminated more than 90 percent of the Native American population in the Pacific Northwest, the river people along the Columbia might have caught as much as forty million pounds of salmon in a year, a figure that's nearly equivalent to the height of the white industrial fishery in the 1880s.

Not long after published accounts of Lewis and Clark's expedition appeared, white settlement in the Columbia Basin began, led by fur traders and Christian missionaries. By the 1830s, mountain men chasing furs had trapped out much of the territory. In 1846, the United States ended its land dispute with England, claiming everything south of the forty-ninth parallel; the Mexican War, which had begun that same year, concluded in 1848 with the spoils of California and the Southwest. Soon after, the Oregon Trail saw a steady increase of wagon trains, with a peak of seventy thousand settlers migrating west in 1852. Isaac Stevens, territorial governor of Washington and superintendent of Indian Affairs, persuaded (i.e., coerced) tribes of the Pacific Northwest to sign treaties in 1854 and 1855 that ceded sixty-four million acres of what would become the states of Washington, Oregon, Idaho, and Montana to the "Great Father." The first cannery started packing Columbia River salmon in 1866. By 1883 there were fifty-five canneries on or near the river. Advances in the canning process and completion of a transcontinental railroad opened new markets, encouraging an ever-greater catch. The white newcomers enjoyed technological advantages, such as the fish wheel, an ingenious mill-like contraption that turned in the current, scooping up salmon in the process. It was so effective that both Washington and Oregon eventually abolished it.

Even more effective was the use of political power to wrest traditional fishing sites away from Native Americans. Within a few decades, the Columbia River's mostly subsistence fishery was fully transformed into a market fishery, with displaced Indians working in the canneries in addition to putting up their steadily shrinking subsistence quantities. The year 1911 saw the peak commercial catch, with nearly forty-seven million pounds of salmon packed, but the river was already in decline by then. In fact, some observers believed the decrease in chinook, the most economically valuable species, had begun as early as 1886, just a few short decades after the arrival of the first white settlers. The 1893–94 edition of the Fish and Game Protector Report compared the State of Oregon to a profligate: "For a third of a century, Oregon has drawn wealth from her streams, but now, by reason of her wastefulness and lack of intelligent provision for the future, the source of that wealth is disappearing and is threatened with complete annihilation. No private individual so wasteful and improvident of his resources would receive the least sympathy from his fellows if he died in poverty and was buried in the potter's field."

While overfishing was the first threat to the Columbia's prodigious salmon runs, darker clouds hovered on the horizon. On September 28, 1937, President Franklin D. Roosevelt, fulfilling a campaign promise from five years earlier to electrify the Pacific Northwest, dedicated a new hydroelectric facility on the river. Bonneville Dam, forty miles east of Portland, was the first step in his vision for unifying an entire region via cheap electricity, irrigation, and shipping. The dam went online with much pageantry from local boosters, most of whom had called the place home for only a generation or two, and few at the ceremony would have given much thought to a small gathering of people off to the side, who watched grimly as their way of life was engulfed by unstoppable forces.

In 1941, the Bonneville Power Administration, the federal agency that markets Columbia River electricity, hired a folksinger to exhort the virtues of hydropower and jobs. Woody Guthrie, or anyone else, for that matter, could not have guessed how much the New Deal and World War II would transform the basin over the next twenty years. That same year, on the eve of war, Grand Coulee Dam went online. Located on the Columbia Plateau nearly six hundred miles from the river mouth, it remains the largest electricity-generating facility in the country—and since no provision was made for fish to pass, twelve hundred miles of spawning grounds above the dam are now closed to salmon. A 1947 memo from the Department of the Interior put it bluntly when it came to dams versus salmon: "Overall benefits to the Pacific Northwest are such that the present salmon run must if necessary be sacrificed." Between 1954 and 1971, eight more hydroelectric dams were built on the main stem alone (plus another three in Canada between 1973 and 1984). Large tributaries of the Columbia, such as the Snake River and the Clearwater River—watercourses that play starring roles in the founding narrative of America—received their own impoundments, flooding a wealth of ancient artifacts and slowing their dash to the sea. The newcomers, for the most part, didn't worry about the salmon, and they certainly didn't worry about the people who had lived along the Columbia "since time immemorial," as it was usually put (because no one really knew how long it had been). They looked to the future, not the past, and the word *progress* trembled on their lips. The spring chinook that had nurtured countless generations slipped into obscurity.

JOHN DIDN'T SEEM TOO INTERESTED in hearing about the First Salmon ceremony at Celilo Village, though he did agree that springers were the finest eating of all the salmon and what a damn shame it was that they were so pitifully squandered. If anything, he said, it was a crime so many still ended up in Indian nets today, and what's more—

He jumped up from his seat at the tiller and pointed to the screen of his high-tech fish-finder. "That's a fish right there!" We watched a red line scroll horizontally across the screen, and it was nearly as exciting as seeing the thing itself. The lone salmon was at a depth of about twenty-seven feet, a good ten feet below my offering. But a glance upward and it might just decide to suddenly give its powerful tail a shake and rise through the water column to grab the offending lure. We waited, motionless, watching the screen. The red line vanished.

By the time the sun poured over the northeastern rim of the gorge and into the bay like molten lava, the main body of Drano Lake was done for the day. We'd seen exactly one fish landed among the dozens of boats trolling back and forth. I reeled in. John cut off the Mag Lip and switched to bait, which involved tying on a heavy round weight about the size of a Ping-Pong ball and a bright-green reflective plate called a flasher, to attract attention. It was a setup that could just as easily hook a guide as a fish. "Don't hold it up in the air," he warned me, "or it'll end up a kite." With an east wind blowing—the near-daily result of low-pressure weather systems on the coast sucking all the hot desert air out of eastern Washington and Oregon through the gorge—hats, tarps, tents, and anything else that wasn't nailed down, flashers included, was at risk of taking flight. At last he threaded a brined pink shrimp onto a hook and secured its tail with a loop of line. We made straight for the Toilet Bowl.

Drano Lake's outlet flows under a railroad trestle and Highway 14, where it meets up with the wind-tossed main stem of the Columbia. The Toilet Bowl is right at this outlet, where migrating salmon entering and leaving the lake are funneled into a narrow channel. Fishermen have learned how to exploit this conflation of natural instinct and man-made impediments, and with so many of them jostling for position in a small area, an informal system has evolved. Boats slowly circle counterclockwise, making one pass after another at the sweet spot near the bridge, dragging their lures and baits as they go. Today it was relatively calm; there were only two dozen or so boats circling. At the height of the run there might be twice that, all lined up, nose to tail, endlessly rotating this piece of high-value watery real estate. "You should see it," John said. Some days there could be near bedlam, with simultaneous hookups, fishing lines knifing through the water, boats locking horns, words exchanged, anglers and guides frustrated with their fellow human beings. And that's just among the boaters. A whole different contingent was busy flinging its enticements from shore. The bank anglers were like an aggrieved minority—they had no claim to power as they hurled their neon-colored Mag Lips and Wiggle Warts from the firmament with a mixture of hope and resentment, trying to penetrate the wall of boaters for a few seconds before reeling limply back to land. Occasionally one of the bankies hooked a fish despite the odds, and it was cause for celebration up and down the shoreline.

We took up our position in the line of boats and started circling the bowl, waiting—hoping—for a bite. "I had a real job once," John said. He'd worked construction, until an injury relegated him to a desk job. I tried to picture him this way, dressed in a button-down shirt, staring at a computer monitor. His craggy, sunburned features were handsome in the way of someone who works a physical job outside, a cowhand or housepainter. I couldn't imagine him interpreting a spreadsheet for his boss, adjusting his bifocals rather than a pair of menacing wraparound sunglasses. That job didn't last, he went on. The company "changed direction" and he decided it was time to jump from hardcore recreational angler to professional. He resisted the urge to go to Alaska and guide for a lodge. That was a young man's game. This way he could stay relatively close to home and his family. Even so, he still spent weeks away in the spring, renting a house with a couple of other guides, getting up at three in the morning to cure bait, tie knots, and beat the crowds at the boat launch. The dirtbag fisherman's life, some called it, a mix of admiration and dread in their voices.

With a high-noon sun slowing the already sedate action even more and putting a few anglers visibly to sleep, chins tucked into chests, their heads lolling with the swells, I got my first and only strike of the day. It was a few minutes past the hour when the rod tip bent savagely once, twice, and I felt the pull of a strong fish. Why would an animal with no desire to eat be fooled by a preposterous pink shrimp? Whether this is a territorial behavior or some sort of muscle memory from a predatory life at sea, no one can be sure. In any event, there was no point dwelling on such unanswerable questions in the moment. The reel strained, and my guide demanded that I not let the fish get under the boat. Now it was his turn to stand with a long-handled net as if ready to plant it like a victory flag in the bilge. Once I had the salmon tired out and close, he dredged it up in a spume of water and quickly knocked it over the head with a little wooden billy club. We both sat down and caught our breath. It was a beautiful fish, about twelve pounds, its opalescent sides shimmering in the glare as the faintest crimson spot pooled at the jaw. I looked a little closer. The fish was missing a small, thumb-shaped nub of flesh between the tail and dorsal called an adipose fin. The adipose is a vestigial fin that gets snipped off at a fish hatchery, to mark its man-made origins and distinguish it from a wild fish. Only fin-clipped spring chinook can be kept on the Columbia. The wild fish—those hatched naturally in gravel beds, adipose fin and all—have to be released, because they're in such short supply. A majority of the Columbia's salmon these days are of hatchery origin.

I wasn't surprised. The river is hemmed in by major arterials on either side for much of its length. We were fishing next to a busy highway and a railroad line. I could hear the roar of long-haul truckers and the whine of freight trains on the tracks. Across the river, Interstate 84 chugged along, its four lanes busy with traffic. Both banks are made of riprap. More than a dozen hydroelectric dams on the main-stem Columbia alone have transformed a brawling river into a series of reservoirs more suited to transporting goods than salmon. Barges plow downriver, carrying wheat from Lewiston, Idaho, to Portland. Given all this, who would expect to catch a wild spring chinook in such a place?

Unlike other types of popular seafood, salmon spend a crucial part of their life cycle among us. They push deep inland to spawn. South of Canada, those spawning grounds are seldom far from outposts of humanity. I was reminded of what my old friend Rene Henery, a fisheries ecologist in California, likes to say: The world we give to salmon is the same world we must live in. He likens the homogeneity of the human landscape—endless sprawl bending nature to its needs—to the homogeneity of hatchery salmon. One begets the other.

Take these Columbia River springers. They're all about the same size and shape: cookie-cutter fish produced in a fish factory, the piscine equivalent of strip-mall architecture. In a landscape that's been homogenized, we've populated a tamed river with a domesticated run of salmon. But without them, the argument goes, there would hardly be any springers at all. Having just caught one and looking forward to seeing its thick red fillets on my grill, it was impossible to not have mixed feelings. The fish itself would taste just fine—would, in fact, be indistinguishable to the palate from a wild fish, since both have to feed and survive in the ocean. And certainly it was better than a farmed salmon, one raised in captivity, never knowing the freedom and danger of the sea. Still, the more I stared at that empty space where a small fin should have been, the more I had to concede that hatchery salmon are an illusion. An illusion that everything is okay. The missing adipose is all too obvious. It signifies loss. If people understood this, I wondered, would they stand for it? What if all those Copper River kings and sockeye were hatchery fish rather than wild? Would the marketplace still be mobbed? The issues facing salmon all over the world are complex, and hard to unravel. Just about every fish market in the country sells farmed salmon. You can catch a hatchery salmon in the Columbia nearly any day of the year. Why so much fuss, one might ask, over these fine distinctions between the wild ones?

TUMBLING RIVERS TURNED INTO reservoirs; spawning grounds replaced by hatcheries; the deep blue sea scaled down to a salmon farm. Recently scientists have begun revising their theories about the adipose fin, this supposedly inconsequential limb that gets lopped of at the hatchery in a process called, unfortunately, marking. Studies suggest it may in fact have implications for how salmon choose their mates, making it one of many cues in the ongoing drama of natural selection. The little adipose might as well be a blinking billboard trying to get our attention: There is no substitute for natural ecological processes.

Like me, John would prefer to catch and eat a wild fish, adipose and all. That isn't possible any longer with Columbia River spring chinook. The deal, our bargain with the fish, has changed. Instead of husbanding wild runs, we now make facsimiles in a lab. Perhaps this is why their reputation as the best eating of all salmon is a thing of the past. You rarely see Columbia springers in the market now. Commercial gillnetters are allocated few openings in the spring, for fear they'll take too many wild fish in their indiscriminate nets, and both Oregon and Washington have agreed to phase out gillnetting on the main river altogether. Sport fishermen are ecstatic, of course, because their long, contentious battle with the commercial fleet over the Columbia's shrinking resource is almost won. But the fight is mainly over hatchery fish, the figment that keeps my guide and many others like him in business.

John would also like to see the river cascading over Celilo Falls again, he confessed, but the sight of Indians netting salmon out in the middle of the river—an area closed to non-tribal anglers—now, *that* was an affront to him. Why should they get any special dispensation, he wondered aloud. The Indian Wars are history. Times change. Had I seen all those welfare redskins selling salmon under the Bridge of the Gods downriver? What a racket. He held up my springer by a gill so I could admire it. "Congratulations," he said, putting it away in an ice chest. "Now you don't have to go buy a salmon under the bridge."

CHAPTER 4

BRIDGE OF THE GODS

THE BRIDGE OF THE GODS IS A WONDER OF GEOMETRY. COMPLETED in 1926, it spans the Columbia River Gorge from Oregon to Washington where the river cuts through the Cascade Crest, its steel trusses converging at every conceivable angle like a kid's Erector set gone mad. Drawn back to the Big River mere weeks after catching my first spring chinook, I parked my car in the bridge's complicated shadow and started walking into the town of Cascade Locks, Oregon. The Columbia, that famous wind tunnel, was surprisingly calm on this summer-solstice morning. Barges pushing downriver contended with neither whitecaps nor errant sailboarders. Mount Hood's melting glaciers looked dirty and spent as turkey vultures made low, listless turns on the horizon. A phalanx of skyscraper-sized wind turbines on a far ridge stood motionless. The power, as usual, was in the river.

Beneath the bridge, a dozen or more Native American fishermen from different tribes tried to sell me a salmon. Despite what I'd heard from white anglers about "old boots rotting in the back of a pickup," these fish looked good—and at $8 a pound, the price was right. The memory of my springer—how it tasted grilled with a little olive oil and rosemary—was still with me. Martha called it the best piece of salmon she'd ever had, even if it was a hatchery fish. But I kept walking, ignoring the sales pitches, until I came to Brigham Fish Market at the west end of WaNaPa Street, in a choice location across from the Cascade Inn and down the block from the Eastwind hamburger stand. The two-thousand-square-foot building, designed by Kim Brigham Campbell and built by her husband, was made of stone and cedar and embellished with fish-themed metalwork by a local artist. Colorful steelhead wind socks dangled from the eaves. A crowd had gathered outside the new storefront, completed a few months earlier, waiting for the blessing to begin.

Campbell was behind the counter with her sister, Terrie Brigham. They looked a little frazzled. The place was jammed, and more people kept coming in off the street to see what was going on. Brigham's was selling freshly caught chinook fillets for $10 a pound—cheaper than a farmed salmon in nearby Portland. Someone asked where the fish came from, and Campbell glanced over her shoulder at the back door.

"More and more these days, people want to know where their fish and their food comes from and what's in it," Terrie Brigham quietly explained to me. "We can tell you when our fish was caught and who caught it." She said that the family's relatives and friends did most of the catching. I pointed to a fillet with a deep-orange color. "I caught that one!" she exclaimed. Usually Brigham was on the river fishing while Campbell ran the store, but today was different. Everyone in the family was here for the ceremony.

Their mother, Kathryn Brigham, sat by herself at a lunch table by the window, chewing on some chinook jerky. She offered me a piece—maybe I'd want to buy a few bags for the road, she suggested. Air-dried and leathery, the way it would have been generations ago, the preserved meat was updated with spicy chili peppers. "It has some kick," she said approvingly, smacking her lips. The commerce of salmon was nothing new to her, even if ceremonial and subsistence fishing came first. "When my mom was alive, she'd trade salmon for vegetables and canned foods. People come down to the river and they give you a box of apples or a box of cherries." The fish have a higher purpose, though, she said. The commercial part comes later, when enough salmon have been put away for the year and the many spiritual rites performed, like the First Foods ceremony in April. Though the tribes mostly use modern methods these days—motorboats and gill nets—there are still plenty of traditional fisheries up and down the Columbia and on suitable tributaries such as the Klickitat, where the river people gather to net salmon in a roaring basalt slot canyon that's nearly narrow enough in spots to jump across. "Our goal is to keep those scaffolds open," she added, referring to the scaffolds that hang over the Columbia in a few places where Indians can work a dip net in the old way. About 15 percent of the salmon in the store came from the scaffolds, the rest from gillnetting.

Kat, as she's called, is a well-known figure in the Confederated Tribes of the Umatilla, a union of the Cayuse, Walla Walla, and Umatilla tribes. That day she wore tinted glasses and a necklace of dentalium shells of the sort that would have been especially valuable as a trade item for her ancestors. She knows a lot about the fishery because she's served as chair of the Columbia River Inter-Tribal Fish Commission three times. Not everyone appreciates a woman in a high position, she admitted. "When my husband first started fishing, it was considered bad luck for a woman to be fishing and touching the gear. The men would give you a look."

"I still get that look," her daughter said. Broad-shouldered and wearing a football jersey, Terrie Brigham looked capable of handling any sidelong glances.

Kat Brigham is Cayuse, her husband Walla Walla. Like most Native Americans living along the Columbia, the family has always fished. There was a time, though, when the fishing life seemed in doubt. The Columbia's salmon runs had plummeted, and the Umatilla River, a tributary that ran through the tribal reservation near Pendleton, Oregon, was entirely barren of salmon by the 1920s. While the reasons for the decline are many and complex, everyone knows the crux of it is the massive hydro complex that transformed the river and the region in the twentieth century. As the river's traditional resource diminished, competition increased. Brigham experienced firsthand the wrath of white fishermen during the Indian-rights movement of the sixties and seventies. "We used to leave our boats down at the marina, but non-Indians would come down and sugar the tank, cut the cables. To this day my husband always brings his boat home." She remembered other insults from that time. Their Boston Whaler was shot full of holes. At a sit-in in Portland, a white woman shoved her. "I was gonna take her on, but my husband drug me out of there." One event she didn't remember, perhaps the biggest insult of all, was the flooding of Celilo Falls by the Dalles Dam in 1957. "I'm glad I didn't see it," she said. She was a little girl at the time. As Native Americans on the banks wept at the sight of the rising water submerging one of their most sacred sites, her parents took her away to higher ground, away from the river. In 1987 she brought her own children to Bonneville Dam's fiftieth anniversary, to witness the pomp and ceremony.

"Is that when you made us protest?" Campbell interrupted from behind the counter. All three women broke into peals of laughter.

"Yes, and when they had the seventy-fifth anniversary they made sure to invite us."

"Back then we thought we could change everything and make it better," Terrie Brigham said of the dams. By *we* she really meant the newcomers, the white people; they were the ones who looked at the river and saw something different, something better, that didn't involve salmon and fishing. "I hope we've become a little more humble. We can't make anything better than what nature has already put out there." Her mother nodded. Kat Brigham didn't expect to see any of the Columbia River dams taken down in her lifetime. "We'd like to see the dam operations change, though," she said. This included spilling more water in the spring and summer months to aid young fish migrating to the ocean, something that the Bonneville Power Administration is reluctant to do unless forced by lawsuits.

The battles their mother fought, Campbell said, were a far cry from their new problems—good problems. Now they have a business to run. Product to move in and out. Debt payments to make. They're part of the American market economy. Terrie Brigham, for one, didn't think it was useful to read too much symbolism into this. Columbia River Indians have been participating in the Euro-American market economy for a century and a half. They charged Oregon Trail emigrants to portage their boats and belongings around the Cascade Rapids. They sold salmon to the first canneries. It wasn't as if capitalism was considered a dirty word. Could the salmon survive in a market system? All of them thought so, as long as there were hatcheries.

OUTSIDE, NEXT TO A half-finished fire pit, family friends moved picnic tables aside for the ceremony, as more people arrived and curious bystanders came off the street. From my position I could catch a glimpse of the river. Beyond it in the distance rose the broad escarpment of Table Mountain, its sheer red-rock face the remnant of a fifteenth-century landslide that cleaved off the south flank and swept much of it across the Columbia. The natural dam that remained backed up the river for miles and formed what Native American lore called the original Bridge of the Gods, a story confirmed by modern geology. Indian legends tell of fair maidens, jealous rivalries, and the wrath of vengeful kings—stories that tried to make sense of the erupting volcanoes, landslides, floods, and other natural phenomena that once framed their lives. When the river finally broke through the Bridge of the Gods to reclaim its channel, it scattered boulders downstream like a broom sweeping away a pile of dust, creating the Cascade Rapids, at one time one of the most desirable fishing sites in the gorge. Though Bonneville Dam destroyed the Cascade Rapids, many of the river people, the Brighams included, continued to fish traditional sites in the area that had been handed down for generations.

A dark-skinned middle-aged man wearing braided pigtails and a salmon-colored dress shirt asked everyone to put away their cameras and segregate by gender. Behind him stood four drummers. "Today we come here to show our hearts to our creator," he began. "As Indian people we try our best to follow examples of the people before us. This belief was given to us way before the white man came here." He explained that today the assembled would sing three songs—one for the body, one for the heart, and one for life—to bless this ground, this new building, and the family that owned it. He rang a bell and the drumming began.

From my place among the men, I watched the Columbia below while listening to the percussive rhythms of the drummers. It was hard to believe the river wasn't always flat and nearly featureless, and picturing it roaring through a rock garden of its own making took effort. I tried to imagine the legendary watercourse as Lewis and Clark had seen it: a mile-wide beast raging toward the ocean, a wild river like no other. Wouldn't it be something to see that again? But such a fantasy is probably a minority position today. The river, such as it is, *rolls on,* in the words of Woody Guthrie.

Chanting voices and drumbeats brought me back to the little parking lot high above the south bank, where a Native American family was busy making history of a sort. When the three songs were over, the pigtailed man addressed the crowd again. "Our old people have told us this land was created first. The land spoke and said, 'I have prepared myself for the Indian people. I will take care of them.' This is what the land spoke when time was new."

Hearing these words and looking across the gorge, at the mountains and the river that parted them, at a rock face suddenly and irrevocably created several hundred years ago and still visible today—even if the results of its formation, the Bridge of the Gods and the Cascade Rapids, were now buried beneath Bonneville Pool—I felt myself fall into a sort of vertigo, a feeling of tumbling through time. The speaker told of the creation of man and woman, how the salmon came next. "Today we honor the salmon as sacred to our religion, to our language, to our tradition and custom. This is what our old people have taught us. Since time was new, salmon has been a part of our life, and today the salmon is still part of our life." Boys played a game of pebbles in the dirt as he spoke. A man in work boots and a flowery vest came over and told them to knock it off. The sun continued to rise high above the river on this, the longest day of the year, and I heard the ringing of another bell. Brigham Fish Market, the first Native American brick-and-mortar fish market in the Columbia River Gorge, a place where people have been fishing for ten thousand years, had been blessed.

AFTER THE CEREMONY, still feeling the odd sensory confusion of centuries condensed into a droplet of time, I walked on slightly unsteady legs down to the former locks to take a closer look at the river. This stretch was one of the first to be transformed by American industrialists. Lewis and Clark portaged around the Cascade Rapids in 1805, calling it the "Great Shute," with water "foaming & boiling in a most horrible manner." It was an equally treacherous passage for steamships trying to move goods and people upriver and down. The locks were started in 1878, finished nearly twenty years later in 1896, and became obsolete with the completion of Bonneville Dam in 1938.

Today a museum and park mark the site, with a concrete-lined channel where Kim Brigham Campbell's fifteen-year-old son, Brigham, was fishing from a traditional Indian platform suspended from a stone retaining wall. He figured he'd been fishing since he was six or seven. The scaffolding that supported him hung over the river, connected by high-tension cables. With one hand gripping a long pole, he sank a net ten feet down, while his other hand held a line tied to the back of the mesh. "Sometimes on the pole I get a little tweak sideways or it'll shake a little bit," he explained of the technique. "But mostly I feel it on the string." And just like that, he pulled up on the line and hauled in his net. Several shad thrashed in the mesh, their large silver scales lighting up like strobes in the sun. He dumped them in a bucket and continued to fish. Earlier that morning he had caught a seven-pound steelhead. Sockeye are harder to catch. "It's lucky to get just one. Two is really good. My mom got two yesterday." Spring chinook require extra vigilance; otherwise, they can do damage. "Your pole shakes. You've got to get it up fast. If it gets its head down and shakes, it'll break the net." The steelhead and sockeye were all filleted and sold in the market. The shad got pulverized into fish cakes or sold as bait to sturgeon fishermen, who fished for the prehistoric-looking bottom-feeders in the deep pools behind the dams.

Everyone in Brigham's family fished. For his grandparents, the fishing life had been fraught with problems for many years. As the era of big-dam building came to a close, a pair of landmark court cases re-invigorated Native American salmon fisheries. The 1969 Belloni and 1974 Boldt decisions clarified language stretching all the way back to the original treaties of the 1850s, which guaranteed the tribes' fishing rights at "all usual and accustomed grounds and stations . . . in common with all citizens of the Territory." Consequently, the tribes in Washington State and along the Columbia River can once again fish at their traditional sites—and perhaps more significant, as a result of linguists unpacking the nineteenth-century terminology "in common with," they get half the total catch, with the other half split between non-Indian recreational and commercial fishermen. Years of acrimony and general lawlessness followed these decisions. White fishermen protested, and state officials allowed a free-for-all flouting of fisheries regulations to go on in Puget Sound and elsewhere, prompting the U.S. Circuit Court of Appeals to call Washington State's role in the controversy "among the most concerted official and private efforts to frustrate a decree of a federal court witnessed in this century."

Now the tribes work with state and federal fisheries officials to manage the harvest. The early years of co-management were difficult. The tribes didn't have any scientists. The white technicians laughed, Kat Brigham recalled, when a tribal elder said the salmon were coming because the dogwoods were blooming. "How tribal people saw the world was not technical. It was based on Mother Nature's signs. The non-Indians didn't see it that way. Rather than try to understand it, they made fun of it." Undeterred, she joined a tribal fish-and-wildlife committee and began meeting with state fisheries managers. "I used to drive my grandfather and father-in-law to meetings." They had to make their way through crowds of angry people carrying signs that said BELLONI IS FULL OF BOLOGNA and SAVE A SALMON, CAN AN INDIAN. Brigham remembered meeting a sport angler who said he'd rather have zero fish than share the catch with Indians. The comment made me think of white anglers I've met through the years who think nothing of maligning Indians for their fishing rights, anglers who would never utter disparaging words about African Americans or Asian Americans—"That's racist"—yet somehow feel that the first Americans do not deserve the same consideration.

In recent years, to ensure an adequate supply of ceremonial and subsistence fish, the four main treaty tribes along the Columbia—the Yakama, Umatilla, Warm Springs, and Nez Perce—have actively pursued a strategy of building salmon hatcheries, much to the chagrin of environmentalists. This is one of the central ironies on the Columbia River. One might think the tribes and environmentalists would be natural allies, but it hasn't turned out that way. "We work with the environmentalists, but at the same time we're not environmentalists," Brigham told me. "Because of the dams, these hatcheries have to mitigate for the losses. There will always be a need for hatcheries. As tribal leaders we're willing to sit down and talk, but always in the back pocket is that treaty right. We stand on our treaty right. If we don't, our kids' children and their children won't be able to fish."

Listening to her, I was reminded of an environmentalist I had met recently, a biologist by training who, I suspect, loves salmon just as much as Kat Brigham does, but for different reasons. When I asked her opinion of Kathryn Brigham at a fundraiser, she smiled enigmatically, drained her vodka martini in a single gulp, and composed herself. "Kat Brigham," she said finally, "has been a very strong leader for her people." With that, she looked at her empty glass and excused herself to the bar.

WALKING TO MY CAR to head home, I passed beneath the man-made Bridge of the Gods one more time, where a small bazaar of Indian goods was for sale in its shadow. A gaunt, toothless man who said he'd driven over from the Warm Springs reservation had an eight-pound steelhead for $7 a pound. I told him I'd already bought some salmon at the market. "That's okay, I know those people," he said. His Bonneville scaffold a few miles downriver was next to a Brigham scaffold. "They're good people. I've watched their kids grow up."

Nearby, in the shade of a canopy, a Yakama man with a long ponytail jumped out of his beach chair to show me what a June hog looked like. He threw open his big Igloo cooler and grabbed by the gill the lone fish that lay in its ice bed, hoisting it up with tensed biceps. "This is the real deal." It was an impressive fish, maybe twenty pounds, lustrous with just a hint of rose beginning to show underneath, and deep in the belly, just the way Kevin Davis likes them. Historically, the June hogs, as they were called by white settlers, were summer chinook bound for the highest headwater tributaries of the Columbia, sometimes as far as a thousand miles upriver from the ocean, all the way into Canada. At Kettle Falls, whose Salish name means "noisy waters," Native Americans from many different tribes would catch the hogs in baskets lowered into the boiling river, an ancient fishery erased by Grand Coulee Dam. Like the spring chinook that preceded them, the hogs were known for having high fat concentrations to see them through a long migration and many months in fresh water without feeding. They were also known for being exceptionally large. Fish of fifty pounds were common, and tales of June hogs tipping the scales at a hundred pounds were not unknown. I'd seen black-and-white pictures: white men predating the dam era, dressed in their finest dinner suits and standing next to a salmon as tall as themselves dangling from a hoist. As far as I knew, I'd never tasted one. Most people hadn't. Grand Coulee snuffed out the run of June hogs, and even though many anglers swear there are still a few to be found below the dam, fisheries biologists question whether the strain that gave rise to these tremendous fish is still in the gene pool. Hatcheries on the upper river tried to maintain the stock, but their efforts came to naught.

I looked the fish over. Experienced anglers say they can tell June hogs by sight. They have more girth than spring chinook, blunter faces. They're heavier overall for their size. A few are rumored to be hanging on in unnamed tributaries just downstream of Grand Coulee. This stocky salmon fit the bill. At $10 a pound, it was a $200 fish. I studied it more closely. The salmon had an adipose fin. A wild hog, possibly? It was easy to feel conflicted about the taking of a wild fish, especially one from a run that was veiled in such myth. But then I thought about it within the context of Native American fisheries and ten thousand years of salmon fishing—and I continued to think about it as I drove away, my wallet $180 short of a sale. That big fish stuck in my head. Exits went by, and each time I considered jamming on the brakes and turning around. I could find an ATM somewhere. . . .

Several miles west of Cascade Locks, my phone rang. "When a star explodes," the voice on the other end said, "one of the last things it does is expand exponentially at an astonishing rate, using up all the matter around it before collapsing back upon itself into a black hole." It was Rene Henery, my ecologist friend in California. He was calling from the road, on his way across the Sierras for a fisheries meeting with other scientists, wanting to hear about my trip to the gorge. "I think we're seeing the exploding star right now," he said, "and while collapse may be imminent, the dawn of recovery could also be right around the corner." Despite his work as an ecologist, which seemed to me to be an exercise in occupational depression, Rene was always trying to see the bright side of an otherwise dreary picture. "There are multiple paths," he liked to remind me. I told him I was wrestling with the tribal paradox in the Columbia Basin. Money, lots of it, was flowing into salmon restoration efforts, some of it considered dirty money. Conservationists were frustrated with the tribes for taking payouts from Bonneville Power in exchange for their silence on the hydro complex—the Fish Accords, as they were known. The amount was something like a billion dollars over ten years. "Selling out" was the expression I heard a lot.

"You know, that's funny to hear," Rene said, "because down here in California the Columbia restoration is being held up as a model for the future. Down here we're envious of all the money and resources the Northwest has in salmon recovery. We don't have any. The idea is simple: Make the resource extractors pay for salmon recovery. Make Big Ag and its federal enablers pay for it in California."

"A lot of people are upset," I said.

"Well, something that conservationists need to wrap their heads around," Rene continued, "is the connection between salmon and people. For thousands of years, Native Americans were the ultimate stewards of salmon populations. It may well be that we can't have salmon recovery without the recovery of indigenous cultures."

We said goodbye and I turned around. But instead of returning to Cascade Locks and the Bridge of the Gods, I took the exit for Bonneville Dam on a whim, driven by a feral dream, and followed the crowd of visitors. A greeter working the front desk at the interpretive center understood the main attraction. "You can see the turbines and generators and all that stuff later," he said to several of us as we came pushing through the front door, our faces full of intent. "First you want to take the elevator down to floor one." Floor one was the place to see the fish ladder.

As soon as the elevator doors opened, I heard the clamor. A group of tourists pressed their faces to the glass as chunky chinook salmon, dozens of them, moved silently through the ladder, a galaxy of bubbles rushing backward in the current. A few of the salmon sported fleshy adipose fins. "I'd like to have a couple of those in my truck," murmured a man in coveralls. Nearby, a docent spoke to a tour group, gushing about the latest forecasts. Columbia River fishermen had their hopes pinned on a very favorable estimate of returning salmon, she said, a "potentially historic run," in the words of state fisheries managers.

Well, historic since 1938, at least. It was true that charitable ocean conditions were aligning to promote a larger return than usual, maybe a million fish or so. But it was unlikely that salmon runs on the Columbia would ever approach anything like the pre-dam numbers, even with all those hatchery fish and the ongoing habitat-restoration work by the tribes.

As the chinook passed through the viewing room of the fish ladder, I watched them closely, falling into a trance. Flash of scale, glimpse of dark beady eye. The form of persistence. They moved through, several at a time, a few falling back in the current to try again. Did the salmon recognize differences among themselves as they schooled? The presence or absence of a little nub of flesh we called an adipose fin? In the ladder, the wild fish and hatchery fish come together like children on a school bus, innocent of what lies ahead, but upriver the wild ones will bypass the hatchery facilities and disperse across a watershed larger than many European countries, each tributary giving rise to its own slightly distinct strain of chinook, many of those strains now extinct. Some of these fish might even be the last holdouts in their particular stream, receptacles of rare DNA that might disappear entirely if they fail to spawn. Their ancestors survived countless generations—through flood, fire, and ice—in part because of all that genetic diversity. Diversity made them stronger. At one time, king salmon pushed as far upriver as northern Nevada. Now their spawning grounds in the Columbia Basin had been reduced by half, in less than a century. The man in coveralls went up to the docent. "Seriously, where can I get one of those?"

"The Bridge of the Gods," she told him, a hint of skepticism in her voice. "You can get one under the Bridge of the Gods, if you really want to."

CHAPTER 5

OF ZOMBIES AND STRONGHOLDS

Guido Rahr doesn't hate hatchery salmon. Not completely. He'll admit they have their role in a landscape overrun by civilization. But Guido, who pronounces his name *Gee-doh,* with a hard *g* like *guitar,* is devoted to wild fish, and in this way he is just the sort of environmental activist who is at loggerheads with Kat Brigham. Youthful at fifty-four, with tousled blond hair and a winning ability to laugh at both himself and the absurdities of salmon politics, Guido knows the Columbia Basin won't be losing its dams or hatcheries anytime soon, so he has washed his hands of the greatest salmon river of the past to focus on the rivers of the future—the smaller, lesser-known reaches where a wild salmon might find a gravel bed to lay its eggs, far removed from the schemes of humanity. Such watersheds still exist on the Kamchatka Peninsula in Russia, for instance, and even here on the Oregon Coast, where we were presently navigating the serpentine bends of an estuary in a small johnboat, puttering to one of his secret spots.

Guido Rahr is first and foremost a fisherman. "If you tell anyone about this," he cautioned, "just say a North Coast river. Nothing specific." Like prized mushroom patches, his fishing holes are the result of determination and detective work, adding up to a cache of streams *whose names shall not be spoken*. It helps that, as the president and main architect of the Wild Salmon Center, a nonprofit based in Portland that has worked to protect more than eight million acres and ten thousand river miles of Pacific salmon habitat in both North America and Asia, he enjoys privileged information about where and when these fish might be lurking. And though Guido is as wily as they come as an angler, he likes to think of his professional presentation in boardrooms and fundraising banquet halls as totally aboveboard. "I'm not tricky," he stressed to me. "My style is open and transparent. I'm not organized enough to be anything but candid. The first rule about running an organization like the Wild Salmon Center is to find someone else who can help run an organization." Guido has several of these people, including scientists, researchers, and policy wonks, who do the running, which gives him the time to strategize on two continents—and take well-heeled potential donors fly-fishing when time allows. Today's trip with me wouldn't add anything to WSC's coffers. It was more like a vacation.

The water, greenish and slightly opaque from recent rain, was more unassuming than I expected. These coastal rivers don't have far to go to reach the sea. From mountain source to lower estuary might be thirty miles or less. To cross them on Highway 101 is to pass sluggish, blackberry-choked sloughs in the blink of an eye. But closer to the salt they spread out and meander through tidewater—the place to drop a crab pot or reach for your birding binoculars. After anchoring the boat, Guido pulled out an assortment of large fly boxes. One fell from his threadbare tackle bag with a thud, revealing a hundred identical flies inside; all of them were chartreuse and tied to look like a small baitfish, a pattern known to fly anglers as a Clouser Minnow, after its inventor. "I like to find something that works and stick with it," he said, laughing abashedly. A second box had another hundred identical flies, carefully aligned in rows, only red. He called those Red Devils. After taking a glance upriver and then down, and then up at the sky (which was clear), Rahr made a decision. "Try one of these," he advised, plucking a sparsely dressed chartreuse fly out of a box and passing it to me.

While I tied on the fly, he explained the rules. These were almost certainly all wild fish. Females would be released, should we be lucky enough to catch any, because they had eggs. Males over fifteen pounds would also be released, because they were big, and chinook have been steadily shrinking in size for the past century and a half from intensive commercial harvest that selects for the largest fish. "And smaller bucks?" I asked. It's a judgment call, Guido said. "I'm not doctrinaire. We can keep a small male if we feel like it when the time comes, if the Pleistocene hunter-gatherer in us is up for it. Let's see what happens. A fifteen-pound chrome-bright buck eats as well on the plate as anything that swims."

Guido took the rod from my grip and stripped several yards of line off the reel in quick bursts, checking the drag tension. The coils settled about his feet in the bottom of the boat. He handed the fly rod back to me, a stout 10-weight. "These are powerful fish. You can't pussyfoot around." We were anchored beneath an overhanging tree, with little room for a back cast. He told me to roll-cast downstream and not worry about the presentation. Chinook are notorious bottom-huggers. The trick is to fish deep without getting snagged up on a rock or root wad—and to find a willing fish. If salmon are difficult to hook once they enter fresh water, they're especially difficult to hook on a fly. Flies tend to rise in the current even when they're attached to sinking lines, passing over the recalcitrant fish. But occasionally a chinook will chase a fly out of instinct or territorial aggression. To improve my chances, I had a thirty-foot head of fast-sinking line to get the fly down. Everything about the setup—the fly, the line, the downstream presentation, the retrieve—had been puzzled out by Rahr and his companions over the course of many years of fly-fishing Oregon's coastal streams for big wild kings. While the average guy hoping to stack salmon fillets in his freezer trolls cut-plug herring or drifts gobs of smelly roe through a hole, Rahr and his friends have figured out

how to catch kings on a fly, a pursuit that most anglers consider quix-
otic at best. This sort of fishing isn't a numbers game. The satisfaction
comes from that one fish outwitted by a likeness of nature, using an
ancient technique refined over centuries.

With Guido's counsel in mind, I roll-cast my fly downstream, raising my rod tip just high enough for it to flex forward without tangling
in the branches behind me. The graphite rod's surprising force sent a
rip curl of line unfurling across the water. I gave it several seconds to
sink and then started slowly stripping it back toward the boat, my
fingers nervously registering every little twinge on the line that might
be a big fish nipping at my fly.

EARLIER THAT MORNING, Rahr and I had crossed the Coast Range
from Portland to Tillamook Bay in his Land Cruiser. On the far side
of a squirrelly mountain pass, we caught our first glimpses of what
would become the river. It was just a headwater creek at this point in
its journey to the sea—small, dark, and mysterious, dodging in and
out beneath a soaring canopy of conifers that rose like a green wall on
either side of the winding two-lane blacktop. Guido pointed out old-
growth Sitka spruces looming over the road. The "beauty strip" of
unlogged trees gave way to reasonably large second-growth forest
that marched down the hillside into a ravine, where it gave adequate
shade to the salmon-bearing stream percolating below. Yes, most of
the forest in this corner of the coastal mountains had been cut, but it
had also been given a chance to recover, and now it was part of a functional ecosystem. This was why Rahr's organization had staked its
hopes on the Oregon Coast. Though heavily logged in the past, this
swath of territory, which runs more than two hundred miles from
north to south along the left-hand margin of the state, differs mark-
edly from places like Puget Sound and the Willamette Valley in a couple of salient ways: a lack of people and a smaller hatchery footprint.
Urban development is confined to a narrow strip along the ocean
beaches, with Newport the largest city north of Coos Bay at ten thou-

sand people. At the other end of the watershed—the mountain head-waters, twenty or more miles inland—the landscape is only affected by timber harvest. And while there are salmon hatcheries on some of the rivers, other coastal rivers have little or no hatchery presence. For Rahr, the success of wild salmon in this part of the world depends on limiting the influence of hatcheries and promoting the influence of healthy forests.

In his twenties, when he was taking a crash course in Pacific North-west salmon and steelhead, Guido would drive the same route on a Friday night after work and sleep on the dusty floor of a dilapidated Tillamook Bay bait shop so he could get up before first light and catch the dawn bite. The bait shop is gone now, burned to the ground, but the memory of that cold floor lingers. "I did a lot of crazy stuff in my youth," he said, as we surveyed the bare foundation of his former crash pad from the road. The river flowed beyond it, larger now and more purposeful. Looking at him—this married father of three, in scholarly spectacles that hardly diminished the boyishness of his features—I wondered how far away that youth and those crazy times really were. Guido took one more look and stepped on the gas. "That's where I learned how to fish for coastal steelhead and salmon, down there with all the curing bait. It stank. I was just a fishing bum for a while. That's how you learn. Locals were skeptical about the fly-fishing thing for salmon, that's for sure. They still are." He'd had a fishing show in college, on local cable TV, called *On the Fly*. With typical self-effacement, he described it as "pretty primitive stuff, one long take of me standing there wearing a khaki shirt with a fly-tying vise. 'Today we're tying a Woolly Bugger' or whatever." Later he be-came a reporter for the ten o'clock news, doing little outdoor features. Guido enjoyed poking fun at himself. It wasn't hard for me to picture some big-shot captain of industry, whiskey flask tucked into his wad-ers, taking a shine to him out on the stream and handing over a small chunk of the family fortune to the Wild Salmon Center after Rahr got him into his first chinook on a fly.

A few miles down the road, near tidewater, we stopped to look at the river again from an abandoned lot near a convenience store that advertised ICE on its large faded sign. Dark green now, the river had gathered the strength of countless creeks and rivulets along its mountainous course, and it sauntered across the floodplain with the slower, more languid confidence of an elderly flâneur out for a morning constitutional. No sooner had we looked over the chain-link fence than a fish rolled in a lazy bend where trees leaned over the river as if to spy on the current's secrets. Rahr ran back to his car, begging me to hurry up. No boats! The hole was empty! We jumped in and took off once again. A couple more miles down the road, we crossed a plowed field where he had an agreement with the farmer. He backed his trailer down a rough launch, and in a few minutes we were motoring upstream toward the hole where we'd seen the fish roll.

Guido Rahr comes from a well-to-do Midwestern clan that made its money from beer—the family business is called Rahr Malting— though he's careful to point out that most of what was left for his generation of siblings and cousins was in the form of shared vacation homes rather than banknotes. In the past, this sort of lineage might have come with a rustic getaway lodge on a Canadian Atlantic salmon stream, in New Brunswick or Quebec, where angling is divided into "beats"—private sections of river that can only be fished by one or two anglers each day, and strictly on the fly. But Rahr had gone west instead, following the family's maternal line (his mother was from Portland), and fallen for Pacific salmon and public water (albeit keeping the slightly upscale trappings of the fly angler). His inclination to work for the family business was nil, and he hadn't forgotten the day his own father was called back to Minnesota to take up the reins, how heavily that decision had weighed on him.

As Guido fussed about in the boat, rigging up an assortment of rods and reels for our day on the water, I asked him if he'd ever eaten a wild Atlantic salmon. It was a question that surprised people, one they had to think about. Rahr was sure he had. He told me about some connected friends of his who owned a cottage on Quebec's Gaspé Peninsula, home of the Grand Cascapédia River, one of the most famous and storied Atlantic salmon rivers in the world. In 1995 he got an invitation to visit and managed to catch a very nice wild Atlantic salmon on a fly, which he released. A few of the other fish weren't so lucky. Their fillets were laid in rock salt and brown sugar overnight, then rinsed and bathed in Grand Marnier, after which they were cold-smoked in an old wooden smokehouse at eighty degrees, where they hung for forty-eight hours. Rahr closed his eyes. He could taste the smoked fillets. "They came out with a little bit of a crust, and oh my God. You thin-slice it and you just want to eat it by the handful. It was so good I only ate half a fillet and froze the other half. I thawed it out two years later and it was still amazing." At the time, having a bite of wild Atlantic salmon didn't seem like such a noteworthy event. But despite plenty of money and elbow grease, salmon populations on the East Coast and in Europe have not recovered. If anything, their age-old claim is as tenuous as ever.

Which brought us back to Pacific salmon. I stripped in my fly and cast it out again, trying for more distance. Guido said there might be thirty or forty wild chinook milling around in the deep pool below us. Such a gathering of native kings is a rarity in Oregon these days. No one wants to see the Pacific fish go the way of the Atlantics, yet the forces arrayed against them are basically the same, if only ramped up. "Starting at a hundred thousand feet," he said, speaking with the authority of someone who has given this speech before, even as he used his teeth to tighten knots, "we're seeing the steady erosion of wild salmon populations going from south to north, climbing up both sides of the Pacific Rim, just like they did along the Atlantic. What's driving it is global population going from seven to nine billion within fifty years. Even more of a threat is the emergence of two-plus billion people into the new middle class. They're going to have the same patterns of consumption and same expectations we have. If you look at available protein, fiber, and so on, within fifty years there just won't be enough to go around. The globe can't deliver. We're standing on a burning platform."

Like many successful environmentalists, Rahr has a knack for delivering bad news without judgment. The reasons for the pickle we're in are self-evident, and—let's face it—we all have a hand in it. "From a salmon's standpoint," he continued, "everything that's happening now is going to get a lot worse and start happening a lot faster: increased competition for water, increased competition for land—we'll see the steady fragmentation of timber and agricultural land and steady pressure on public lands—and also pressure on the fisheries themselves. And then you have the impacts of climate change. Tillamook Bay was almost seventy degrees this year in June. That's lethal for salmon. The places we're targeting are those we think have the best long-term chance of making it."

This requires money, he added, and money tends to follow the problems, not the opportunities. In many ways, the Endangered Species Act, though absolutely essential for environmental protection, is something of a hindrance when it comes to salmon conservation. "The ESA is driving policy. We're spending hundreds of millions of dollars in the Columbia Basin trying to restore wild salmon and I'm not optimistic it's going to succeed, in large part because no matter how much habitat restoration you do, if you can't get wild fish back into the system, it's not going to work." The problem, in a word, is hatcheries.

THE U.S. HATCHERY SYSTEM began as an act of Congress in 1871 and broke ground in California a year later, when Livingston Stone, a former Unitarian minister, began serving the new U.S. Fish Commission by building the first national hatchery on the McCloud River, a tributary of the Sacramento River snatched away from local Indians. (That same year Stone published his life's work, *Domesticated Trout: How to Breed and Grow Them.*) The hatchery location is telling. The Sacramento was one of the world's premier chinook nurseries before white settlement, but a mere two decades of gold mining had already taken its toll by the time Stone arrived, to such a degree that the original pioneers of the canning industry, Hapgood, Hume & Co., had decamped from the region for the Columbia River to the north in 1866. Stone's job was to restore the lost productivity, even if he couldn't reverse the decline of the river itself.

Born of ingenuity, sweat, and a spirit of exploration, the idea of making salmon was a product of its time. The root philosophy held so much promise: improve nature for the benefit of mankind. Fittingly, Stone's first shipment of salmon eggs went east on the fledgling trans-continental railroad, in an effort to prop up the failing salmon fisheries of New England with non-native Pacific salmon. The McCloud River hatchery tried to raise chinook but found more success with rainbow trout, and so began the export of that game and food fish all over the world. Nevertheless, the know-how to produce all species would come shortly, and before long a belief metastasized that you could mitigate any insults committed against a river and its fish by building a hatchery.

The key word is *mitigate*. They became known as mitigation hatcheries. Erect a dam? Build a mitigation hatchery. Clear-cut a forest? Build a mitigation hatchery. Dig an open-pit mine? Build a mitigation hatchery. Irrigate a river to death? Build a mitigation hatchery. Today one of these hatcheries is named after the country's original aquaculturist. The Livingston Stone National Fish Hatchery squats in the shadow of Shasta Dam near Redding, California. There, hatchery employees are busy keeping the Sacramento River's declining run of winter chinook on life support. Winter chinook are unique among Pacific salmon for a life history that involves migrating up the Sacramento in the winter months and then spawning in the heat of summer. This is possible because the Sacramento Basin once had tributaries fed by cold springs that kept the water temperature down. Shasta Dam (and Keswick Dam a few miles downriver) changed this. Now the winter chinook from those tributaries are all mixed together into a single population that spawns in the main stem of the Sacramento below the dams. Historically the population numbered about two hundred thousand returning adults; today it averages ten thousand, a 95 percent decline, mitigation hatchery and all.

The dawn of modernism has many symbolic markers: railroads, machine guns, abstract painting. Add to the list the fish hatchery. Though it has its roots in Roman times two millennia ago, and even in dynastic China a couple of thousand years before that, the hatchery as we know it today is a largely American invention of the Industrial Age that coincided, not coincidentally, with dam building, hydropower, large-scale irrigation, and the taming of the West. Fish didn't need a river and Americans didn't need nature. A notion emerged—and still survives today—that the environment could be plundered endlessly for profit, and all you needed to do was mitigate the damage with a hatchery. Just as the canneries moved north from the Sacramento to the Columbia, so too would the burgeoning hatchery effort. By the close of the twentieth century, the Columbia Basin, with more than four hundred dams large and small, would become the most hydroelectrically developed river system in the world—with the largest complex of fish hatcheries to show for it.

Most salmon hatcheries never fulfilled their promise and quietly got mothballed. Even those with some initial success required regular infusions of wild genetics to keep their stock from "wearing out," beginning a reckless cycle of sacrificing a wild run in order to preserve its hatchery replacement; that sad process was supported by politicians promising more fish to their constituents, compliant fish-and-game agencies, and university fisheries departments caught up in the lucrative hatchery schemes that funnel money in and graduate students out. The cycle continues today despite widespread condemnation from wild-fish advocates. It turns out that the life histories of salmon are much more complicated than Livingston Stone—or generations of his adherents—realized. A chinook from a coastal rainforest isn't the same as a chinook from the high-desert plateau. Though the same species, each possesses a site-specific set of adaptive genes that make it more fit for a certain sort of habitat or run timing. Even in the same river system, stocks from different tributaries have genetic makeups that give them an advantage in their particular niche. Hatcheries can't possibly address all this genetic variation. Meanwhile, with the advent and proliferation of hatcheries, the hereditary diversity that has made salmon such vigorous survivors up and down the Pacific Rim—through volcano, earthquake, and Ice Age, through drought and disease—is now dwindling, as stocks go extinct in little tributary after tributary, victims of dams, overfishing, and development. Even more alarming, scientists now know that the hatchery fish themselves are hastening the demise of the last wild holdouts. They compete with the wild fish for food and territory, and sometimes they even spawn with the wild fish, diluting their genetics in the process.

It's not an easy case to make, the case against hatcheries. Most people assume the hatcheries are saving salmon. My daughter came home from school one day with exciting news. The entire fifth grade got to skip classes and go on a field trip to a fish hatchery. They piled into a bus and drove east from Seattle across Lake Washington to the suburb of Issaquah, nestled in the Cascade foothills in the shadow of Cougar Mountain. There they visited the Issaquah Creek salmon hatchery. The hatchery has been operating since 1936. It was built to address depressed fish runs after the completion of the Lake Washington Ship Canal. But the fish runs continue to slide even as the hatchery pumps out more and more juvenile salmon. Some of the state biologists promoting the hatchery effort say they just can't understand why this is so.

"There was a big black bucket with more than two hundred fish in there," my daughter reported. She got a paper cup with two babies with very different personalities. One hardly moved. "He was shy." The other was active and tried to jump out of the cup. She walked down to a calm stretch of the creek, where the temperature was fifty-five degrees—ten degrees warmer than usual, someone said. One of her fish jumped out of the cup and made "a huge splash" and was gone. The other was reluctant to leave the cup. He finally swam out and he "just sat there." Then the shy salmon met another fry and they swam away together. She beamed with the telling. A happy ending.

What was I supposed to say to that? Explain to my daughter that this hatchery was promulgating a lie—that we can engineer salmon just the way we engineer our cities? In some ways, a hatchery is a kid's dream, the ultimate do-it-yourself science experiment. I have a friend, a grown-up, who has his own illegal hatchery. He's raising steelhead. The fry live in ponds on his property. Wires strung across the ponds discourage kingfishers, herons, and gulls. When the fry are ready to smolt—the process salmon go through to prepare for salt water, which includes changing into a new silvery set of clothes—they leave the safety of the ponds via a creek that flows through my friend's property and leads to the main river. Of the hundreds of fish that vacate his ponds, only a few make it back each year from travels at sea, as six-, seven-, even ten-pound adults. Imagining a steelhead of this size propelling itself up a tiny stream to reach its rearing pond is a thrill. Each summer, my friend wakes up one morning to find a small school of giant fish in his backyard. It isn't difficult to see why he's breaking the law.

Guido listened to my stories. He heard this sort of thing all the time. He understood the appeal of my friend's trout ponds, of the school field trip. Children are exposed to so little nature as it is; how can you possibly complain about a visit to a salmon hatchery? His critics like to cast him as a villain determined to take everyone's fun away, when in fact his opposition to the hatchery complex is more nuanced than that. But nuance is the first victim in today's contentious politics. If anything, Rahr is fighting for a compromise.

Today, just about everyone committed to the idea of wild fish wants to see the hatchery system overhauled. The exceptions are commercial fishermen, who can't make a living without the hatcheries, sport-fishing guides (same reason), and Native Americans, who depend on salmon for ceremonial and subsistence purposes. In San Francisco I met a commercial fisherman named Larry Collins, a community organizer who has advocated on behalf of beleaguered Bay Area fishermen for decades. On the issue of hatcheries he was clear: "Gotta have 'em." Without fishermen, the argument goes, Big Ag would claim all of California's water for itself, and Collins agreed. "When I started fishing, there were five thousand salmon boats in the state," he said while unloading bushels of Dungeness crab from one of the boats in his co-op. "That was in eighty-four. This last year there were nine hundred boats and only about half those fish. In thirty years we've lost ninety percent of the fleet. If you look at the amount of water taken out of the Sacramento–San Joaquin system and the amount of acreage of almonds and shit that's planted, it's a direct correlation. They've made a decision about what to use the water for. The farmers got it all and the fleet got fucked. Water is everything." For Collins, building hatcheries to pump out catchable salmon is a no-brainer.

The hatchery system, at its heart, was designed to give people fish to catch, not to save or enhance native fish populations. Hatchery fish behave differently from wild fish. Confinement teaches them to crowd together rather than spread through the system. They nip at one another and compete aggressively for food. Studies show that their bullying pushes wild fish out of the best habitat. Yet this aggression doesn't help them in the long run. Untutored in the ways of nature, they end up on predators' menus more often than their wild counterparts do. Whereas the shadow of an osprey or merganser passing over the surface will scatter wild salmon fry, the hatchery fish might mistake such cues for the hand that once fed them and swim right toward their fate. Because they survive at a lower rate, hatchery fish have to be produced in the millions. Certain genetic traits—or lack thereof—are even visible to the naked eye, the sort of traits that take thousands of years of evolution and local adaptation to show up. Hatchery steelhead, for instance, rarely exhibit the burly "shoulders" that characterize large male fish and presumably make them more attractive to female steelhead. They look like clones, all about the same size and shape in any given plant. Anglers sometimes call them zombies. When the zombies go feral and try to spawn with wild fish in the river, the result is a dilution of genetic variability in the offspring. Hatchery fish left to their own devices dwindle over time, each generation less fit than the previous one. So even in quality habitat, a run of hatchery salmon will require regular infusions of genetic material to remain viable.

As Rahr pointed out in an editorial for *The Oregonian,* the largest wildlife-restoration effort in world history has so far been a failure: "Despite the investment of $15 billion since 1978, no race of wild Columbia Basin salmon or steelhead has recovered enough to be removed from the federal endangered species list." Meanwhile, there are still wild runs that don't require anything more than a functioning river to keep coming back year after year, a remarkable gift from the sea. Why, he asked me, isn't there any investment to keep those runs healthy? "Every hospital has an emergency room, but that shouldn't be your first line of defense. If you really want to have salmon in a hundred years, you have to target strongholds, get in early, and prevent bad things from happening. It's easier to prevent a dam from being built than to tear one out."

The river we were fishing that morning was one of those strongholds. It had stable populations of wild salmon in a functioning ecosystem. The *stronghold* concept is a key part of what Rahr and the Wild Salmon Center are trying to do. "It's a concentration of abundance and diversity that's stronger than the surrounding population," he explained. There are global strongholds, such as the sockeye salmon of Bristol Bay, Alaska, and regional strongholds, like the salmon of the Tillamook. In both cases, the fish have access to a high-quality habitat. The Tillamook is interesting from a conservation point of view because in some ways it's a forgotten forest. Though parts were logged, large tracts of old growth burned in the early 1900s before they could be set upon by industrial timber harvest, and when the chain saws moved on, the forest was largely abandoned by the forces that would transform most of the Oregon Coast Range. Many believed that the fires had burned so hotly that dense woods would never return. It was during this period that Rahr's mother, in her Portland girlhood, helped reforesting efforts by planting hundreds of conifer seedlings. The efforts paid off and the burned areas, all told more than five hundred square miles, slowly recovered. Now the Tillamook is once again full of merchantable timber, the same sort of timber that provides good salmon habitat.

For more than a century, the forests of the Pacific Northwest were ruthlessly logged with little regard for salmon. Clear-cut logging dumped egg-smothering sediment into the rivers, and a lack of shade warmed the water beyond the fishes' thermal tolerance. Loggers built splash dams to transport timber; when the dams were dynamited, the resulting flood surge moved the cut logs downriver, scouring the streambed. Despite a fever pitch of work that transformed the great old-growth forests into tree farms in less than a century, the logging communities remained poor and rudderless. By the 1990s, with just small remnants of old growth left—less than 10 percent by most accounts, mainly in high-elevation wilderness preserves—the timber heyday came to a close, with the implementation of the Clinton Administration's Northwest Forest Plan and a call to action to revitalize communities in timber country with job retraining and environmental restoration. Even so, twenty years on, the timber interests are still crying out for more wood to cut. In Oregon, politicians on both sides of the aisle want to open the woods again to increased logging. Unlike Washington State, Oregon doesn't have Boeing, Microsoft, or Amazon. State legislators believe its well-being is still dependent on Old Economy resource extraction. Once again the Tillamook has been put on the chopping block. "It's like the 1950s," Rahr said. "To really understand what we're up against, you need to attend one of the state forestry meetings."

ROLL-CASTING THIRTY FEET OF heavy sink-tip line from underneath the branches of a fly-stealing oak tree was less than balletic, but after a few false starts I managed to get my fly out into the riffle, and the current did the rest of the work, pulling another thirty feet of line through the guides until my fly was deep in the hole several pool lengths away. Now I started to very slowly strip it back in. All at once the rod turned in my hand and I felt slack. Rahr pushed his glasses back on his face. "You need to lean into these fish," he said calmly. A few casts later and the rod jumped again. I lifted the rod tip to set the hook, then watched helplessly as line raced through the guides and the line went limp once more. "You *really* need to lean into them," he repeated a little more firmly. "These aren't normal fish."

Rahr first learned how to fly-fish for what he calls "monster chinook" in Alaska. "There's a place on the Kenai. They're giant, the biggest in the world. A few of the local guides were fly-fishing. They turned me on to it." After getting a tip from one of them, Guido watched the river more carefully. Every now and then a massive king rolled on the surface, showing its broad silver flanks—and, more to the point, revealing its lie. Guido would cast and let his fly swing through the salmon's holding water. "My fly came across and then stopped suddenly. I lifted my rod tip and lost the fish." He gave a little shudder, as if the loss was still painful. "The guides on the bank said, 'You idiot, what were you thinking? Don't do that. That's not how you set a hook in these kings. When the fly stops, you take two steps back and, with your whole body, you pound that hook. Pound it, pound it, pound it—until you think the rod's gonna break. That's how you set the hook in a big king.'" The next morning he went back down to the riverbank. A huge fish rolled right in front of him. He cast his fly across and felt it stop once again. "I took two steps back and went *wham*. I look at the rod and I hear this buzzing sound. All of a sudden, *boom!* The rod shatters just above the cork. It was like a gun going off. The tip slides down the line into the water and boinks the chinook right on the nose and the thing just explodes. It cartwheels out of the river and takes off on a screaming run. I've just got a reel. The rod's gone. The line's gone. The fish is gone. Everything's gone."

"You're saying I need to set the hook more forcefully? So the rod detonates?"

Guido took the rod from my grip and demonstrated on an imaginary fish. With the full force of his body, he nearly jumped out of the boat while yanking the rod back with both hands. The maneuver made him stumble over his tackle bag and we rocked dangerously, fly boxes scattering across our feet. "See what I mean?" he said, handing the rod back to me.

"I'll try not to flip us."

Guido reminisced about his Alaskan adventures as I got ready to cast again. Soon, I told him, I would have similar tales to tell. I was going to Cordova, the small fishing village that had made such a big name for itself with Copper River salmon. Guido suggested a few little-known streams where I might want to cast a line. The big state to our north, he agreed, was rightly a place of myth and yearning— yet even Alaska, he said gravely, was susceptible to the forces working against the wild. "And you don't have to go there to catch a monster king. You can do that right here." That's when I noticed a slight disturbance with my fly, a little *tic-tic-tic* that might have been some debris near the river bottom or possibly an annoyed chinook swiping at my fly. When I felt a distinct pull, I struck as savagely as I could without destroying the rod or swamping the boat. There was a long pause, during which I might have reflected on the high blue sky that morning, the wind whistling through my guides, white gulls wheeling in the distance. The boat dipped on one side, then the other. After what seemed an eternity, I felt the weight of a fish realizing it's hooked. It blasted across the river and went to the bottom with most of my line. Ten minutes later—which felt more like an hour—Guido helped me net a bright twenty-pound hen with a conspicuous adipose fin.

This was just the sort of fish that Rahr hoped to protect with his stronghold initiative. We took a photo and watched it slip from my hands and disappear back beneath the surface.

ON THE DRIVE BACK to Portland, Guido told me a story to illustrate how nuanced and also how acrimonious the salmon-conservation game has become. He views the hatchery system as the most pernicious obstacle in the way of restoring wild fish runs. Everyone is addicted to the hatcheries, he said, and it's easy to understand why elected officials from the Oregon Coast see it as politically expedient to whip up a frenzy in favor of more hatchery production. A feature documentary on hatchery fish was even made, with a bunch of talking heads from the fishing industry appearing in support of a system that directly benefits their own economic interests at the expense of wild fish—although they don't put it that way. Rahr went to opening night of the film at the Mission Theater in Portland—in disguise, wearing a camo hat pulled low over his face, because it was hostile territory. Nevertheless, he was recognized and called out during a post-screening Q&A (he declined to engage at the time, something he now regrets).

It was in this climate that the Wild Salmon Center, working with the Oregon Department of Fish and Wildlife, managed to pull off the amazing feat of setting aside multiple watersheds up and down the Oregon Coast as wild fish refuges in 2014. As with most rules that get enacted in a state of polarized contentiousness, compromise was required of the WSC. In this case, they agreed to a boost in hatchery production on some rivers in exchange for no hatchery production on others. "The plan came out and some of the local legislators went crazy. 'This is an attack on hatcheries. Blah blah blah.'" When it came time to go to the mat for the compromise, Rahr contacted his allies at other fish-conservation organizations, asking them to play ball. He told them he wanted to create the largest wild fish preserve south of British Columbia but would allow for some hatchery production, and he asked for their support. The other groups balked. "They couldn't help themselves," he told me. "When they saw the increased hatchery production on certain rivers, they attacked the plan with both guns blazing. I was livid. But guess what happened? The coastal legislators, seeing that orgs like the Native Fish Society were attacking the plan, thought maybe this was a good thing after all. So they ended up supporting the plan and we got it passed. It's a microcosm of the crazy salmon politics."

The new salmon-management plan could be seen in action all around us. Half the rivers that flow out of Tillamook State Forest are now set aside for wild fish. The Nehalem, Salmonberry, Miami, and Kilchis are wild fish only. Only the Wilson River allows hatchery steelhead. A few rivers that already had hatchery salmon, such as the Trask and Nestucca, will see additional hatchery plants, but those without hatcheries will remain that way. "We did it," Guido said proudly. "We froze the hatchery program. It's the biggest network of wild fish rivers south of Canada."

———

ON A WET FRIDAY MORNING a few weeks later, I met Rahr in Salem, the state capital of Oregon, where he planned to testify at the Department of Forestry. "Look at this place," he said as we walked up the path. "They've built themselves a nice little clubhouse with all their timber dollars." Backing up on a creek that flows into the Willamette, with neatly trimmed grounds, the building reminded me of an English manor house. (Later, one of the administrators would joke that the department had been criticized for not using enough wood in its construction.) Inside the spacious conference room, sepia-toned portraits of Oregon's state foresters hang on the wall, dating back to Francis Elliott, the first. It happened that the Elliott State Forest, named in his honor, was on the agenda today. County commissioners wanted to sell off this ninety-three-thousand-acre parcel of public land, which still held a few rare patches of coastal old-growth timber, to the highest bidder. The Eugene *Register-Guard* called the move "embarrassingly shortsighted," noting that Oregon legislators were still "seeking ways to privatize public forests, all the while making archaic claims that more logging will create more prosperity. Neither history nor unbiased economic analysis supports their claims."

The first agenda item concerned the Tillamook State Forest and other state forests on the North Coast. The advisory panel, seated at tables in the center of the room, wanted to hear public comment on its plan to accelerate logging on state lands. The "70–30 plan," as it was known, would open 70 percent of the Tillamook and other North Coast forests to industrial logging while maintaining 30 percent for conservation purposes. The chair called on *Gwee-doh* to speak. "Did I say that correctly?" he said fatuously. Rahr corrected him and launched into his testimony. As he spoke of passing down a natural heritage to future generations, the county commissioners and foresters fidgeted and looked on indifferently, one even shaking his head. They all stood to benefit from logging every last stick out of the state's public lands, with the counties receiving two-thirds of the revenue and the Department of Forestry a third. Since the panel would recommend a plan to the Department of Forestry, this was an obvious conflict of interest, but it's how things are done in Oregon.

"In California the runs are collapsing," Rahr reminded the panel. "Willamette Valley runs are in trouble. The Columbia Basin is an absolute mess. Puget Sound is a mess. The Tillamook is this amazing little refuge where things are still working." Guido paused. Did he notice the bored looks on the faces before him? "The question for all of us is what we want this place to look like in the future. The region is changing. Portland will be twice the size in forty years. All the pressures, demands, and expectations are accelerating. People's expectations for the forest are changing. It's not just about how many timber dollars you can generate from this forest. It's about other things too. I want to see old-growth forest—giant old trees like my grandfather saw when he went fishing there. I want to know that my grandkids can come here to see that."

Guido looked up from a page of notebook paper that had the barest of scribbled notes. He pushed it aside. "Personally, as you know, I love this place. I've been fishing here my whole life. My family has been involved for generations. It's where I take my children. Floating down the Kilchis River in my little boat, the water so transparent it's like a pane of glass, with chinook circling underneath . . . No one in California has this chance anymore, no one on the East Coast. Seventy–thirty will take this away. I'm asking you: Make pragmatic decisions, but don't go to seventy–thirty. Let's work together to diversify revenue for the Department of Forestry. Let's end this long-running arm-wrestling match in this beautiful place. If we do these things, all of us can be proud about what we've left for the next generation."

Rahr's lieutenant, Bob Van Dyk, a former professor who had renounced tenure to be the Wild Salmon Center's technical arm, showed slides depicting the result of a 70–30 plan. Huge swaths of red— logged forest—stretched across acreage owned by Oregonians, with tiny little blips of green illustrating the protected tracts. Van Dyk had gone through the difficult and time-consuming process of accumulating all the data on proposed changes to timber management and then overlaid it on maps of the current management plan, which was closer to a 50–50 split between logging and conservation. The difference was stark. No one said anything, but he'd made his point. Defenders of the logging testified next, including a representative from Hampton Lumber. They spoke of *inventories, revenue, board feet,* and so on. You wouldn't know that a bunch of trees were involved, a forest. When the testimony was over, the chair polled county commissioners on the plan. One commissioner, from Clatsop County, was on the fence, but the others were vigorously in favor of the 70–30 plan and took the opportunity to discredit their opponents.

It was at this point that a curious interchange took place. At first I thought it was a joke, a bit of lighthearted theater. One of the county commissioners spoke disparagingly of "habitat," saying that when trees are allowed to get too big, they're under threat of being set aside for wildlife such as the secretive marbled murrelet, a small seabird whose life history had only recently been sleuthed out. Though they spend most of their lives at sea, diving for baitfish, the murrelets build moss nests during the breeding season on the stout limbs of old- growth trees along the coast. Such trees are harder and harder to find these days, and now some of the birds fly miles inland looking for suitable nesting grounds. As a result, marbled murrelets have declined precipitously with the clear-cutting of the Pacific Northwest. The commissioner warned his colleagues that leaving such trees as habitat was like having a cancer, and the cancer would spread. "We have age stands that are greater than sixty-five years old that are starting to come online since the original cut. This is millions and millions of dollars' worth of commercial timberland." Older stands like this, he suggested, were in jeopardy of being permanently protected. He called them the camel's nose under the tent.

The chair agreed. "What happens is, if you start creating old growth, it'll spread across the landscape, just the way it did in the Elliott."

"It's a disease that grows," his colleague reiterated. I was amazed. Had a couple of Oregon's county commissioners, including the chair of the forestry panel, just called old-growth forest a cancer? And then, in a bizarre bit of self-consciousness, perhaps guilt or shame, the chair raised his voice and pointed toward Rahr and Van Dyk, who were seated in the gallery. "We've been taken to task by the folks in the back of the room. I read their stuff—I hear what they say."

But the other county commissioner had worked himself into a lather. "Well, I don't care," he declared. "We're elected to represent the people. I have to be accountable to the people I see at the grocery store. There's a train wreck waiting to happen, and I don't want to see those revenues go." It was a foregone conclusion that this advisory panel would recommend increased logging in Tillamook State Forest—would recommend, in effect, a revenue increase for their own counties and the forestry department.

AFTER THE MEETING, on our way back to Portland, Rahr filled me in on one of the testifiers, an employee of Hampton Lumber. When he was a child, Guido was best friends with one of the Hampton kids. Now they were on opposing teams. Hampton Lumber had built a new mill next to the Tillamook State Forest with the expectation of having plenty of timber to cut. As in a high-stakes chess match, the Wild Salmon Center was making its own countermoves to ensure that as much forest as possible remained intact. It was right out of Ken Kesey's *Sometimes a Great Notion*. "Sometimes I go to these meetings and there's my old friend David Hampton." Guido sighed. "I grew up with David. We used to zoom down the hill together under the chair-lift at Mount Bachelor as ten-year-olds. He's a wonderful guy, but now there's this tension. He sees us as a huge obstacle."

The timber wars, the salmon wars—they take a huge toll. And the fighting today is over scraps. In the Pacific Northwest, most of the big trees are long gone. The salmon runs are a fraction of their former size. Nature's grandeur has been cut down. Guido shook his head, in sadness more than anger. "We'll be at this a long time. David Hampton is as committed as I am, and I'm going to fight this until I'm an old man. My kids are going to fight it." He was confident that a compromise could be worked out to conserve fisheries and still provide timber for the mills, but in the climate of constant acrimony that has spread across the country, the art of compromise is no longer seen as a skill. "Who knows," Guido said at last, "maybe it'll be my kids fighting his kids."

CHAPTER 6

LAST RUN OF THE
MIDNIGHT EXPRESS

WE LEFT THE HARBOR A LITTLE AFTER 6:00 A.M., THROTTLING up to join a line of boats heading toward the fishing grounds. It was late August and in the forties. I was a long way from the dams and mitigation hatcheries and busy highways of the Lower 48, as Alaskans often call the rest of the country. Behind us, the town of Cordova was waking up, lights flickering on, pickup trucks idling on steep streets. I could see a few dark silhouettes of people, maybe spouses, standing on the Reluctant Fisherman's outside deck in their Xtratuf boots, watching the exodus. The night before, I'd stood on that same deck at sunset, looking down on the harbor and having a beer with some of the fishermen I'd met in town. Michael Hand, wearing a Red Sox cap, and his wife, Nelly, were there, along with a friend of theirs from Texas who now made his living as a gillnetter. The seduction of Cordova is like that. A certain type of person can't resist it. Nestled snugly between water and mountains—with its own ski slope on the outskirts of town—Cordova fits the popular image of an Alaskan fishing village. It's one of those anachronisms still viable even as the rest of the world busies itself with fiber optics and cloud technology. The day before, I'd gone hiking with the Texan. He wore an enormous .44 on his hip, and I was glad for it. The grizzlies like the place too.

There's no road into Cordova—you arrive by either boat or plane. Snowcapped peaks of the Chugach Range surround the place like a fortress. For years there was talk of trying to connect this beachhead of two thousand year-round residents to Alaska's highway system, but the effort foundered. The most common bumper sticker in town expresses the sentiments of many in two simple words: No Road. I myself had flown in, arriving into Merle K. (Mudhole) Smith Airport, named after a legendary bush pilot who would become a director at Alaska Airlines. On the short drive to town I passed scores of anglers—some of them visiting sportsmen, others locals getting their annual allotment of salmon—and one moose.

I had come to Cordova to see where all those Copper River salmon that cause such a stir in Seattle came from and also because it's one of a handful of communities still around with an economy that revolves almost entirely around wild food—salmon, of course, and to a lesser extent recreational fishing and hunting, which keep a number of residents busy as guides. All the fishermen I know, recreational and commercial, talk about the magnetic pull of Alaska. You can't avoid it. At some point you have to go north. Guido Rahr, Jon Rowley, Kevin Davis—they all speak of the forty-ninth state the way some people talk about church. Rene Henery yearned to organize a wilderness float trip with a bunch of his biologist friends and spend a couple of weeks rafting a remote river from headwaters to salt, recalibrating his own shifted baseline. This was a dream for him, a fisheries ecologist who had never seen a properly functioning river ecosystem. Few have. Alaska is the last place in America where you can get into real wilderness, see nature the way it existed before white settlement.

To someone like Micah Ess, who was steering us toward the fishing grounds, the place means a chance at a livelihood that isn't circumscribed by pavement, glass, or cubicles. But even here, the creature comforts of modernity exert their centripetal tug. He checked his cell phone for email messages and tossed it back on the dash. "These have made the job safer, no doubt," he said, almost apologetically. Commercial fishing has a reputation for danger, as hyped on reality TV.

But for plenty of born-and-bred Northwesterners I know, the Alaskan salmon fishery was just another summer job, an exciting and lucrative one to be sure, provided you didn't get stuck on the slime line, cleaning fish. When I think about my own summer jobs as a teenager on the East Coast—caddying at a local country club comes to mind—there's no comparison, except that maybe both involve the outdoors, one on freshly mowed fairways and the other on the remorseless ocean. Every now and then a kid falls overboard or loses a hand in some infernal contraption designed to guillotine fish heads. Those are the stories Martha remembers. She knows I'll suggest Alaska when it's time to ship our son off somewhere to make some college tuition, and I'll probably have to put him on the night flight to Cordova while she's asleep.

I ate a Dramamine and washed it down with coffee. Though the weather forecast was for clear skies and sun, with calm seas, I didn't want to take any chances. Ess fiddled with a hunting knife. Fishing was almost over for the year, and his mind was elsewhere. He'd already earned his keep from the sockeye run. Now he was fishing for silvers, the last of the five species of Pacific salmon to spawn in the Copper River region, but there wasn't much money to be made this late in the season. He was earning little more than a dollar a pound for the silvers—less than half the price paid for sockeye. Soon he would put the boat, a twenty-eight-foot bowpicker, to bed for the winter and rejoin his wife in Colorado. And then next year, if everything went according to plan, the *Midnight Express* would be someone else's and he'd have a shiny new boat. Or, more likely, a shiny used one.

The bowpicker is the boat of choice for Cordovan gillnetters. First designed for the Columbia River fishery, it's built to fish its net from the front. The fisherman stands in the bow, picking fish, while a hydraulic reel the size of a fifty-gallon drum gathers up net. Today's bowpickers are a far cry from the early days of the Columbia's commercial fishery, when gillnetters powered open boats by oar and sometimes with makeshift sails, pulling in their nets by hand. Modern bowpickers have a pilothouse in the stern for shelter, usually with an oil cookstove that doubles as a heating source, and a couple of bunks. Seeing the procession of boats that morning—a long line of them lit by running lights—reminded me of a muscle-car rally. All hood, with horsepower that put you in the back of your seat. Bowpickers had to be tough to perform in a place like this.

"The morning commute!" Ess said brightly, with a sardonic grin that said he'd spent enough time in the Lower 48 to know the difference. He gripped his coffee in a yellow enamel camp mug and ate a donut. Uncombed brown hair poked out from beneath his ball cap, and he pushed it out of his eyes. Short and trim, he looked younger than his mid-thirties, with sharp, almost elfin features and a wispy beard. Another boat paralleled us across the channel, off our port side. "That's an angry little boat," Ess said, refusing to make eye contact with its captain. He had words for the man. *Gruff. Uncivil.* "I was gonna squeeze him a little bit, but you can't go there. We went toe-to-toe at the board meeting the other day." The meeting was for fishermen who were trying to work together to keep their livelihood prosperous in a time of increasing mechanization and competition. This sort of collaboration had already helped to make Copper River salmon the most recognized wild salmon in the world. The fishery had come a long way since Jon Rowley first approached a few gillnetters with his ideas about bleeding and icing the catch for the fresh market. Now other wild salmon fisheries in Alaska were retooling in the same way. Ess said it was crucial for his fellow fishermen to work together.

The Cordovan fleet has gone through expansions and contractions through the years. Recently it's recovered from a slump spurred by farmed salmon in the nineties. With consumer education and renewed market interest in wild salmon (and higher prices), the fleet is gearing up again—with bigger boats, bigger catches, more skin in the game. There are more than five hundred boats in the gill-net fleet, and each year the price to buy in increases. While Ess thought his fellow fishermen had done a good job of banding together to promote their fishery, there are always, in a place like this, the go-it-alone types who revere the "last frontier" narrative about Alaska and masculinity and what it means to work in the outdoors. To Ess, the captain of the boat across the channel represented a throwback of sorts—a guy who was resourceful and independent on the one hand yet had trouble with the basic skills of getting along with other people on the other. "He's just an asshole, is what he is," Ess said finally.

For many Americans, especially those on the West Coast, it's this rough-hewn, antediluvian aspect of the place that's most appealing. Alaska is the ace in the back pocket, the place to escape to when every-thing finally goes to hell elsewhere—politically, socially, economi-cally . . . environmentally. Just build a little cabin somewhere and live off the land. Alaska is essential to the American perception of itself. Without it, we're just another vote in the United Nations. I wondered how much of this is true. Certainly Alaska is still big and mostly empty, but is it as immune to the pressures of civilization as is gener-ally believed?

Bald eagles glowered from rock piles that stood up out of the water like haystacks. Ess called them pigeons. To our right was Hawkins Is-land. It rose steeply from the shore to dark, forested summits. Ess studied its contours as we passed. Hunting season was just around the corner. "That's the mountain I've been scouting," he said, pointing to a dark knob outlined against a purple sky. Whenever he went by Hawkins, he looked for deer. A pair of binoculars hung from a peg, but it was still too early to see much. He'd whittled down his target to a couple of large bucks that stayed high. "It's this time of year I look at the tops of those little mountains. I just love to get up into that high country. It's rocky, with ponds where the deer come down to drink, and all the trees are like bonsais because they're so windswept and close to the ground and gnarly. It feels like a fantasy world up there, a land of gnomes." On our left we passed a derelict clam cannery. Be-fore the salmon fishery, Cordova was known for its copper mines and its shellfish, razor clams in particular. The copper mines played out eventually, and the shellfish, I would learn, came to an abrupt, earth-shattering end. A line of green and red markers guided us through the channel, narrowing to less than a hundred feet wide. The depth was barely double-digit.

We passed a much larger boat, a tender, with booms sticking out like the arms of a scarecrow to operate hydraulic winches, which transfer and weigh the bowpickers' catch. It rocked gently at anchor, its lights still out. This was one of many tenders currently on the water to buy fish, most of them owned by large seafood processors like Trident and Ocean Beauty. Back in the harbor, the fishermen could also sell their catch directly to local land-based processors. At Copper River Seafoods, a huge workforce of mostly immigrants—Mexican, Filipino, Vietnamese, more than fifty of them in orange waders and white hard hats—brought the fish into the processing plant from containers via big vacuum tubes to a conveyor belt, where each salmon was headed, gutted, and graded before being shipped off to market. It's a bloody business, the slime line, with one employee continually hosing down the floor. There was even a room devoted to making ikura, the cured salmon roe beloved in Japan. The processors dictated the terms. Each fisherman had a relationship with a particular company, one based on time, experience, and loyalty. Usually all the buyers were fairly close on price, so other perks might make one more attractive than another, and some of the buyers enforced fidelity through loans that the fishermen had to pay off. Ess didn't want to put himself in that position, but next year, with a new, bigger boat, he might have no choice.

Ess radioed his half brother, Ashton, who was a quarter mile ahead of us. "How's it look?"

"*Wide open,*" crackled the voice on the other end of the two-way. Though younger, Ashton owned one of the nicest boats in the fleet, a large aluminum state-of-the-art bowpicker with big inboard jets that could muscle through some of the rougher water the flats routinely doled out. Ess laughed at himself. He'd put his money into a little farm in Colorado, where he and his wife had a peach orchard; his little brother had bought a nicer boat. Ess wasn't ready to decide which was the wiser choice.

Up ahead, the water boiled and sprayed and made a commotion as we approached a shallow bar that marked a psychological boundary of sorts between the protected inner coastline and the wide Gulf of Alaska. Ess told me to brace myself. "We'll shoot through a tiny gut between the beach and the breaker patch. Sometimes these waves can be six, seven, eight feet, and you need to be on your game so you don't get smashed in the side by one of them. It'll be exciting." Even though today's swells were only three feet, it still seemed slightly iffy. "If you add a little wind, they can get big quick." Ess throttled up and punched through a regiment of standing waves, crossing a turbulent stretch about the width of a football field, and that was it. We'd crossed the bar.

Following the southern shore of Hinchinbrook Island, we headed west. "This is a really powerful place for me," Ess said. He's seen grizzly cubs scampering along the beach in the past, and he considers the island's bear population to be one of the most ferocious anywhere because they'd adapted to hunting deer. "You've got to be careful packing out a kill from here. I carry a little chunk in a game bag that I can sling to the bears." Right now there was just a lone raven, jet black against bone-white sand, looking around mischievously. Bears, ravens, eagles, salmon. It's a land of totems. Virtually every living thing is freighted with myth and meaning. Ess repeated an old tale, the story of the Woman Who Married a Bear, which taught generations of Tlingit children to respect the bears that lived in the forest among them. He figured he was about one-eighth Native American—White Earth Ojibwe—from his mother's side of the family in Minnesota. "She came up here from the res when she was eighteen." Ess said she had decided to face the natural environment rather than an abusive relationship at home. Directly or indirectly, nature is the arbiter of all fates in a place like this.

═══════

ON GOOD FRIDAY, MARCH 27, 1964, the Pacific and North American tectonic plates collided. In what's known as a subduction-zone earthquake, the oceanic plate dove under the continental plate, causing a magnitude 9.2 "megathruster," with an epicenter seventy-five miles south of Anchorage. It was the strongest earthquake ever recorded in North America. It rumbled for four and a half minutes, and when the initial shock was over, solid ground from Anchorage to Kodiak Island had liquefied. Thirty people in the town of Valdez died when the ten-thousand-ton freighter S.S. *Chena* listed and destroyed the city docks. A tsunami swamped the native village of Chenega, killing another twenty-three. In Seward, an oil-tank field exploded in a ball of fire, incinerating twelve. Landslides rearranged the city of Anchorage, demolishing schools, toppling the airport's control tower, and obliterating some neighborhoods entirely. Buildings in Seattle swayed. Even Houston, Texas, hopped up for a moment. One source reported that for two weeks "the entire planet vibrated like a giant gong as the seismic waves circled the globe." In all, nearly 140 people lost their lives. Cordova, the self-proclaimed razor clam capital of the world, saw its waterfront upended. Tidal flats disappeared in an instant—and the shellfish economy with them.

Twenty-five years later, on another Good Friday, March 24, 1989, a different sort of environmental disaster struck, its effects still felt today. The *Exxon Valdez* ran aground in Prince William Sound to the northwest of Cordova and disgorged its cargo of crude oil. The tanker hit Bligh Reef (named after the ill-fated captain of the *Bounty*) with a hull filled with 55 million gallons of oil, spilling anywhere from 10 million to 32 million gallons, depending on which source you believe. This time the fishing economy of the region was even more devastated. Herring and shrimp fisheries vanished overnight in a plume of muck. For months, TV-news cameras flashed images of oil-soaked sea otters and blackened shorebirds; they were many Americans' introduction to the wild beauty of Alaska and its mighty oil industry. A quarter century later and oil still clings to beaches. "We had an Alas-kan dream, and that dream was intact for several thousands of years," an Eyak tribal member from Cordova told NPR on the twenty-fifth anniversary of the spill. "Our way of life and our Alaskan dream was stolen from us."

These are the twin events that shaped modern Cordova's fishing economy and undoubtedly its psyche. The first ended its renown as a shellfish producer, and the second threatened to take away everything else. Copper River salmon had not yet become a recognized brand name when the oil spilled. Micah Ess was a little boy at the time, living in Prince William Sound. His memory of the disaster, especially what would follow in its wake, was hazy. It was more of a feeling that he kept inside, the feeling that his place in the world could be taken away in an instant. He and Ashton were being homeschooled on a house-boat while their parents shrimped. "My dad had a big huge beard, long hair. He looked like the Creedence Clearwater Revival guy. My mom was totally hippied out. I was a little snot-nosed kid. Super patchy, woolly, old hand-me-down clothes. We were dirt-broke." There was no money in shrimp, and it was hard work. The family could barely live off their meager earnings. "When we went to town we'd shy away from people. We were homesteaders." Instead, Ess learned to love the wildlife that surrounded him. "I've got this great connection with the earth and animals. Humans are my sticking point." Shrimping ended with the oil spill. Ess and his brother left Alaska for college in Colorado, but neither could stay away. "My head was always out the window, in the trees. I have a hard time with the teacher–student relationship, probably because I'm a know-it-all and I don't take directions very well. I didn't handle the classroom politics. Plan B was staring me in the face. I could just go fishing." Now he was in business for himself as a gillnetter, married, and ready to start a family.

I suppose I imagined the populace of Cordova—of Alaska in gen-eral—to be mostly born-and-raised frontier folk, springing right out of the womb in flannel and side holsters. And it's true that the town can seem like a regression to simpler times, full of resourceful citizens living off the land and its bounty. But it's also full of seekers from all over the globe, armed mainly with a willingness to work hard and learn. Earlier that week I met a young woman named Blair, who had graduated from college in Seattle and was now working to promote the fishery. She arrived with fifty dollars in her jeans and pitched a tent at Hippie Cove, the free camping area just outside of town. Before signing on with the Copper River Marketing Association, she went to work for a hunting outfitter. By the end of the season Blair could dress a moose and make an excellent camp dinner with a freshly killed Dall sheep. Now, a year later, she had traded her tent for a house on the hill shared with a fisherman named Curly and a couple of other folks. Curly, with a sonorous voice that suggested a former radio career, had been fishing the area since 1968 and was eligible for Social Security, not that he wanted a government check. He lived half the year in Portland, Oregon, where his wife was a schoolteacher. In between salmon openings we went mushroom hunting together. He introduced me to the nagoonberry, a blackberry relative that grows close to the ground and has a tropical flavor that belies its tundralike habitat. Later that night Curly grilled up some of his home-pack salmon with a wild cranberry barbecue sauce. After dinner someone played a YouTube video of commercial sockeye fishing in Bristol Bay to the west, arguably the most famous salmon fishery on the planet, and we all gathered round, marveling at the proximity of the fishermen to one another in a little inlet jammed with boats. The intensive competition in Bristol Bay was not for them, though they admitted that tensions could mount on the Copper River flats too.

Curly's son, Alec, tall and lanky like his father, was also in town. I found him one afternoon mending a net on the docks. "This isn't what catches fish," he said, pointing to a fancy new bowpicker moored next to him. "This"—tying knots and fixing holes—"catches fish." Alec hadn't planned to be a gillnetter. "I got a degree in economics. I tried working in that world for about a year." This was a common refrain among many of the gillnetters. Then he taught English in Japan. "I wasn't outside all day long. That's when it clicked that my dad had it figured out. Part of the allure is being your own boss. You have your own boat. You fish when you want to fish. You're a business owner, running your own operation." When he told his mother, she had a look of complete and utter disappointment on her face. "She's coming around since I bought in with my own boat," he quickly added. His bowpicker was called the *Cheryl and I*. He bought it for twenty-five thousand dollars from a fisherman who'd named it after his ex-wife. "I had every intention of changing the name, but there's a lot of bad luck associated with changing boat names if you don't go about it the right way—if you're superstitious." Come wintertime, Alec teaches snowboarding in Girdwood, an hour east of Anchorage.

Dennis, another gillnetter, had also tried the straight and narrow. "I was going to college to be a mechanical engineer and realized I'd probably be wearing a tie, sitting behind a computer." The summer before his senior year he came up to Cordova and got on a boat. "Within two weeks of being here I fell totally in love. I went back, finished my degree, then came up the day after I graduated." Besides selling to the processors, Dennis was trying to market smoked salmon directly. Michael and Nelly Hand, whom I'd joined for sunset on the Reluctant Fisherman's deck, were trying to do the same thing, with a new business called Drifters Fish. You could make a lot more money selling direct, but it also required time to package and ship the salmon and even more time to market and build a clientele. Sometimes in the off-season Dennis ran a trapline. He also guided for moose, brown bears, and sheep. "This is a harsh country in the wintertime," he said. "Everything's looking for something to eat." Another gillnetter I had hoped to meet, a friend of Curly's, was in the hospital. She'd been torn up and nearly killed by a grizzly a few weeks earlier, while walking a friend's dog.

Many of Cordova's gillnetters head south in the winter. Before returning to Colorado, Ess dry-docks his boat for four hundred dollars in a gravel lot up by Six-Mile, on the road to the airport. Each year he writes a letter to himself at the end of the fishing season, with a to-do list. Then, when he arrives back in Cordova the following spring, he knows exactly what needs fixing. He uses the lead time to make purchases or fabricate metal parts for the boat. He has friends who own a machine shop in town. "I can weld aluminum and do some machining. I drop off a case of beer and they open their doors for me. If I see anything that's cracked, I'll pop it off the boat and throw it in the truck and take it up there and hammer on it."

This year he gave himself only a week of lead time. There were no big projects. The boat was musty, of course, and needed to be dehumidified and scrubbed. He washed linens and restocked food. The atmosphere around town crackled, as usual. He loves the run-up to the first opening. "People are pumped. We're all getting together and talking." The season opener is usually in mid-May, which is before it gets really good, so there's time to iron out any issues. "You want to be on your game and get some fish. This year the opener had some weather, which was disconcerting because you don't trust the boat the first time out after winter storage."

The season starts with king and sockeye. By the end of July the sockeye fishery is over and there's a brief lull before the silver season gets going. Most of the fishing takes place around the Copper River Delta, one of the largest contiguous wetlands on the Pacific coast of North America. From the air it looks like a boundless marsh, nearly fifty miles wide at the mouth, where the river empties into the Gulf of Alaska with countless braided channels. It's wild country. The day before, I'd taken a bush plane over the delta for a bird's-eye view. A mama grizzly with two cubs stood up on her hind legs and stared at us as we went by, her massive head turning in the direction of our props. The pilot wondered if this was the same bear that had been surprising recreational anglers on the Ibeck River outside town and pilfering their catch. "I wouldn't fish too far from the road down there," he said.

The gillnetters work just outside the Copper River mouth in an area known as the flats, where barrier islands take the brunt of the storms blowing in off the Pacific. To the immediate northwest, in

Prince William Sound, another salmon fishery is at work, using different boats and gear. The purse seiners dwarf the bowpickers and require multiple deckhands. Seiners target pink and chum salmon, species used by the canneries rather than the fresh market. The seiners will locate large schools and circle them with a net, using a smaller support skiff. The net is then pulled tight like a purse, hoisted out of the water, and emptied onto the deck. When the fishing is hot in a particular area, seiners will line up and take turns, one after another, with each haul in the hundreds of thousands of pounds. Today, at the end of August and with only a few openings left, Ess was after a different species: coho salmon—or silvers, as they're called by almost everyone, whether you're on the Oregon Coast, Puget Sound, or the Gulf of Alaska.

On the Pacific salmon's evolutionary tree, silvers occupy a branch closest to chinook. Like their larger relatives, they spend more time in fresh water after hatching than other species, a strategy that won't serve them well as the Anthropocene era progresses, with increasingly degraded river habitat a barrier to their success. They're the second-least-abundant species, after chinook, but in much of Washington, British Columbia, and Alaska they're the chief saltwater game fish. Puget Sound in a good year will see close to a million returning silvers in the late summer and fall, split about 50–50 between wild and hatchery fish. Clayoquot Sound to the north, on Vancouver Island, is another place where anglers from all over the world travel to tie into a strong, hard-fighting silver. Fast and streamlined, these pursuers of baitfish are voracious predators that rely on speed to chase down their prey. They're the cheetahs among salmon, averaging six to twelve pounds, with the largest on record weighing in at twenty-six pounds. Anglers call the big males hooknoses because of their distinctive *kypes,* a biologist's term for the elongated and hooked snout that gives the Pacific salmon genus its name, *Oncorhynchus*. It's thought that the larger and more pronounced the hook, the more likely a male is to attract a mate. No surprise, then—or it shouldn't be—that wild fish have demonstrably larger kypes than do hatchery fish.

Silvers are aggressive and sometimes foolhardy. They're known to chase flies and lures with abandon near the surface, sometimes right into the beach in just inches of water, and once hooked they're the most acrobatic of all the Pacific salmon, going aerial and testing a fisherman's tackle with hard-charging runs. I've taken silvers at my feet on a Seattle beach, standing in ankle-deep water, and stripping my fly practically to the tip of the rod. One time I surprised another angler next to me, a recent immigrant uneducated in the ways of silvers. A small school flashed by in the breakers just a few feet from us. They turned and came back. I put my fly in front of the pod and watched as three fish all attacked the hot-pink confection at once. Feeling a tug, I struck hard and landed one of them in the same motion, right on the gravel behind the other angler. "These fish are crazy, mon!" he exclaimed in a deep East African accent. They're also tasty. Though not quite as admired as kings and sockeye, their flesh is firm and bright red with orange tints, and perfect for the grill.

Though silvers will spawn in the tributaries of large rivers, they're best known for using small coastal streams, some of them barely seasonal rivulets. This makes the silver a popular fish among kids up and down the Pacific coastline, who find the adult fish and their progeny in little neighborhood streams and even urban creeks clean and cold enough to support salmon. As every kid knows, a stream with a bunch of fallen trees in it is much more fun to explore than one without. Yet, for more than a century, the parents of such kids have been busy cleaning and manicuring these streams, removing the woody debris to make the water courses more navigable or, in their eyes, more pretty. A stream without logjams, however, is also one without deep pools, braided meanders, and gravel bars. Lacking structure, these creek beds are scoured and channelized by winter storms, which wash out the spawning gravels. The result is a fishless stream.

At one time, silvers were synonymous with the north coast of California. Fisheries ecologists like Rene Henery think of them as the redwood fish. Silver salmon and the great fog-shrouded coastal forests evolved together, with the salmon making use of all those redwood-shaded streams that purled and pooled off the coastal hills. The big trees created slow bends and deep, sanctuarylike holes where they fell, slowing the gradient of the rivers cascading down from the mountains and allowing spawning gravels to accumulate in the tailouts. Before the timber industry logged out these unique riparian zones up and down the California coast, silvers spawned in hundreds of small creeks from Monterey to the northern limit of the Redwood Empire just over the border at Brookings, Oregon. Colored up a garish pink in the spawning season, sometimes rolling about in streams that couldn't even cover their backs, the fish were easy to spot.

My first salmon hooked from a beach was a silver, caught on a rod-and-reel combo that I bought at the now-defunct Warshal's Sporting Goods in downtown Seattle for about thirty dollars. I took it one weekend to Whidbey Island with Martha. A local tackle shop supplied me some lures, the ever-popular Buzz-Bomb, in neon shades of pink and green. "Just walk down to the beach," the clerk at the tackle shop advised. "You'll see what's going on." He was right. I could see what was going on. There were fishermen up and down the beach, flinging their lures out into the chop, and every now and then someone would yell—"Here they come!"—and we'd all look down the beach to see a parade of jumping and splashing advancing toward us. The silvers were swimming right on by, close to the shore, announcing themselves. With any luck, you could put a lure right on one's nose. Anglers on either side of me did just that and hauled in beautiful salmon, and then it was my turn. A fish grabbed my lure and took off. I apologized as I staggered out in front of other fishermen, trying to avoid their lines. Eventually I got the fish under control and fought it into the shallows. "Haul it up," someone advised. This dragging of the fish out of the water and up on the cobbles struck me as somehow unsporting, but it was clearly the only choice with a seven- or eight-pound silver that leaped and thrashed like a hellion. Moments later I had my first salmon on the beach. The fish flopped on its side and then over again, its gills gasping for water. Martha looked at me. "Now what are you going to do?"

WE IDLED IN JUST FOUR FEET OF WATER, holding our position a few hundred yards offshore with a five-knot breeze blowing against a five-knot current in a comfortable stalemate. I was still getting used to these unlikely depths. The coastline around Cordova is like a big bathtub. You can hop out of the boat a mile from shore and land in knee-deep water. At low tide the place is a huge mudflat. And the water: Take away those mountain vistas all around and you might think you were bobbing in the Gulf of Mexico, not the Gulf of Alaska. Aquamarine as far as the eye can see. Ess told me to not be fooled. "That's unadulterated ocean out there. We're fishing in some of the biggest tides in the world. All of this water in a matter of six hours flows out of here, and it's riverlike conditions." He pointed to the south—Pacific Ocean for thousands of miles. "It's like *Hawaii Five-o* out here." And virtually all of it within our line of sight was open. Ess could go another eight miles offshore—over the horizon line—to fish.

I studied the beach. Behind it, a flank of snowy peaks rose in the distance like a white wall—and indeed, those mountains, part of the Chugach Range, receive more snowfall than anywhere else in the world and proved impenetrable to explorers for a long, long time. Even today they reward arrogance with their own special form of vengeance. Recently a friend of Ess's had tried to backpack from Cordova north to Valdez, about fifty miles as the crow flies but much longer on foot. He showed up back in Cordova a few weeks later, emaciated and clinging to life.

Since the season was nearly over, Ess was fishing closer to town than usual today. "Everybody's got their little spot they prefer. I like to go really far away. Once we come around the corner here, you start heading down the coast of Alaska. You can go all the way down to Juneau. I love that feeling of being on the edge of the world. So I go way down past everybody, way southeast. It takes a couple three hours to get to where you want to fish; that's why we've got to wake up so darn early." Not today. A six o'clock departure was downright civilized. In a few minutes—right at 7:00 A.M., as determined by Alaska Fish and Game, and not a second earlier—Ess could start rolling out his gill net. The opening was twenty-four hours in all, though he didn't plan to fish past dark; the change in tides would work against him, and there was no point in dealing with shallow bars and darkness for just a few extra fish. Three days had passed since the last opening. The fishermen call it cleanup—they're cleaning up the fish that have accumulated in the area over the last few days. The salmon come in from the North Pacific and follow the beaches, schooling up and loitering off points. "They're following the current, and once they smell a little Copper River mixed in the surface lens of the water they start keying in, and depending which way the wind is blowing, they angle in and pile up on the beaches. Silver salmon like to hang out for a while. Sockeye push right through, so you can miss a big wad of fish if you're not in front of them."

Ess pulled on his bright-orange fishing bibs, not bothering with a jacket. It looked to be the first sunny day in a while. The *Midnight Express* rocked in the breakers just off the beach. He shifted a gear knob on his reel into free-spool mode, attached a big red buoy to the front end of his net by a carabiner, and tossed it overboard. Now all he had to do was put his boat into reverse by activating a second set of controls, mounted near the bow, and the gill net would pay out from the free-spooling reel. The net was 150 fathoms long—about nine hundred feet—and twenty feet wide. Small Styrofoam buoys painted white and yellow floated on the top of the net—this was called the cork line—and weights sank the bottom of the net—the lead line—so that it hung in the water like a curtain. Ess motored backward away from the breakers until all 150 fathoms stretched in a line nearly perpendicular to the beach. Salmon swimming easterly along Hinchinbrook's southern shore toward the Copper River would entangle themselves as they tried to pass through.

Contrary to popular belief, the fish often sense the net. "They know it's a barrier," Ess said. They can feel it, almost the way we might hear something that alerts us to danger. "Their lateral line is a giant eardrum. They can sense the net is in front of them by the vibration the net's making just from the water passing over the filaments." But that input doesn't save them. They're headstrong, with a place to be. They try to pass through the net and it snares them. Sometimes they'll run into it and try to back away, catching a gill plate. Other times it's just the tip of a fin or a lip, enough to become entangled. Struggle makes it worse, as they get wrapped up in the mesh. You can see the fish splashing from the boat. On a good day, fish will start hitting the net as soon as it's laid out, and there will be sloshing and corks bobbing up and down the line.

Right now we were fishing the net, as Ess put it. It was still tied onto the boat, and he maneuvered his outside controls to make small adjustments to each of his engines. This way he could tweak its shape as it hung in the water—give it a C shape or an S shape, depending on what the wind and current were doing. Sometimes he disconnected from the net and let it drift freely in the current. Early in the season, while fishing for sockeye, he looks for big splashes. These are kings. He'll disconnect and steer in the direction of the splash, nosing his bow up to the disturbance and using his dip net to bring in the fish. "The big suckers don't last long in the mesh. They don't get caught by much more than a fin or a lip. Luckily, they're fairly docile creatures. When they hit they just lay in the web and they're not too motivated to get out. If you do everything perfect—you get up there and pull the cork line and get the dip net around them . . . and then . . . ahhhh . . . get him before he gives a couple big kicks—you've got him. Losing a king is a pretty emotional experience. Sometimes the wind will drift you onto the net and you'll have to reach back and hit reverse. The net stretches out and you lose the fish and curse a little bit. I got about a dozen big kings this year. I kept them all. They're a good bargaining fish. I give them to my doctor, my chiropractor, people who I feel I need to reciprocate with something special. I don't try to target them. The guys who try to catch kings are missing out on a lot of sockeye. This year the lion's share came from sockeye." In early

June, battling eight-foot seas, Ess made thirty thousand dollars in just two days by hauling in fourteen thousand pounds of sockeye.

Several hundred yards away, a boat that had been idling now started laying out its net. Ess said it was a Russian. He could tell by the hull, which stood out of the water with a high, sharp profile. "They build their own boats. They look like *Terminator* boats." I gathered there was some friction. Fishing communities, like other communities dependent on natural resources requiring careful husbandry, can be insular. In such a climate, any small act—even if unintentional—takes on a larger significance. Technically this was an Alaskan Russian to our port side, a U.S. citizen, probably from Homer, where there were a couple of Russian Orthodox communities; these were populated mostly by fishermen who had left their native country long ago, in a diaspora that included migrations to Portugal, South America, and even China, before they formed tight communities in Alaska. I'd read about them in *The Atlantic* before coming to Alaska. The article referred to the Russians as "Old Believers" looking for a remote place where they could be left alone—a commonality among Alaskan homesteaders of all kinds. It also said "the Russian fishing fleet today has a reputation for aggressive tactics and self-policing. Americans in the surrounding communities can share stories about the Russian fleet setting nets too close to other boats, ignoring calls from the Coast Guard, and only responding to help if it comes from another Russian." I asked Ess if this was true. He thought about it for a moment.

"They went the long way around the earth before ending up here. They're refugees from a pretty gnarly regime, still shell-shocked. They won't even look you in the eye. Part of their identity is to not integrate." Ess was annoyed by the fact that the boat had waited to see what he would do. Now it was upcurrent from us and would intercept any fish coming our way. Though not close enough to qualify as corking—when a fisherman lays out his net right in front of another—it was still an irritation, given how spread out the fishery was today. "I'd hold him to a higher standard if he wasn't Russian," Ess said finally, letting it slide. He ate another donut. Today's fishing wasn't going to change his annual income too much, so there was nothing to get stressed out about, though it still irked him. The money was in sockeye, not silvers. He took a look through his binoculars. It was probably a teenager, barely old enough to drive a car. "Most of them are kids, eighteen, nineteen years old. They're out here because their dads make them."

Nearly half the gill-net fleet in Cordova is now made up of Russian Americans. "They perceive prejudice. They think we think they're weird. If he was drifting on top of me, I'd say, 'Hey, can you give me some room.' Start mellow. And if he goes, 'Ahh, fuck you,' if it's a young guy, I'd say, 'You're being a dick and I'm gonna be a dick right back to you, if you don't mind.' So I'd set right in front of him. He'll pick up and set in front of me. I'll go talk to him. When I go to talk to him, I'll take my engines out of gear but I'll still be going forward and I'll lay up right against him, ram him a little bit, scratch the shit out of his boat. It's a psychological thing. I have a boat I don't care about— well, I do, but what I want him to know is that I'm willing to take crazy to the next level. It's the whole 'mutually assured destruction' thing, so I kind of feign on that. If he knows I'm willing to trade some paint, he'll back off. Even though it's a ruse."

Ess poured some coffee from his thermos and fell silent. Maybe he'd told me too much. We both watched the boat to the west rising and falling in the swells. "It makes me all anxiety-ridden," he said at last. "I'm not a confrontational guy, but you have to go there in your head. Otherwise it will always happen. Earlier this year I bumped someone. You never call it ramming. 'Oops, sorry. My bad. I'm not very good at steering.' It just lets them know you're not happy and you're not gonna be pushed around. Word gets out. 'The *Midnight Express* came over and bumped me.' It's scary. You never know if they'll pull out a gun and go, 'No, fuck you!' Some of the non-Russian guys in town, the heavy drinkers and old-time salts, they'll pull a gun on you. They know the game. All of a sudden you're playing a game you don't want to play." Ess's wife gets protective when she comes aboard, despite being very non-confrontational in other aspects of her life. She yells at fishermen who cork her husband. The fishing life is like that. One's livelihood is on the line.

At 8:00 A.M., Ess put his foul-weather gear back on and went outside to haul in his first set of the morning. On a busier day he might make half-hour sets or even ten-minute "flyer sets" to sample a spot; today he could see already that fishing was slow and there was no point in making faster sets. He reattached the net line to his reel and put it into gear. With his foot on a trip wire to control its speed, he watched his net as it came off the water and over a roller before winding onto the reel. When a fish appeared, he cut the power. The first salmon was bright and silver, about twelve pounds. It was already dead, its gill plates forced shut by the net. Ess untangled it and used his gloved hand to rip the gills so it would bleed out. He gently dropped the fish to the deck and it slid toward the hold in a watery pool of its own blood. The next fish was a flounder, requiring careful extraction due to a poisonous spine behind its fin. Ess flipped it back out into the breakers like a Frisbee. "You wouldn't believe how tough those guys are," he said with admiration. He'd caught and released the same flounder multiple times in the past, none the worse for wear. The next salmon was a male, about fourteen pounds, and active. It kicked its tail and tried to free itself, to no avail. Ess picked a few more from the net and knocked some jellyfish out. Six fish in a set was pretty sad; not even a hundred dollars' worth. He hauled up the rest of the net. The reel moved back and forth laterally on a spindle—just like the reel of a spinning rod—winding up the net evenly. Ess didn't need to worry too much about today's small haul. Fortunately, his season was already made.

It was time to prepare the hold. Ess shoveled flake ice and mixed it with buckets of seawater. Slush ice is the industry standard for keeping the fish cold. Each fish is laid in the slush and covered with more ice. Later they're put into brailer bags, large mesh totes that can be hoisted out of the hold by the tender. On the next set, a sea lion surfaced right where a fish had just hit the net a moment before. "Thief," Ess said without malice. You had to give them credit: They could pick a net faster than any fisherman. A few minutes later the sea lion was back. It cruised the length of the net, coming surprisingly close to the boat. There was nothing to be done. Though he had a pistol some-where on board to scare away predators, Ess rarely brandished it. He used to use M-80s, but 9/11 had made that harder. "They know we don't like it," he said of the seals and sea lions. "They're diabolical. I have a lot more tolerance than most fishermen. Can you imagine try-ing to catch a salmon with your mouth, no opposing thumbs to help you out?"

Sea otters are a different sort of problem. "Once they learn about the net, they'll pop over the cork line. Before they get trained up, they go through a learning stage when they get tangled and you have to help them out." This means trying to gingerly unwrap a furious ball of fur and fangs. No one wants baby sea otters in their nets. But dog-fish are just about the worst. The three-foot sharks come through in large schools that can destroy a net. "They'll tear it in half. You can't really pick 'em. There's no market." Ess looked out at the beryl-colored ocean, seemingly so benign. "There are a million ways to spend ten thousand dollars out here."

And there are also plenty of ways to die. Every year a few boats—and sometimes lives—are lost. Peeing off the boat is an easy way to fall overboard. "If I was smart I'd have a tagline all around, something to grab on to." There's this impression, popularized in the media, that half the fleet is on drugs. I asked him about it. "There's a few," Ess agreed, though not as much meth as some think. "You can't perform out here on drugs—not that kind of drug. Meth people burn out. You have to be a smart thinker to stay on edge." No, what weeds out the fleet isn't so much drugs or alcohol or carelessness but work ethic. "Some of these guys will throw their net out and go to sleep or watch a movie. Everybody's got a different way of doing it. Maybe ten per-cent of the fleet is really aggressive and works really hard to get tuned in."

Ess checked in with his radio group, a bunch of friends in the fleet who talk to one another over a scrambled frequency. They use code names. Ess is Mowgli, the feral child from Kipling's *Jungle Book,* the one raised by wolves. His brother is Tenakey, a sly reference to one of Ashton's first forays into the business world. "I just watched a sea lion steal a fish," Mowgli reported. "I'm gonna pick up the net. I think they're blowing off the beach for us. Getting some wind out of the cutoff. We're hanging okay, but I don't think it's good fishing." The idea is to share information with a small number of trusted partners—and also to stay safe. A gillnetter with the name Woody chimed in. He had just torn his net on a stump, an accident that would probably cost him a hundred dollars, paid to a net mender in town. Now he was to the south, doing short sets. "Pretty consistent. Ten fish every fifteen to twenty minutes. There's a jumper here and there, but it's chocka-block full of boats down low. Kooky crowded. If you come up high on the east side, there's room."

"That's what I was expecting," Ess told his friend. "We're just hanging out and having fun."

"Yeah, it's a nice day for that," Woody agreed. "I'm just paying for propellers and web. We'll do that after this water. A hundred fish. We're almost done. Not getting rich, not starving." Before signing off, Woody said that their engineering project—fixing Ess's gas tank in his welding shop back on the mainland—would take only a few more beers. It's a good business model, he added, one he could work with. Ess signed off and took a slug of coffee. "Woody's a good aluminum fabricator and has a nice shop. He's a benevolent father figure for a lot of guys and a good influence on the younger crowd." Not everyone in the radio group works out. Ess could think of at least one guy they had to cut loose for sandbagging. "It was a tough call. He was a lifelong friend of ours. But he was always downplaying how many fish he was catching. 'Oh, it doesn't look like much, maybe thirty or forty.' Two hours later he's like, 'Yeah, I had two hundred on that one.' Finally we said, 'Dude, give us the radio.' He was kind of a dandy and didn't fish very hard. His heart wasn't in it. Now he's got a bookstore in Homer, he's got a coffee shop and a B&B, and it's totally up his alley. It all works out."

The radio buzzed again. Another member of the group was way southeast. The tide had picked up and he was averaging a fish a minute. At least someone was catching fish.

THE RUSSIAN BOAT HADN'T moved in a while. Ess wasn't surprised. "He hasn't picked his net once. He's watching movies or playing Xbox." Ess wasn't sure what to make of the Russians in general. They stayed to themselves. "There's a lot of prejudice because they come flying into town and it's bling-bling. The first thing they do with their money is spinner rims on their trucks and big sound systems. They can be quite a nuisance in a small town, peeling rubber everywhere." Ess paused and thought about it. "We've got American kids that do that too. But the Russians tend to piss off a lot of people with their unruly behavior, with the fireworks and gun shooting, and it doesn't help them out with their public perception. I think there are some universal laws to being a good human. I know culturally there are differences. But if you're an asshole, you're an asshole in every culture. I can't really tolerate it. I try to keep them lined out."

It's a good idea to have friends on the water. Ess was pretty sure he had a buyer for the *Midnight Express,* a young woman from Anchorage who was fairly new to the fleet and had struggled with mechanical issues with her boat, the *China Cat,* all season long. She was done for the year, having skipped today's opener to go camping with her mother. "She's making mistakes that beginners make. Not only do you lose out on fishing time but you need to pay for your mistakes. Ashton has taken her under his wing. She's awesome and we like having her around. We want her to be successful, because we want people like that in our fishery. If she sells her permit, the person who buys it isn't likely to be as awesome." For his new boat, Ess had in mind one of the big inboard-jet boats that are popular on the flats. He expected to pay somewhere between a quarter and a third of a million dollars for it, the sort of money that required him to be ready when next year's season opened in mid-May. Already he was drawing up plans for how he would tweak it with personal touches that fit his fishing style. "There's a saying: The first boat you build is just a boat. The second you build is *your* boat."

LATE-AFTERNOON SUN WARMED OUR faces as we sat outside on the deck, shooting the breeze. Loons taxied across the flats. A seal popped up and looked at us with its innocent-seeming brown eyes. On the next set Ess untangled a hen chum salmon, a different species. After picking up the net and laying it out again, he tended to a half dozen silvers and then found the chum wedged beneath the reel, already colored up with the telltale tiger stripes that distinguish chums from other Pacific salmon. Ess slit her open and pulled out two skeins of pearly red eggs. These went into a Tupperware and the rest of the fish went overboard. "I know it doesn't look good," he said, referring to the wastage, "but no cannery will buy a chum in that condition." The fish was already in its spawning colors; the meat would be soft, all its vitality now in the eggs.

The chum salmon is a conundrum. Less commercially valuable because of its lower fat content and softer flesh, it still represents the biggest catch percentagewise. That's because chums are the second-most-plentiful species after pinks, which are the smallest and least valuable of Pacific salmon, and they're the second largest by weight after chinook. Chums might have been the most abundant salmon historically. Their geographic range is the widest. Formerly they spawned as far south as Monterey, California, with as many as a million in the lower Columbia River, and their northern range includes more of the Arctic than any other species. The Columbia runs are a thing of the past, with only a few thousand fish in an average year, and though they're the most abundant species in Washington State, several runs around Puget Sound are extinct, with a generally downward trend in population size. Chums tend to spawn in the lower reaches of estuaries near tidewater, habitats severely degraded by urban development. In Alaska there are also chum populations that make long migrations, notably in the Yukon and Mackenzie Rivers.

Along with pinks, chums are the main target of the Prince William Sound seiner fishery, with most of those fish-hatchery origin. Though the bulk of the catch goes to canneries, there's an increasing demand for fresh-market chums—provided they're still silver and haven't begun to change into their spawning colors. They're sold as "keta" or "silverbrite" salmon, at a fraction of the cost that you'd pay for chinook or sockeye. Lower in fat and oil, fresh chums from the salt have mild, flaky meat. Once they start to turn, however, the flesh quickly softens. Their skin changes from silver to green, with a red and black calico pattern of stripes down the flank, and males develop a slight hump and a snaggletoothed kype with canine fangs. They look fierce and not at all palatable. Chums are also called dog salmon, because northern peoples feed them to their sled dogs. For all these reasons, chums have historically been less valued than other species, but this was changing. In Japan, chums are revered for the eggs, with brined and seasoned roe fetching a premium at specialty fish markets and sushi restaurants. The large red orbs pop in the mouth with a salty taste of the sea. Sometimes I make my own salmon caviar at home. A wire cooling rack—the sort used for cookies—is a handy way to separate the eggs from the stringy tissue of the skein membrane. I rub the skeins over the rack and then brine the eggs in canning jars. Added salt gives them an attractive semitransparency. For ikura, I add soy sauce, aji-mirin, and dashi broth. After a night curing in the fridge, it's ready to eat. The Japanese consider chum roe the sine qua non for ikura.

Guido Rahr once told me that pinks and chums were Alaska's "dirty little secret." While most of the country's so-called wild salmon harvest comes from Alaska, the word *wild* is slippery. It's used, unsurprisingly, to draw a distinction between the Alaskan catch and the farmed salmon that have taken such a big economic bite out of fishing communities since the 1980s. But if we want to get technical about it, a large percentage of Alaska's salmon harvest is actually hatchery fish, with most of those fish being pinks and chums. The state has made a concerted effort to boost its hatchery production. The result is an increasingly complicated issue for wild-fish supporters to dissect. For commercial gillnetters in Cordova, who target mostly wild runs of Copper River sockeye, silver, and chinook, the pink and chum seiner fishery to the north in Prince William Sound is a blessing. The relatively small fleet of purse seiners can scoop up huge hauls of these less valuable hatchery fish and sell them to the canneries, taking the pressure off the wild fish and allowing the gill-net fleet to keep fishing. It's like having a neighborhood Walmart that doesn't put all the small local stores out of business.

David Reggiani, a biologist with the Prince William Sound Aquaculture Corporation (PWSAC), told me that this homegrown Alaskan effort had learned from past mistakes to the south. "We're a supplemental hatchery program," he said, drawing a distinction between that and the mitigation hatcheries in the Pacific Northwest, which are meant to compensate for salmon-killing dams and habitat destruction. "We're just trying to make more of the local salmon." But local conditions in the rugged terrain around Prince William Sound aren't always favorable to salmon or fishermen. Reggiani pointed to two main limiting factors: extremely cold temperatures in winter that can kill salmon eggs, and torrential rainstorms that periodically scour the spawning beds. Because of these natural events on the ground, every few years the salmon runs crash. The nonprofit PWSAC started in 1974 as a result of one of those busts, when the pink salmon fishery collapsed. It began with a low-budget, grassroots effort by the fishermen themselves, carrying gunnysacks of concrete on their shoulders to build rearing ponds along a creek and forming a bucket brigade to seed these initial efforts with fertilized eggs. This stab at increased salmon production grew into a complex of five hatcheries, which now produce six hundred million smolts annually. The fishermen themselves voted to impose a two percent tax on their catch to fund an annual budget of $11 million. Of the five hundred million pink fry released each year, about four percent survive to adulthood, providing commercial fishermen a catch of twenty million.

Even Alaska, it turns out, is tampering with the natural order of things. I had to wonder about all those hatchery fish. Nature always has a way of reminding us of the law of unintended consequences. Ess agreed with that logic. "We're out here as environmentalists," he said. "It's hard to imagine that, because we get lumped in with coal miners and loggers, and it's hard to imagine that we actually care. But we've been raised to care. There's a lot of people like my brother and me that would shut down in a heartbeat if it meant saving this ecosystem. We've got a lot of options. There's untapped bounty." He ticked off a few products that an entrepreneurial sort might try to market: composted sea kelp, mussels and clams, wild berries. "There's hardly any export out of Alaska for our wild blueberries. They're everywhere." So was driftwood. For now he was on the fence about the hatcheries. "I'm split down the middle," he said, mulling it over. "For lack of any real evidence, I think it's a good thing, but I'm willing to change my mind if I start catching fish that look dumb. I can tell how smart a fish is. If they start acting a little inbred, I'll start worrying."

A long silence followed; I noticed a warm rosy bloom beginning to form along the jagged top of the Chugachs as the sun went down over the Pacific. It was a gorgeous sight. The mountains and the sea: It all looked perfect, unblemished. Ess perked up. "I'm trying to keep my environmentalist perspective in check, because I naturally gravitate to the opinion that we shouldn't be fucking with any of it. If it's good enough for nature, it's good enough for me." We watched the day's last light creeping down the peaks. "I don't want to be on my deathbed thinking back over my life, wondering if my moral decisions were influenced by economic gain." A note of self-doubt crept into his voice. "We're still a frontier town up here. I haven't seen any problems with hatcheries in my life, so I can't just jump on the anti-hatchery bandwagon. I do like having augmented fisheries. I can make my living right here on the flats. Part of the reason I'm successful is because the fleets are divided up. If the hatcheries weren't here, there would be a lot more competition. So I guess my opinion is skewed by the economic incentive of having the hatchery."

Ess put his coffee cup down with a thud and swiveled in his seat to face me. "I'm definitely swayed by the money," he decided at last. "It's probably not a good thing, to be honest. But it could be worse."

IT WAS DUSK WHEN we delivered our load to the tender back in town. Much of the gill-net fleet was already in the harbor, even though another twelve hours remained in the opening. Ashton was back, and so was Curly. Another year of fishing on the flats was winding down. Ess had hunting, not fishing, on his mind, and he was eager to get back to Colorado to see his wife. They had decisions to make. Lately he'd been thinking about selling the peach orchard and finding a new home. He wanted to be in a wetter part of Colorado. The climate was changing—anyone could see that. Water would be increasingly important. He wanted to be surrounded by moist woodlands, in a place where he could raise a family.

As for me, I had already decided I would go south before the year was out, where even more profound changes in water usage were under way. Little more than a century ago, California was the Alaska of today. Resource rich, sparsely populated. A grizzly bear still lumbers across the state flag, the Golden Bear of legend. Between 1848 and 1849, the city of San Francisco grew from a mere thousand residents to a population of twenty-five thousand, in a spasm of excitement that reached from coast to coast and beyond. My friend Rene Henery said exciting things were happening again in California. He wanted me to see the fish in a way I never had before.

CHAPTER 7

A TENEBROUS FUTURE

WE SUITED UP QUICKLY BENEATH THE HOT SUN OF TIMBUCTOO, the old Yuba River mining district that, as legend has it, was named for an escaped slave turned gold panner, originally from Timbuktu, Mali. It was a good day for a swim, another one of those high blue California mornings, lately a specialty of the drought-stricken state, and I was eager to get in the water before succumbing to sunstroke in my heavy neoprene wetsuit. Already a thin veneer of perspiration had formed on Rene Henery's brow below his hood. He wiped the sweat from his eyes and took a few tentative steps in his rubber booties down to the waterline.

We weren't the only ones feeling the heat. Ghost pines in the foothills looked ready to burst into flames at the slightest provocation. A gauzy yellow haze hung suspended in the valley bottom below, with its implication of fallow fields and dust storms. In front of us, an improbable roller coaster of white water thundered past, too much and too fast. Rene, a rock climber in his spare time, with a compact, muscular frame, pulled himself atop a large boulder to get a better view of the river.

"My nature is to scout for obstacles and then look for a way through," he said from his perch. "But this is sketchy."

He slid back down and we picked our way up the cobble-strewn beach. Rene had invited me to California to get a glimpse of both the past and the future. The former was on display all around us. Up-heaved earth and piles of rock and gravel told a story right out of the history books. The Gold Rush started within fifty miles of here. Forty-niners worked this stretch of Yuba riverbank in the 1850s, stamping their signature on the land in ways that are still visible today. Wielding enormous hydraulic hoses that could reroute a bend in the river and blast a man to smithereens, they peeled back layer after layer of geologic time to reveal its secrets, then leached precious discoveries out of the rock with mercury mined from the coastal ranges. Today the river's wealth is simply the water itself. The state was in the middle of the worst drought on record. Meanwhile, its farmers were bawling for more water. And swimming up this liquid gold? As fanciful as it seemed, salmon. In some circles, I was learning, they had no value at all.

Around the next bend we found calmer water. My wetsuit hadn't seen action in a while. A beat-up Farmer John model, four millimeters thick with reinforced elbow and knee patches, I mostly use it in Puget Sound to dive for shellfish. Metal hooks at the crotch are corroded from salt, and my gloves have holes left by irate Dungeness crabs. I spat in my mask to keep it from fogging, then waded awkwardly into the current in my flippers before falling backward into the river's cool arms. Icy water rushed in where it could, forming a thin layer under the suit that warmed against my body. Rene dove ten feet down to the bottom of a deep-blue pool, and I followed him. A shoal of suckers with large yellow scales drifted backward at our approach, reluctant to leave the dinner table.

I didn't need a fisheries ecologist like Rene Henery to tell me we were too late for this stretch of river. The salmon were already gone from the riffles and stacked in the sandy bottoms of pools, where cur-rents had arranged their spawned-out carcasses, pale white and stiff with rigor mortis, into morbid formations that were at once grotesque and beautiful. Suckers fed on them greedily, like inheritors at a wake.

The shapes of smaller fish hovered on the periphery, barely visible and always close to shelter, no doubt taking advantage of this feast when an opportunity presented itself. These were young salmon, hatched in the spring, and their presence went a long way toward answering the question: Why do Pacific salmon die after spawning? So the next generation can live. A few jacks scooted by too, looking for live females on nests. These were precocious males, smaller than fully adult salmon but still able to spawn. Returning to the river a year or two earlier than the rest of their cohort, they were a hedge against disaster, nature's insurance policy. Rene was reassured to see all these variations of the salmon life cycle: spawned-out adults, jacks, and juveniles in one stretch. This was what you should see in a working system.

We explored a few more pools with the same results, each of them decorated with carcasses. You had to admire these fish even in death—especially in death. A spawning run is a suicide mission, the biological imperative a toe tag. Here in California the rallying cry of "Spawn till you die" was complicated by a litany of obstacles that, in Rene's view, made the Columbia Basin to the north seem almost functional. Yet a few wild salmon continued to hang on after decades of abuse, and this tenacity, this failure to go quietly, was setting the stage for a showdown. As we bobbed in the slow current, Rene talked excitedly through his snorkel. "The fish are on a downward trajectory and doing everything they possibly can," he said. "The same can't be said for us. We need to do more. We all need to work together." This is Rene's worldview in a nutshell. Yes, he's a scientist, but his true calling is in the art of building bridges. Every day he has to insert himself between warring factions of people—farmers, ranchers, urbanites, environmentalists—and try to coax them into taking a shared responsibility for what happens on the landscape, to help them see commonalities rather than differences. Though hard science is his vocation—research, data, peer-reviewed hypotheses and conclusions—it's the softer science of the sort utilized by his wife, a psychologist and counselor, that he finds more useful in some ways: the ability to talk to people, to find common ground, to work through problems with nothing other than a conversation. He's also ungoverned by the conventions—the walls, you might say—that typically separate the object of study from the studier. Pacific salmon culture in North America is a dance between fish and humanity. For that dance to continue, the human partner needs to pay attention to nature's music. What's more, the human partner might need to take some dance lessons from the salmon themselves, which thrive on diversity, adaptability, and resilience. Nowhere is this more on display than in California.

Even after years of conservation efforts, salmon populations are continuing to decline in the Golden State, while water is more precious than ever. The specter of federal action looms. Listing these fall chinook as endangered would effectively end commercial salmon fishing in the state, hamstring agriculture, and pit Big Ag directly against the Endangered Species Act, with far-reaching repercussions well beyond California's borders. Even environmentalists want to avoid such a listing, fearing blowback of game-changing proportions. "Nobody on either side wants it," Rene admitted of his biggest tool in the toolbox, the ESA, as everyone calls it. "It's a big wuzzle we've tied for ourselves." But the fish need help, and writing off as insignificant even a single run—such as this struggling Yuba population—has larger implications. For one thing, a diverse group of stakeholders that includes Rene's employer, Trout Unlimited, has already gone to the mat for the river, signing the Lower Yuba River Accord in 2006; the landmark deal ensures a safe supply of clean, cold water in the river, where the salmon need it. If local advocacy-minded coalitions can't reverse the decline without federal action, who can? Besides, the Yuba is just a single piece in a larger puzzle.

"It's easy to say we might not be able to restore this or that particular river," Rene explained, "not fully recognizing that the entire Central Valley is one watershed, a giant portfolio of salmon populations. Historically they were all connected and intermixing." Formerly the biggest wetland in North America, the valley is fed by countless rivers and streams coming down out of the mountains and foothills of the Sierras, for hundreds of miles up and down the state, all of that water converging at the Sacramento–San Joaquin Delta before heading out to the Pacific through the Golden Gate. The salmon that survive their oceanic odysseys and pass back through that same gate return to a river system very different from that of 165 years ago. Take the Yuba. It has seen more streambed excavation than the Panama Canal. Fish-blocking dams hold back deadly mine tailings. And a toxic inheritance will continue to contaminate river sediment for years to come with high concentrations of heavy metals such as arsenic and mercury. Yet this ravaged stream remains one of the last holdouts for wild chinook salmon in the Central Valley—and it's an example of fish-friendly coalitions thinking creatively. For all these reasons, the implausible run of Yuba River chinook is on Rene's radar.

We got out of the river and drove a few miles downstream to meet another biologist at a public campground. Duane Massa stood in the middle of an aluminum skiff in his waders, waving around what looked like a giant pair of hedge clippers. The tool, it turned out, was homemade. He used it to decapitate the corpses of spawned-out salmon on the river bottom, collecting tags from their heads as well as a small piece of piscine anatomy called an otolith, the fish's inner-ear bone, which helps date a salmon the way rings date a tree. Tall, with a ponytail and a laid-back demeanor, Massa welcomed us aboard. "Hop in, but don't sit over there," he advised merrily. Over there a pile of fish heads stared blankly back at us. Earlier in the day Massa had used his makeshift clippers to neatly sever a dozen chinook heads from their decomposing bodies. After cleaning weeds from his jets with a screwdriver, he fired up the engine and took us a mile upstream. "Don't worry," he shouted above the noise as we skipped over tight-fisted rapids, "you'll see some spawners."

This stretch of the river looked like a Montana trout stream. Surrounded by dry hills, the stream alternated with riffled straightaways and deeper bends, taking its time to wander back and forth across the valley. Massa kept a firm hand on the tiller as he guided us through a rock garden at full speed. Rene caught my eye. "Duane is the man." Though Massa worked for a large interstate agency, the Pacific States Marine Fisheries Commission, and Rene for a nonprofit, the world of salmon scientists is a small one, with collegial bonds that stretch across political borders. "There's gotta be some reason why I do this," Massa yelled over the roar of the jets. "It's not the boatloads of money." Like so many in his profession, he's made sacrifices to unravel the secrets of fish. Below a steep embankment where the river makes a slow turn, he cut the engine. "Have a nice swim, boys—but don't miss the takeout. It's five miles of angry water after that." We slipped off the stern and let the current take us back down into riffles where the river spread across a wide tailout, bumping chest-first over the sort of baseball-sized cobbles that chinook prefer for their spawning gravel. I saw my first live fish holding beside a dead tree in the river, in just a foot of water, its pectoral fins working like frayed Chinese fans to keep it upright, the delicate lavender color turned a jaundice yellow. At twenty pounds, this fall chinook salmon seemed all out of proportion to its surroundings. The fish had turned dark, its snout nearly black, while white scars from obstacles encountered in its 150-mile journey upstream from the ocean stood out in sharp relief. Only a few days from death, and it was still a master of its underwater medium. Pelvic fins twitched slightly, making minor adjustments in the current. The salmon shifted to one side and I drifted past it, held tightly in the river's grasp.

The nests, called redds, were just a couple of feet beneath the surface and easy to spot—some as big as a king-sized bed, their gravel bright as a window in the sun where algae had been scraped away by the female's vigorous tail-scouring. Some of these redds might have contained as many as five thousand eggs, deposited by a single female. Rene surfaced downstream with his hands in the air. "One just swam right under my armpit!" he shouted like a kid. Though almost forty, he still got carded whenever the fisheries biologists lifted a pint at the local, and even now, after years of handling salmon, a close encounter was a thrill. Most days were spent at a desk. I kicked over to him and together we floated downstream through light rapids, counting salmon as we went. Some of the fish, nearly spent, barely moved to the side to let us pass, while others, still alert and vigorous, darted out of the way, startled by the unexpected encounter. I suppose I felt a melancholy sort of joy at the natural drama unfolding here, one repeated annually for millennia. Considering how much abuse had been heaped upon this river in just the very recent past, to see any fish at all seemed beyond astonishing.

THE YUBA RIVER IS a tributary of the Feather, which is in turn a tributary of the Sacramento, the sprawling river system that drains a good portion of interior Northern California between the Sierra Nevada and the Coast Range, more than twenty-seven thousand square miles in all. Spanish explorers were so taken by the valley's "chattering birds," its big fish "darting through pellucid depths," its "champagne air," to quote from an early expedition, that they "drank deep of it, drank in the beauty around them," and christened the river "Most Holy Sacrament of the Body and Blood of Christ." The Sac, as modern-day users know it, is the state's largest river and was once a salmon producer on par with the Columbia and Fraser Rivers to the north. Today it's thought of as one of California's two main faucets, the other being the San Joaquin. Together these rivers irrigate the Central Valley, the agricultural region that stretches more than 450 miles, from Red Bluff to Bakersfield, and provides Americans, by some accounts, with nearly a third of what they eat.

The transformation from wilderness rivers to irrigation plumbing happened quickly enough that no one, save a few proto-environmentalist worriers, put up much of an argument. Explorers and early settlers in the mid-nineteenth century found a valley that looked considerably different from the one that exists today. The Sacramento and San Joaquin were so braided and meandering at their outlet to San Francisco Bay that it was nearly impossible for boatmen to find a main channel deep enough to proceed upriver. In 1844, explorer John Frémont reported seeing elk "running in bands over the prairie and in the skirts of the timber" along the San Joaquin. This might have been the high point for game animals in California. With Native Americans nearly

wiped out from disease and war, and the Gold Rush, white settlement, and market hunters still a few years off, herds of deer, elk, and
antelope roamed the grassy plains of the Central Valley in herds more
typical of an African veldt. Grizzlies and wolves patrolled the perim-
eter. Waterfowl blackened the skies. California was a land of plenty,
the salmon numerous enough to be an afterthought. They returned to
the Central Valley by the millions. Then the whites arrived.

Trappers and miners came first. Trapping out the beaver changed
the hydrology of the mountain streams, eliminating structure that
gave salmon fry places to hide, while gold mining destroyed the rivers
wholesale, a legacy that's still with us. The settlers came next. Much
of the valley was either too arid or too marshy for the first homesteaders. The Mediterranean climate meant hot, dry summers and cool,
wet winters. Rivers reduced to trickles by fall would roar back to life
with spring floods from the melting mountain snowpack. But soon
the farmers figured out how to drain the marshes, impound the rivers,
and irrigate the desert. They waded into streams with pitchforks to
waylay an easy source of fertilizer. The Central Valley flowered with
new crops, and the salmon began their swift slide into irrelevance.
Today, with anthropogenic climate change as the newest challenge
facing salmon, the question was not just whether past damage could
be undone but whether such efforts would make any difference at all
in a hotter world.

I stood up in the middle of a riffle and took my bearings. Salmon
surrounded us. To my right I could see the dorsal and tail fins of a female on her redd. Closer to the bank, a large male wallowed in a
pocket of slow water, listing from side to side, fins worn down to
cartilage and white fungus covering much of his dorsal side. Native
Americans have a name for big old warriors gone long in the tooth:
mossback. Just the same, he sprinted out of his pocket at my approach
with several quick tail shakes and glided easily into the middle of the
river, where the current swept him backward. These were his final
hours. Without DNA testing it was impossible to know the genetic
makeup of these fish. Though they looked and acted like the sort of

chinook salmon that people in the Central Valley might have encountered a century ago, in the intervening years so many runs have been influenced by hatchery efforts that skeptics call them mutts and wonder whether truly wild salmon still exist in this part of California at all.

Mining, agriculture, hatcheries, climate change. It's so easy to just throw your hands up and cry surrender. People like Rene Henery and Duane Massa are not about to do that, and I admire them for it.

AFTER OUR SNORKEL, we drove into town for lunch. To the west, the Sutter Buttes reared up out of the haze like shark fins. Unique for being the smallest mountain range in the world, the buttes are the remnant lava dome of a Pleistocene volcano—exactly the sort of geologic activity that caused salmon to evolve the way they did, using both fresh and salt water during their life cycle, vacating habitat as it gives way to cataclysm, reclaiming it as it reemerges. Rene shifted his gaze from the far-off buttes to modest ranch buildings on the other side of the road. Somewhere around here was a lunch spot he wanted to find, but it was proving elusive. The last time he'd eaten there, one of the waitstaff had served up a surprise. She was an old Chinese woman, very possibly a descendant of the coolies who built the railroads to California and later dug all the irrigation canals, work deemed too menial for even the most dirt-poor of whites. "Do you want to see the dragon?" she had asked cryptically. He and his colleagues had nodded—yes, they did want to see the dragon. "She takes us out back and there's this insane—I mean, amazing—huge junk sculpture of a dragon. It's super ornate, with old musical instruments built into it. We're looking at it and we're like, this is incredible. And she says, 'Yeah, I thought you guys would appreciate it.'" As Rene and his companions were marveling at the dinosaur-sized sculpture, the old woman reached her hand inside it and flipped a switch. The dragon started to move, blowing smoke out its nostrils. Though he left it at that—what storyteller wants to explain the moral of his tale?—I wondered if the dragon somehow represented for him the triumph of creativity over adversity in a harsh place. Certainly the Chinese woman had been tested throughout her immigrant life. The dragon might have been a link to her past and also a view of the future.

Lately, Rene had been thinking a lot about imagination and the environment, how human beings needed to envision a landscape of possibility that included both people and salmon. When he wasn't studying fish, one of his favorite pastimes was hunting for and displaying natural objects as found pieces of art. Hanging from his living room wall was a skeletal spread of driftwood manzanita. It looked like a shade tree in miniature, the sort you might see in winter—bare of leaves and bony-fingered, an oak or maple—yet it was worn entirely smooth by water. He had found it in a subalpine lake near Castle Crags to the north, where he sometimes worked with graduate students on fisheries projects. The icy lake had preserved the tree branch in all its dendritic intricacy until it began to resemble a leafless bonsai. Collecting it without damaging any of the limbs had been a painstaking operation. In Rene's kitchen gurgled a water feature built from volcanic rocks gathered in the channeled scablands of eastern Washington. An owl's wing took flight over the fireplace mantel. Nature's artworks decorated every room.

WITH THE SMOKING DRAGON nowhere in sight, we settled for the local taqueria and a plateful of Rene's favorite comfort food, Mission-style burritos. Not a surprising choice, since he grew up in San Francisco's Mission District ("when it was still the Mission," as he likes to say) and later in the Western Addition. Though comfortable in a solid middle-class way, his parents encouraged their son to expand his horizons beyond their tidy home. Rene liked to get out of the city to go fishing, usually for panfish in one of the many foothill reservoirs, or for larger quarry in the salt. One summer his uncle rowed him out into Bodega Bay in a little dinghy, where he hooked a bright coho salmon within sight of Highway 1. He clammed and crabbed too and then watched as those places closed, one after another, because of pollution. Sometimes he visited rural areas with the Sierra Club, an education he would pay back later as a trip leader for Inner City Outings. Rene's father is black, originally from Guyana, the "land of many rivers"—also a fitting description for a man whose ancestry included African, native South American, English, and even Chinese. His mother is white, a Californian of both Western and Eastern European descent. One of the things that Rene realized at a young age is that city people of color seldom venture beyond the urban boundary. In contrast, he fell in love with the wilderness. His grandfather on his mother's side, a Unitarian naturalist and writer in the mold of Thoreau, was a major influence in this way, having homesteaded in Alaska's Brooks Range, where he learned to outsmart Arctic char with lures made from old can openers and later taught his grandson to catch trout by twisting a cigarette rolling paper into a moth. To this day, Rene's single most vivid image of angling skill is the memory of his grandfather coaxing a thirty-inch char from the depths of the icy lake behind his cabin with nothing more than a kiddie rod and four-pound test.

When he was older, a teenager, Rene backpacked with friends into Hells Canyon of the Snake River in Idaho, the deepest gorge in North America. The weather was perfect, but the boys didn't bring enough food. That evening, weary from a long day's march, they came upon a small stream that emptied into the river. At the mouth, large silvery fish floated up and down in the billowing current, behemoths heaving into view and then dropping again just as quickly, like emanations from beyond. Rene could just barely make out the rosy hue of a gill plate before one of them vanished again. It was a mesmerizing sight. The boys pooled their gear and contrived to make fishing tackle with whatever presented itself. "I think someone had a couple hot dogs left or some jerky." Amazingly, the biggest rainbow trout they had ever seen took the bait. "We were falling all over each other on the bank. Pandemonium in Hells Canyon. We hauled that big-ass fish out of the river and went to bed with full bellies." Not until much later would

Rene realize they had caught an endangered Snake River steelhead. Retelling the story, he motioned with his arm like a referee throwing a flag. "Young and stupid, guilty as charged."

The memory of that steelhead dinner in the high-desert wilderness stayed with him. As did more than a little shame.

After college in Portland, Oregon, Rene answered a newspaper ad and soon found himself working on the sixth floor of a run-down office building on 2nd Avenue in downtown Seattle, across the street from a needle exchange, for a little-known start-up called Amazon.com. Stacks of books covered Rene's desk. As quaint as it might seem now, in 1997 his first job at the company, as a member of the catalog department, was to scan every new book cover by hand and put the images on the website. To other employees—such as me—he had the look of a global citizen, that impossible-to-pin-down physiognomy resulting from intermarriage between cultures. He was short, maybe five-seven, with close-cropped black hair and an ebony fang-shaped earring in each lobe. Every couple of days I brought down an armload of books from the editorial department for Rene to scan, and as the books started arriving faster and faster, in ever larger shipments, the wall around his desk grew taller, until I couldn't see him in there any longer. A year later he was promoted to program manager, overseeing technical details of catalog projects at the company. Scientific inquiry suited Rene. Logic was his currency. In meetings he laid out carefully orchestrated point-by-point arguments that would leave his colleagues silent and his bosses, who might have other, less well-formed plans, feeling upstaged.

Outside work, Rene was devoted to the natural world, to climbing and mountain biking and fishing. The Pacific Northwest appealed to him. He started fly-fishing for sea-run cutthroat on the Stillaguamish River, for desert redsides in the Yakima Canyon, and for twenty-five-pound chinook salmon on the Rogue. He loved the rivers and their environments as much as the fish, the meditative pursuit of what one angling writer has called "standing in a river waving a stick."

A couple of years later, right around the turn of the new millennium, he sent out an email to friends and family with the tantalizing subject line "My Tenebrous Future." As is typical with a Rene Henery missive, more than one recipient had to look up the adjective (Oxford: "dark; shadowy or obscure"). In the email he declared his intention to leave his job and pursue as-yet-unknown pastures. Selling a bunch of stuff to millions of people was not, he said, his life's mission. He solicited advice and suggestions. Several replies came back with just one word: "Water."

The next several years were a blur. Rene moved back to California to study salmon, earned his PhD at UC Davis, and managed a summer field station in the headwaters of the Sacramento River, near Mount Shasta. He quit recreational fishing during these years; as long as he was killing as many salmon for research as he was, he felt he couldn't take any more. One of his professors in the doctoral program was a mentor and hero to his fish-crazed students. He reminded them that no one went into this for money. Even jobs in the private sector couldn't offer the sort of compensation that Rene had enjoyed at a profitless Internet start-up. No, they went into it for love. "Do you feel that inside?" this prof would ask his students when they were hard at work on some esoteric branch of piscine biology. "That's your heart."

Rene's first day in the field as a graduate student nearly ended in tragedy. He was helping out on a salmon survey in the Yolo Bypass of the Sacramento River. He joined a biologist to check a fyke trap—a large funnel-shaped pen—that held a heavy-bodied female chinook. "The big salmon was just starting to turn a beautiful copper color," Rene remembered. Once they freed the salmon from the trap and examined it, taking its measurements and some scale samples, he asked the other scientist to snap a photo of him with this great fish. After some fumbling around, during which they had to change camera batteries, they got the picture and Rene waded back into the river with the salmon to release it. Immediately, the chinook listed to its side and started floating back downriver. "Oh well," the other biologist said. "We lose some." Rene was beside himself. He caught it by the tail and tried again. "Don't worry about it," his superior reassured him. "It happens." The scientist said it was part of the work, that the young ecologist would have to get used to this aspect of the job. But Rene wasn't having any of it. He waded deeper into the current with the fish—and that's when he lost his footing in the mud. Water poured over the tops of his waders, anchoring him to a soft river bottom. He still wouldn't let go of the salmon. The other biologist ran back to the truck to get a rope. Meanwhile, unable to clamber out of the mud and onto the bank, Rene felt himself slowly pushed deeper into the current as he cradled the salmon like a baby. The water rose above his chest, to his throat, to his chin. He tried to stand on his tiptoes. At that moment he saw the chinook's gills flare. Its body came back to life, the muscles rippling beneath his hands, and it powered out of his grip into the depths. Rene held his breath, went under, and let the current push him downstream, where he found footing on a rocky ledge and hauled himself out. The other biologist shook his head. "I sure as hell wasn't about to lose that fish because I wanted a picture," Rene told me.

Eventually, Trout Unlimited hired Rene to be their lead California scientist. It was a good fit. Even the organization's name appealed to him, the sense of boundless opportunity. TU, as its supporters know it, is an organization that counts on its strength coming in equal measures from a large membership and science-backed advocacy. It was started in 1959 in Michigan and now has four hundred chapters across the country, from Maine to Alaska. Like its equally successful namesake, Ducks Unlimited, the organization focuses on habitat—preserving, improving, and rehabilitating rivers and riparian areas in North America for salmon and trout. And just as good waterfowl hunting is integral to Ducks Unlimited, good fishing is at the center of Trout Unlimited's charter, the idea being that a lifelong angler will also be a steward of the water.

By joining TU as a scientist, Rene became part of a young new guard taking over key positions in the environmental-science community. As their superiors began retiring—mostly white men who had grown up under the influence of business-as-usual resource extraction rather than ecosystem restoration—the new guard started re-placing them in the U.S. Forest Service, the Bureau of Land Management, and in the nonprofit sector. It was a more diverse group. They weren't dour end-of-the-world sign-holders from *New Yorker* cartoons either. They had a sense of humor, used analogies their peers could relate to. Salmon conservation, Rene liked to say, was like learn-ing to snowboard. "At first it was all about avoiding obstacles—not running into a tree or falling in a hole. After a while it was about pick-ing a line and moving gracefully around the obstacles. Now it's about using those same obstacles for leverage—jumping off a rock and ex-pressing the beauty of the vision."

Sometimes the vision was conveyed with a flourish, a little self-conscious bit of showboating to get attention. Rene's colleague Jacob Katz, for instance, was working on a restoration of the Sacramento River floodplain, in an area that historically flooded during the rainy season of most winters, giving juvenile salmon access to hundreds of square miles of productive forage. With the diking and channelizing of the river to prevent such floods—and to keep cities like Sacramento dry—the survival of young fish has been severely diminished. "We've been sending our salmon to the ocean grossly undersized," Rene told me. "It's like sending a peewee-football team up against the 'Niners defensive line." His colleague Katz is now collaborating with rice farmers in the valley to intentionally flood their fields in winter—or jumping off the rock, to use Rene's snowboard metaphor. It's a pro-cess that's good for rice production and good for salmon. Studies are revealing that young fish in these managed floods grow much faster than those confined to the river proper. Katz calls them "floodplain fatties," and the program was christened "The Nigiri Project," for a variety of rice used in sushi. This is the sort of hook that gets you front-page coverage in the *Los Angeles Times*.

The salmon of California can use a little ink. Even Californians have forgotten that their state once hosted epic runs. The reasons for the collapse, in a little over a century, are not hard to understand.

More than 80 percent of the Sacramento River's historic spawning habitat has been lost behind dams; more than 90 percent of the historic floodplain habitat is gone. As a consequence, the state's most productive salmon river is on life support. The San Joaquin, the other major artery of the Central Valley, has fared even worse. It hardly resembles a river in the true sense of the word. "Ditch" is how some describe it. The San Joaquin has been diked, dammed, channelized, and dewatered. Because more water has been promised to irrigators than actually flows through the San Joaquin in an average year, the river runs dry for more than forty miles between Gravelly Ford and Mendota.

But it's about more than rivers and fish for Rene and his colleagues. It's about people. It's about how human beings living in a society deal with this problem. "We've been avoiding the big issues and trying not to make the real change that's required of us, the change of working together, the change of looking at the ways we've been living and adjusting our behavior." Behavior is connected to values, and neither is fixed, Rene firmly believes. Both can change. "We need to look at our value system. Salmon are always maximizing every possibility nature gives them. We're not doing that—we're not maximizing our survival potential. We're just trying to maximize earning potential."

Not everyone doing the work of salmon conservation is enamored of Trout Unlimited's approach. Because of its large membership and its geographic reach, TU enjoys a position at the center of the fish universe, but a constellation of smaller nonprofits with less to lose revolves around it. A commercial fisherman friend of mine calls these the "Merry Pranksters of salmon politics." Organizations such as the Wild Salmon Center, the Wild Fish Conservancy, the Native Fish Society, and others all take a less compromising view, and their mandate is for the fish themselves, not fishing or fishermen. They have no qualms about suing government to have fisheries shut down entirely in order to protect dwindling stocks of wild salmon and steelhead. TU has to walk a careful line with its diverse membership over fish hatcheries, for instance, which provide angling opportunities at the expense of struggling populations of wild fish. The smaller groups want hatcheries done away with once and for all, and some of these organizations can't be bothered to think too hard about salmon conservation in California; in their eyes, the state is a lost cause.

IN 1867, EXACTLY ONE HUNDRED YEARS before the "Summer of Love," a Wisconsin-raised amateur botanist named John Muir, having recently recovered from an industrial accident that nearly blinded him, embarked on a long, meandering journey of self-discovery that would eventually land him in the young city of San Francisco. It was a course that would be repeated with generational regularity. Unlike adventure-seeking pilgrims of the next century, he used his two feet and a steamer ticket rather than an outstretched thumb, walking all the way from the Midwest to Florida before sailing to Cuba and catching a boat to the West Coast. In 1869, with mountains on his mind and assurances from his new employer that he'd have ample time for high-meadow rambles, he went to work as a shepherd in the foothills above the San Joaquin Valley, setting out with a flock twenty-five hundred strong on June 3 near French Bar, on the south side of the Tuolumne River. He and his sheep gained elevation through the rest of spring and into summer, crossing into the Merced River watershed to the south and finally emerging into the vaulted hanging valleys of Yosemite country, which had been his goal from the beginning. On July 15, 1868, he wrote: "Nearly all the upper basin of the Merced was displayed, with its sublime domes and canyons, dark upsweeping forests and glorious array of white peals deep in the sky, every feature glowing, radiating beauty that pours into our flesh and bones like heat rays from fire. . . . Never before had I seen so glorious a landscape, so boundless an affluence of sublime mountain beauty."

California had been admitted into the Union as a free state in 1850, though many of its first settlers came from the South and brought with them distinctly Southern mores, including a penchant for growing water-intensive crops like cotton. By the time of Muir's arrival, nearly twenty years after statehood, the transformation of California was already well under way. Wrested from Indians and Mexicans, its landscape succumbed quickly to the ministrations of gold miners, homesteaders, cattle barons, loggers, and empire builders, perhaps nowhere more visibly than in the Central Valley.

Thanks to the Southern Pacific Railroad and a host of federal land giveaways, including the Military Bounty Act, the Morrill Act, and the Swamp and Overflowed Lands Act, the place was already more of an oligarchy than it had been under the previous landlord, Mexico; 516 individuals owned nine million acres of land—and under the tenets of Manifest Destiny and all the other unwritten laws of American exceptionalism, no one could tell these pillars of society what they could and could not do with their land. Men such as Henry Miller and Charles Lux ripped this mosquito-ridden country away from nature's grip and made it bloom. They were called industrial cowboys. The vast holdings of the Miller and Lux Corporation and their competitors raised mostly cattle. But the smart ones saw the writing on the wall. They secured the water rights through any means possible and eventually started farming the land instead. I once met a canal manager who spoke with admiration of their pioneer spirit, a spirit that apparently included a willingness to commit fraud. "If you could prove you had gone across this land in a boat, then you could pick it up for practically nothing," he explained. "Henry Miller went across in a boat. The boat was on a wagon pulled by horses, but he was in a boat. That was good enough. He got all this land here."

Draining marshes, irrigating desert, and planting monocultures had the unintended effect of encouraging pests such as the grape-killing phylloxera and that scourge of vegetation everywhere, the jackrabbit. The fledgling communities of the Central Valley organized rabbit drives as a form of animal control and entertainment for valley residents.

By the 1880s, it was common practice for whole towns to gather for a rabbit slaughter and then have a picnic. A phalanx of citizens—

men, women, and children—would march through the fields, flushing the rabbits before them, until they converged on a V-shaped fence that corralled the unruly animals into a pen, at which point the deadly work was done with clubs. In this way, more than 370,000 rabbits met their demise between 1888 and 1895 in 115 separate rabbit drives, a statistic that is as chilling in its exactness (such civic pride in the control of nature!) as in its outcome. Another resident of the Central Valley, the California tule elk, was considered extinct by the late 1870s, a victim of habitat loss and market hunters. While draining Buena Vista slough at the southern end of the valley, Miller and Lux's reclamation crew happened upon a lone pair of the ungulates, thought to be the very last in existence in the San Joaquin Valley. In a grand gesture, Henry Miller demanded the elk be protected—as he continued to drain and plow up their last stand.

Despite the protestations of Muir and his spiritual descendants, including the Sierra Club and the modern environmental movement, the next century saw the reengineering of nature in California on a scale that had never been seen anywhere before, not under the Mayans, not under the Romans, not under the Egyptians, not under any previous society that had successfully—if only for a time—bent nature to its will. In a region where water was king, the state diked, dammed, and exploited virtually every possible drop. The Central Valley Project, a waterworks scheme spawned in the Great Depression and imposed on the land for the next four decades, exemplified this to the point that California managed to achieve what God could not: make water run uphill. As a result, rivers such as the San Joaquin dried up from over-irrigation, and populations of native fish plummeted. In 1988, an organization called the Natural Resources Defense Council, along with a number of other NGOs, had the audacity to challenge this status quo in court, and—to everyone's surprise—in 2006 they won (when the defendants decided to settle rather than face a judge's ruling). The San Joaquin would flow again, or at least a small fraction of it would be allowed to escape to the sea. Downstream farmers and landowners, however, would still be allowed to recapture some of this water for irrigation. In this way, the settlement was seen as a model for balancing the needs of both farmers and fish.

＝＝＝＝＝＝

IF THE YUBA WAS A WINDOW into the past, the San Joaquin River was a look at the future. After our swim, I tagged along with Rene the next day to Fresno, in the heart of the Central Valley, where he planned to join both the plaintiffs and the defendants in the San Joaquin lawsuit to see the court settlement up close—that is, on the river itself—during a bus tour to view the watershed and the many obstacles to restoration that were slowing the process to a crawl. This is part of Rene's job description. Though he is a scientist, he's also expected to take complicated ideas and explain them to professionals in other disciplines, not to mention the public at large. Unlike many in his line of work, he enjoys this aspect of the job. It keeps him in touch with public perceptions and gives him a chance to gauge the possibility of effecting real change, not only in land-use policy but in larger philosophical arenas concerning how Americans actually view the natural world.

We all boarded a Trailways bus together. A heightened sense of anxiety, brought on by increasingly erratic weather patterns that have included sudden shifts from flood to drought, hovered over this caravan of people, all of them connected by the vicissitudes of a natural resource increasingly in demand. There were managers from multiple city, county, state, and federal agencies, people responsible for managing water—the cubic feet per second of water, the irrigation exchanges of water, the reservoirs of water—plus a few worried farmers.

One of those farmers was Joel from Bakersfield—lantern-jawed and tight-lipped, with the broad hands and build of a man who worked the land. Now that the settlement had mandated that 15 percent of the San Joaquin eventually flow downstream, he wanted to see up close what this might mean for his future. He was growing almonds and pistachios, thirsty crops that couldn't weather a sudden dry spell, and right now he was putting carrots in the ground. The farms around Bakersfield supply 90 percent of the country's carrots. As we drove by orchard after orchard, he pointed out a detail I never would have noticed. "See those?" he said, motioning to a grove of small trees planted in neat rows beside the highway. "Those are self-pollinating almond trees. They don't need bees. It's an expensive crop, but we hope it's the future." Farmers like Joel had to plan ahead. Lately, anyone who was paying attention had heard about a new unexplained phenomenon: colony collapse disorder. Planning for a world without bees was his job.

Before our lunch stop, Rene stood up at the front of the bus as agricultural fields whizzed by in a hazy smudge. We had just left Friant Dam in the Sierra foothills and were now passing the fruits of its purpose in the valley below. Rene was allotted a few minutes to speak. Already there had been grumbling about how much money the court-mandated restoration effort of the San Joaquin was going to cost. It always came down to dollars. Yet the cost of *not* doing anything, of making like a scared ostrich, would be so much higher. "We spend a lot of money," Rene began, "trying to engineer things that will allow us to keep behaving the same way." He looked around. Was any of this sinking in? "It's a good thing to keep in mind when you're thinking about the cost of the project."

I glanced over at a few of the water users on board who considered Rene an archnemesis, the irrigators who had gone head-to-head against him in meeting rooms all over the Central Valley. They sat stone-faced. This wasn't the Wild West anymore, and while no one was about to draw a pistol, several pairs of eyes drew a cold bead on the scientist's forehead.

He continued. "In the North Pacific, if there's a keystone species, it's salmon. They move nutrients from the ocean—the origin of all life—to inland areas in the form of their bodies. There are studies that trace salmon nutrients in bears, birds, bats, and redwood trees." He went on to outline some of the restoration goals and then sat down.

An uncomfortable silence filled the bus. At the next stop, as we filed across a gravel driveway, Rene peeled off from the group. He had spied the remains of an animal next to a barbed-wire fence. It was the cranium of a barn owl, ivory white and perfectly cured by the relentless sun, its sharp upper beak still intact. He reminded me of Hamlet pondering Yorick's skull. What had been this owl's fate? A diet of poisoned rats, maybe, or predation by the larger great horned owl, a species that thrives in fragmented human habitats. He pocketed the skull for closer examination later. It would make a perfect addition to his fireplace mantel at home.

Where the Merced River empties into the San Joaquin, not far from where John Muir had tended his flock, we met up with a Bureau of Reclamation biologist named Don Portz, who was netting chinook salmon for an experimental population upriver. These were strays from a hatchery on the Merced. For whatever reason, some of the salmon failed to make a left turn at the tributary, continuing instead up the main stem of the San Joaquin despite a complicated metal barrier across the river designed to keep them out. Securing the fish for this experiment involved an intimate knowledge of the bureaucracy and a willingness to work around it. The salmon were officially designated as "lost fish" once they made it past the barrier. At that point they were netted, outfitted with acoustic tags, and released many miles upriver below Friant Dam, a monolithic 319-foot-tall wall that impounds the San Joaquin into Millerton reservoir and delivers irrigation water in two concrete canals running in opposite directions: one thirty-six miles north to Madera County, and the other 152 miles south, all the way down to Kern County and the outskirts of Bakersfield. Friant, an early component of the Central Valley Project, was the deathblow that dried up the San Joaquin.

So far, Portz had netted and released ten females and thirty-five males. "Everyone knows guys don't ask for directions," he said. Some of the released fish were already building redds. Fry spawned by these salmon would be trapped and hauled away. Those that avoided capture were doomed; they would find a dry river downstream when it came time to migrate out to the Pacific. The data collected from these experimental fish is critical to the restoration effort. One day, if the San Joaquin flows to the sea again, as mandated by the settlement, the biologists will know exactly where in the river the fish prefer to spawn. It was necessary for Portz to use "lost fish" because the hatchery managers on the Merced can't donate fish without local irrigators crying bloody murder and saying there must be enough fish after all for such a program to exist. Declaring the fish lost was the only way to sidestep the politics. "Kabuki" is what Rene calls this dance between agencies.

It had been a long day, and my mind was wandering. As Portz moved about in his waders, tending his nets and scouting for fish, I watched the San Joaquin from a shady bank. The river rolled by with the consistency of spilled house paint. It didn't look real. Everything out here seemed slightly off or even fake. Earlier that day I had stood out in the middle of the flattest landscape I'd ever seen. You could hardly call it a watershed. There were no forests, little in the way of riparian growth. Birds were few, mostly starlings and other non-native species that ruled in a kingdom of diminished biodiversity. Plowed fields stretched to the horizon without a single tree to interrupt the two-dimensional flow. A network of canals and irrigation ditches crisscrossed agricultural land so valuable that most of the farmers' little ranch houses didn't have backyards. A furrowed line of plowed soil wrapped around each house like a boa constrictor. There was just enough room for a gravel driveway out front and a couple of pickups. Kids' play structures stood in the dirt.

Joel, the Bakersfield farmer, told me that about 70 percent of the Central Valley's produce was exported abroad. "We've learned how to sell rice to the Chinese," he said, grinning. Another farmer, Cannon Michael of the Bowles Company, a direct descendant of land baron Henry Miller, swept his outstretched arm before him. He owned everything in sight. Standing amid the clods of newly plowed soil in black cowboy boots and a pin-striped dress shirt, he frowned at the gathering of water managers. "As landowners and farmers who do large projects only when we have the money to do them, we have big concerns," he said. "Over a hundred million has been spent on the river to date and it's still exactly the same. Not a shovel of dirt has been turned and California agriculture is starving for water. As farmers, we take things and we fix them. We don't pretend a magic money fairy is coming down." Everyone nodded. It was true that the river restoration, after being tied up in the courts for years, was taking a long time to gain its footing. If anything, extra care was being taken so that farmers like Cannon Michael would be impacted as little as possible.

"I drove across the Bay Bridge the other day," Rene spoke up. "It was built one day at a time. Same with the Golden Gate."

"What about ruining economies and taking land from people?" the farmer shot back.

Just then a group of white pelicans circled overhead, an incongruous spectacle that offered welcome relief, and I found myself watching the big ivory birds until I could no longer stare into the sun. The first settlers complained about huge flocks of birds. They said they sounded like freight trains in the night, waking them up at all hours with their taking off and landing. Since then, more than 90 percent of the Central Valley's wildlife habitat has been lost. Where there were once 20 million to 40 million waterfowl, now there are a million. "We feed the world," Cannon Michael went on. My head was pounding— several of the participants also admitted to having splitting headaches. A hydrologist quietly said she'd felt nauseated for most of the day. The land as far as the eye could see was being bombarded with chemicals— chemicals to kill the weeds, chemicals to kill the bugs, chemicals to fortify the soil, chemicals to combat the unintentional side effects of other chemicals. It was chemical warfare out here in the Central Valley, and every last piece of artillery was being deployed in this war against nature. At that moment, the idea of eating a single fruit, vegetable, or nut from this place turned my stomach.

Generations of people from all over the world have migrated to California with hopes and dreams. Imagination is a defining characteristic of the state. Rene Henery will tell you it takes imagination to envision a landscape that supports both people and salmon. Like so many Californians before him, he's optimistic. "Is the solution to continue to pour our resources into an unsustainable food-production system that's sucking the life out of everything?" he asked the bureaucrats, many of whom would have had him bound and tied on the next train out of town. "No, let's create better systems and find a balance."

A WAKE APPEARED IN the current, snapping me back to the San Joaquin, this river turned irrigation canal. Don Portz, the biologist, saw it too. "That's a fish!" he yelled, running upstream along the river and pointing. Everyone turned to look. "It's going right for the net," someone called out. The salmon had managed to get past the fish barrier, probably finding a gap near the bottom and using all its strength to muscle underneath. Whether it was simply straying, as salmon are known to do, or whether somewhere in its DNA, muddied by years of hatchery genetics, the allure of the upper, dewatered San Joaquin still exerted influence, no one knew. We all rushed over to the edge of the embankment to see the action, following the fish's progress. The farmer from Bakersfield was there, his hand shielding the sun so he could see better. So was the canal manager who admired the fraudulent land-grabbing technique of Henry Miller. So were all the dam operators, hydrologists, and government pencil pushers. We all stood together on the embankment, watching what would happen next. Portz waded out toward his net, which was shaped like a giant wind sock. The wake continued upstream, heading directly for the biologist. An urban planner from Sacramento let out a gasp and instinctively covered her mouth.

"The pull of these big salmonids is too much for us," Rene whispered to me. He was right. Something about these persistent fish had grabbed me the first time I saw one heading up the Rogue River in Oregon. We all stared at the water as if hypnotized. There was a hush as the wake vanished, then a pause, and finally palpable disappointment. The fish had dodged the net and reappeared farther upstream, swimming into a muddy river that would offer little spawning habitat before going dry altogether. It was beyond a lost fish now. It was a ghost fish. Rene tapped me on the shoulder.

"You feel that?" he asked me.

I did.

"That's your heart."

CHAPTER 8

THE REEF NETTER'S
OFF-SEASON

ONE TIME, DURING A HEATED EXCHANGE BETWEEN RENE HENERY and another biologist about the effects of commercial fishing on salmon stocks, I listened to Rene make an impassioned plea for the ancient occupation. It was true, he admitted, that some species, notably chinook, were getting smaller after more than a century of intensive harvest at sea that selected the biggest fish. But the alternative—no fishing—struck him as a worse fate. "At Trout Unlimited, we don't want the commercial fisherman to disappear," he went on. "One, because we all love fish and respect fishermen, and two, because fishing is one of the main linkages between the public and caring about salmon. People are mostly disconnected from their food these days. The bulk of our seafood still comes from the ocean. If we lose commercial fishermen, we're truly dealing with the wild in abstract."

The wild in abstract. I thought about this as I left the mainland, chasing a rumor. Winter had turned to spring and another salmon season was upon us. For so many people stuck indoors—in their homes, in their cars, in the mall—the changing of the seasons has become an abstraction, even though for millennia it was a way to make sense of that ultimate abstraction, the passage of time, from birth to death. The new season was taking me to an island in Puget Sound with a long history of salmon fishing. The salmon hadn't arrived yet, but preparations for their homecoming were already under way.

I'd been hearing about the reef netters of Lummi Island for years. Supposedly they used a centuries-old technique to catch salmon in a way that was both sustainable and made for an exceptional piece of fish. Most commercial fisheries at sea are not selective—that is, they cannot distinguish between healthy stocks of fish and threatened or endangered stocks. With salmon, this is especially true, since many stocks school together. Whether caught by a troller on a hook and line, in a purse seine, or in a gill net, a salmon from an endangered stock is not likely to survive even the most well-intentioned release. The reef-net fishery, I kept hearing, is an exception. I drove aboard a small ferry near the Canadian border and made the short crossing to Lummi to find out why.

NETTLES FARM IS NOT the sort of place with a blue-chip view of the sound and surrounding islands, not like the Willows Inn down the hill. It's a working farm. The only view is of unkempt pasture and trees. You take the road just past the Willows and climb through a grid of small houses that form a typical beach community, with open lots facing the water. A long gravel driveway leads higher still, entering the dark shade beneath a canopy of second-growth Douglas fir and leading to a cluster of chaletlike buildings in a clearing. Tall thickets of salmonberry and blackberry encircle the houses as if in the final stages of a siege. I arrived to a cacophony of birdcalls. Roosters crowed from near and far. The flutelike song of a Swainson's thrush echoed from the woods in ascending arpeggios. Hummingbirds chased each other about. This was Riley Starks's toehold on the land.

Starks was pulling on a maroon canvas work shirt when I arrived. He had just gotten back from Seattle and needed to feed his chickens. More to the point, he was anxious to check on their welfare. Throughout the spring he had been engaged in a pitched battle with five ravens. Already they had decapitated seven of his pullets. I walked with him through a small orchard of fruit trees to one of his coops. A pair of ravens flew overhead at our approach and made loud croaking noises. "They're pretty raucous. If you know any Native American tales, the Indians really understand the raven. They live to be forty. They're smart. They work together. They probably have a call just for me." He said this with a rueful laugh. He had short-cropped graying hair and a scraggly beard. His glasses were round and wire-rimmed. Dressed in blunt-toed cowboy boots and jeans, he looked the part of a man who worked the land, but the Southwestern belt buckle with its inlaid turquoise suggested whimsy, perhaps a need for the finer things occasionally. He folded back a brown tarp from one of several coops and started counting chickens while filling their water. The pullets moved around nervously, making pitiable peeping noises. They were no match for a corvid, in brain or brawn. Starks said the ravens had figured out how to work as a team—a team of executioners, he called them. One would fly down onto the coop and scare all the pullets into a corner, while its partner waited out of sight on the other side of the fencing until it could grab a cowering chicken and pull it through the pen. Though a whole pullet was too large to fit through the fence, the head was still a prize. The ravens pecked it right off.

Feathers from past depredations lay scattered in the dirt. "I've run chickens here for twenty years, and this is the first year this has happened. I feel bad for the birds—I'm supposed to protect them." His efforts at shoring up the coop seemed to be working, though, and all the chickens were accounted for. We moved on to the incubator, and then the medical coop, where he kept the few survivors from the raven attacks sequestered while they recuperated, their heads bald and bloodied. Starks wasn't much for small talk. As we made the rounds together, he asked me a question. It was a game he liked to play with a new acquaintance, he said, a simple binary question—his way of divvying up the world and making sense of it, on the order of "Ford or Chevy?" Or "Beatles or Stones?" "Matisse or Picasso?" He paused and gave me a look of bemusement, one I would soon realize he'd perfected over years, the slight curling of the lips that suggested his smiles had come at the expense of a lot of experience, then pushed his glasses back onto the bridge of his nose. "I ask everyone the same question. Ready . . . ?"

"Shoot."

"King or sockeye?"

I thought about it. Certainly I loved them both. Choosing one over the other seemed unfair. Each had its own place. Both Jon Rowley and Kevin Davis would choose king—I was pretty sure of that. They knew exactly what they wanted. Me, I wasn't so sure. "Is this a trick question?"

"No, just the answer that lies at the pit of your soul. You're stalling."

"Well, for texture I'd have to go with the fatty silkiness of king. But for taste . . ."

"Sockeye hands down," Starks interrupted, saving me from further equivocation. "On hanging day I'll take a last plate of grilled sockeye, thank you." Something in his voice told me that Starks had been keeping an imagined hangman at bay for years now.

RILEY STARKS'S LIFE COULD be reduced to two totems: fish and fowl. He had spent the better part of a lifetime learning how to produce the best quality of each for the table. Over the years they had oscillated in importance. "I'm actually a homebody," he said to me matter-of-factly. It was a surprising admission for a commercial fisherman. "The thing about fishing is, it's an isolating experience unless you're in a tight fraternity of other fishermen and their wives, because you go away. I like land, a place, an identity. I was fishing Bristol Bay, and you make a ton of money. You mistreat the fish. It wasn't satisfying in a deep way—at least not for me. For other people it probably is."

In 1991, Starks found this piece of logged-over property on Lummi Island in northwest Washington State. It was covered in stinging nettles, twenty acres in all. When he wasn't fishing, he started doing construction. "I was trying to find something to do in the winters that connected me." He built houses and sold off fifteen of the twenty acres. The last five-acre parcel he kept for himself. He wanted to see what five acres could do. Some might call Starks a zealot. Like so many American epicures before him, his on-the-road-to-Damascus moment came in the Old Country, during a vacation in France, eating a tomato in Valence. "It was just the best tomato. I realized I'd never really eaten one before." The juices dribbled peachlike down his chin, and the tug-of-war between sweetness and acidity bowled him over. This wasn't a product of American industrial ingenuity. It wasn't uniformly round for easy sorting or hard as a rock for shipping coast-to-coast. It wasn't even red. Standing there in a French marketplace, Starks took another bite from the misshapen thing, eating it like an apple, and vowed to grow his own.

He sold a thousand pounds of them the first season.

He built greenhouses on Nettles Farm and eventually grew eighteen different varieties of heirloom tomato. "It's all about changing the paradigm of what you expect when you go to the store. Hard to believe it wasn't very long ago, but it was radical." Then he became a chicken farmer. At its height, he ran eight hundred laying hens and six thousand eaters. His wife contemplated a restaurant on the property, then reconsidered. They realized there were too many chickens, too much dust. It just wasn't going to work. The ambience wasn't there. Instead, in 2001 they bought a place down the hill, called the Willows Inn. Starks liked the juxtaposition of the names: scrappy Nettles Farm up the hill and the more refined Willows on the water. The couple built the restaurant into a destination eatery—not that this ensured any sort of financial success. "I used to stand on that deck on a Friday night and the restaurant would be completely empty, or maybe two people inside. The sun was going down and I'd say, 'You gotta be kidding me. This is the best view in the world, and there's no one here to see it?'" And then the Great Recession hit in 2008. One of the last things Starks did before selling the Willows at the end of 2012 (and getting divorced) was hire a young kid named Blaine Wetzel to be chef. Wetzel was a good hire, recently back from apprenticing at

Noma in Copenhagen, a restaurant some were calling the best in the world. "I got to watch him from the beginning, and right out of the gate he was a prodigy." Now Starks was fishing again and selling his salmon to Wetzel at the Willows, the restaurant he had put on the map.

"I'm kind of in the process of remaking myself," he told me as he measured out the chicken feed. He had two marriages behind him and a girlfriend who lived on the mainland. Nettles Farm was now a B&B, his main income for the past year. On the heels of his divorce he had tried to sell the farm and leave Lummi for good. "I never wanted to see this island again. I never wanted to see anybody I knew again. I'm lucky that I didn't get out, because I had to face it. Now I'm friends with my ex-wife and I get to take care of this place. It's had a lot of iterations. We'll see where it goes. I'm getting to where I can enjoy it a little bit." Enjoying it meant paring down his enthusiasms. Salmon season now took first priority. Tomatoes were out and he had cut way back on the chicken farming, running only poulet de Bresse and the Canadian poulet bleu. They take much longer to grow than a typical bird, caged on a feedlot and injected with hormones, but there is no comparison in flavor. He butchered them himself and sold the four-pound eaters fresh and dressed out for about thirty-five dollars apiece. One of his oven roasters, he said, could rival even sockeye for a last meal. Starks also had Asian pears, Jonagold apples, pie cherries, apricots, and strawberries. His asparagus was in demand. And, of course, the nettles: There were still plenty of nettles to pick and eat each spring, just as there had been in the early days, when he lived in a tent and made endless meals of nettle ravioli. You had to be careful with them—the sting was sharp and lingering—but with gloves to handle the bright-green stalks and a quick blanching in boiling water, they were transformed into an intensely flavored food that was bursting with nutrients, the perfect ingredient for a spring soup or pesto. An old French aphorism came to mind: A nettle in the farmyard is worth an extra egg in the pantry. Still true.

Earlier that day he had met with fish buyers at Seattle's Metropolitan Market, a high-end grocery chain that sells organic produce and carefully sourced meats and fish. He flashed his self-deprecating smile as he explained to me that this too was part of his new life. As the so-called marketing director for Lummi Island Wild, a cooperative effort of like-minded fishermen, he was doing more of a desk job these days. Maybe this was appropriate for a man in his sixties. Wasn't life about moving through its various phases gracefully? Though he still thought of himself as a fisherman, now his job was to secure outlets for the co-op's fish. He met with seafood vendors, restaurateurs, and supermarkets. The co-op had created a buying club, with customers all over the country. Starks traveled and sat in on meetings. It was the way things needed to be. Sometimes he had to laugh at the strange turns his life's progress had taken. The sockeye fishery was little more than a month away, and it was his job to secure markets for the co-op's salmon ahead of time. This year, he reminded me, was forecast to be the biggest sockeye run in the Fraser River since record keeping first began. The timing couldn't be better. Starks—and the co-op—needed to make some money. They were building a tender, a $1.4 million boat that would deliver the reef-net fleet's catch to a processor on the mainland. A shipyard in La Conner, Washington, was halfway done, and it was scheduled to be ready for next year's season.

But that was *next* year. This year was the time to show that reef-net fishing was a superior way to catch fish. Part of the deal with Metro Market involved the future: They could have his sockeye—a fish that was in demand—now, but only if they agreed to take pink salmon next year. Pinks are the most numerous salmon in the Pacific; the trick is getting customers to appreciate their relative merits in comparison to more sought-after species. No one likes pinks. They're thought of as a cannery fish—a high-volume, low-quality filler of cans. They have less fat than other species, flesh that's pink rather than a deep red. Anglers like to say, "They smoke up okay," which is another way of saying they aren't fit for the grill like a king or a sockeye. But that reputation is starting to change. If handled properly and rushed to market, they can make good table fare. "Cook them like a trout," those in the know say. Starks came away from the meeting with a handshake, which he considered better than a signed contract.

STARKS BOUGHT HIS FIRST REEF net the same year he moved to Lummi Island. It would take him another five years before he got up the gumption to learn how to use it. One winter afternoon he went for a walk on the beach. It was during halftime on Super Bowl Sunday. Though not much of a football fan, he felt an obligation as owner of the Beach Store Café—a new venture for him—to make sure the island's sole meeting place (other than the pricy Willows) was open for the game, a borrowed TV blaring its traditional rituals from a corner.

That day, as on every other, the water was the bigger draw for Starks. Recently, Puget Sound had weathered a hundred-year storm, and he figured there was a good chance the tide had exposed a secret or two. Though Lummi could boast plenty of beaches, Starks decided to take his halftime walk near Village Point, on the northwest side of the island, a place where Native Americans had gathered for generations in temporary makeshift camps to fish for salmon. The northern end of Lummi is shaped like an arrowhead aimed at Canada. Village Point, a triangular thrust of land jutting into Rosario Strait, forms the left barb on the arrowhead and looks west to Orcas Island. Pacific salmon returning to rivers that empty into the Salish Sea must pass through a deep channel separating Vancouver Island and the Olympic Peninsula—the Strait of Juan de Fuca—and then either turn south into U.S. waters or north toward Canadian territory. Village Point is perfectly situated to intercept Canada-bound fish, especially those headed for the Fraser River, just over the international border to the north.

The Fraser, the longest river in British Columbia, is one of the great salmon nurseries south of Alaska, along with the Skeena to its north and the Columbia to the south. Named for explorer Simon Fraser, it's a huge system fed by a multitude of lakes, draining more than eighty-five thousand square miles, an area larger than Nebraska. Takla

Lake, Chilko Lake, Harrison Lake, Williams Lake, Adams Lake, and Kamloops Lake are just some of the large lakes in its watershed. The river rises at Fraser Pass near the Alberta border and flows northwest along the Rocky Mountain Trench before turning south at Prince George, gaining size and strength as it's joined by the Nechako, Quesnel, Chilcotin, and Thompson, all famous salmon rivers in their own right. The geography of the basin is especially suitable to sockeye because of all those feeder lakes. Sockeye are unique among Pacific salmon in their requirement for a lake environment during their life cycle. While adults spawn in the gravel beds of streams like other species, they can also spawn around the periphery of the lake itself if there's sufficient groundwater welling up or streams emptying into the lake to give the eggs a necessary jolt of oxygen. After hatching, young sockeye rear in the lake for a year or two, until ready to head to the ocean. The world's sockeye concentrations are all in places with large lake systems connected to the Pacific: Bristol Bay, Alaska; Russia's Kamchatka Peninsula; and the Fraser.

Though bright silver like other salmon in their prime, on its spawning grounds the sockeye is equally—if very differently—attractive, earning another nickname: red. When the average person pictures a spawning salmon, this is what they envision: a fish in brilliant Christmas colors, with red body and green head. The sockeye's name has nothing to do with footwear or sight—it's just a bastardization of a Salish Indian word used by people living along the lower Fraser River: *suk-kegh,* meaning red fish. Here on Lummi Island, as in many other salmon capitals, the sockeye is the prize fish. While chinook are heftier and command a higher price in the marketplace, and pinks are more numerous, year in and year out sockeye salmon remain the most valuable species of salmon, because of their high quality and dense concentrations. Larger than pinks, averaging four to seven pounds, sockeye spend longer intervals at sea (up to four years, though usually two) and have a diet that consists primarily of crustaceans, which means their abundance is tied directly to the productivity of the ocean. In years with good upwellings of cold, nutrient-rich water in the North Pacific, the population of free-floating phytoplankton rises, which in turn nourishes burgeoning clouds of zooplankton and the salmon that feed on them. Warmer surface waters associated with El Niño put the brakes on this. The feeding habits of sockeye can be discerned in a particular piece of anatomy: They have more gill rakers—toothy, comblike cartilage attached to the gills to filter krill—than other species of salmon.

In some years the Fraser sees more returning salmon than any other river system in the world, the majority pinks and sockeye. For millennia, indigenous fishermen living along the fingerlike network of waterways that form Puget Sound, the Strait of Juan de Fuca, and the Strait of Georgia—a body of water known collectively as the Salish Sea—intercepted these Fraser-bound salmon using any number of clever devices, from fish wheels to weirs to reef nets. Though evidence of such fisheries is mostly gone, occasionally a relic from the past surfaces. On his halftime walk, just as he had hoped, Starks saw something in the tideline that made him stop and look more closely. A stone among the cobbles was not shaped like the others. It was the absence that caught his eye: He could see through it. Immediately he recognized the form of a reef-net anchor. The smooth granite was round and about the same size as a grapefruit. But what made it stick out was a small hole bored through the middle. This was a rock that had been worked by a human being, possibly several hundred years ago, to be used in an ancient form of fishing called reef netting. Starks figured this particular stone had been chosen because it probably already had a slight indentation at its center that could hold a few agates; it was then likely positioned beneath a cascading stream of water in a creek bed. How many years it would take for the agitation of spilling water and agates to bore through remains a mystery. Such a tool required patience in its fashioning. *Tap tap tap.* Once bored through, the stone could be tied with cordage to hold down a reef, a funnellike contrivance that guided salmon toward Indian canoes, where they could be caught in a cooperative effort that required additional patience and skill. The reef-net anchor was a sign. Starks understood that day where he needed to be and what he needed to do.

As we stood in the dirt outside his home, most of which was now converted into rooms for his B&B guests, he handed me the donut-shaped stone and then disappeared inside a small cottage detached from the main house—his living quarters these days—to make us some coffee. Holding the anchor was like shaking hands with history. Slate-gray, the stone had heft, a sense of gravitas, yet it was smooth and balanced. Starks considered it more than a chance find or a gift from the sea. Both artifact of the past and monument to the future, it represented everything he had been working toward most of his life, as a fisherman and as a person.

He reappeared moments later and we sat down on what he jokingly referred to as his patio—just some old lawn furniture at the edge of the driveway. A song sparrow chittered from a fence post nearby. He inhaled the aroma of his coffee and took a long sip. Starks comes from agrarian stock. His mother's people were Mormons who wagon-trained with Brigham Young. His father was Scottish-English. There was some Blackfoot Indian in the family. He was born in Port Townsend, Washington, and then moved across the sound to Everett, where his father was in the Army. They had a two-and-a-half-acre farm. Daily rhythms back then were less complicated and discordant than today, more Verdi than Stravinsky. "People were intentional about what they planted," Starks said. "There was flow."

Starting in his early twenties, his progression became ever more backward, a steady pace into the past. It began with the boat. After four years of college, he was all set to enroll in law school and the comfortable, respectable existence that would follow. He'd just weathered four tumultuous years, 1968 to 1972, during which the country had gone through wrenching change. He wasn't a radical—more like a hippie. . . . Well, that wasn't accurate either. He was poor. He finished his undergrad degree in the fall and had to wait a year before starting the University of Oregon's law program. Up to that point his life had been governed by an overriding desire to get good grades.

The life of the mind was satisfying, but it lacked an elemental edge. Starks wanted to use his hands. So, with a year to kill, he bought himself a twenty-nine-foot kelper named *Kingfisher* (which he renamed *Asterix,* after the swashbuckling French comic-book character) and went fishing. It was just Starks, the weather, and the boat. No excuses. All up to him. He moored the kelper in Everett, north of Seattle, and then, unnerved by this spontaneous decision, disappeared for a week to figure out his next steps. When he returned, he found the boat half-sunk. A leaking shaft log—the housing of the propeller shaft—had nearly finished him before he'd even started. A taciturn old fisherman on the dock handed him a #10 coffee can and told him to start bailing.

The first time he took the kelper out, he was too embarrassed to try to turn it around in front of the other fishermen hanging around the dock. Instead, he backed the boat a full mile down Ebey Slough to Possession Sound. It was 1973, and his target was Dungeness crab. Before long he knew he wouldn't be starting law school in the fall. The next year, instead of hitting the books, he went after salmon. This was the same year that an obscure U.S. District Court judge named George Boldt handed down a decision regarding the original Indian treaties of 1854–55 that promised Northwest tribes their fair share of fish "in common with" the settlers. Fishermen like Starks had watched this development with interest, most of them opposed to anything that would favor the Indians. When Boldt declared that signing tribes were entitled to 50 percent of the catch, the white fleet exploded and openly disregarded the law. One man with a family connection to the fishing industry, Slade Gorton, based his entire political career on being the "Indian slayer," going all the way to the U.S. Senate and fighting Indian rights to no avail each step of the way—or, as one historian put it, becoming a case study in "failing upwards." Starks, however, was happy for the tribes. "I've always been a liberal," he told me. "I agreed with it then and I still do."

By the mid-1970s, Starks was mooring his boat north of Bellingham in Blaine, Washington, just south of the Canadian border. His first day out for salmon was a rough one and he couldn't pilot the kelper beyond Boundary Bay, where all the other fishermen were waiting for the opening. As luck would have it, wind from the southwest pushed the sockeye in toward shore. For his very first set as a salmon fisherman, Starks hauled in four hundred sockeye, at sixty-five cents a pound. He earned nearly two thousand dollars, half the cost of the boat. In subsequent years he moved around, fishing different species and refurbishing a variety of boats. He kept a modified halibut boat tied up in Sausalito to fish herring in San Francisco Bay. In 1977, after fishing for herring, he was going to carpool home for Christmas with two fishermen from the Swinomish tribe near Anacortes, Washington. They all stood in line at the same bank in San Francisco to cash their checks. "I was out of there in five minutes. It took them forty minutes. All the way home we talked about what it was like to be an Indian in our white culture."

Even back then, Starks was into the simple pleasures of good food and drink. Driving down to San Francisco, he would pull over in Ashland, Oregon, the only place south of Seattle where he could get a decent cup of coffee before reaching the Bay Area. Starks fished Puget Sound and San Francisco Bay. He went up to Alaska and fished Bristol Bay. He fished the Naknek and Nushagak, the Egegik and Kvichak, and watched walruses mating on Round Island. When Mount St. Helens blew in 1980, he and his crewman ran all day and night to make it to a phone in Goodnews Bay, to check on their families back home in Washington. In time, he grew restless. The fishing life had changed him. Looking back, he would say it was like taking LSD for the first time. His whole perspective had changed. Work, food, home. They were interconnected in ways he needed to explore. Finding the reefnet anchor was more than a coincidence.

WHILE THE HISTORY OF reef netting is not well known, it's believed to be a specialty of tribes in the Puget Sound region. Sometime in the first years of the twentieth century, white men watched Native Americans successfully catch salmon using the reef-net method and replicated the technology.

"Look at this," Starks said, guiding me into the main house, the one he now rented out to strangers. In his lightly used living room, he kept a very small library on reef netting, all of two books. The first was a simple sheaf of white paper bound by a rusty clip. It was homemade, all the pages mimeographed. Careful handwriting filled the margins of the first page: "Nestled within the archipelago of the San Juan Islands, there remains a small breed of salmon seekers, ancient in their craft. And though today's tide often turns against them, these fishers cling to their dreams; anchored and steadfast in their way." The text and accompanying photos were by someone named Woody Woodcock. This was one of the few known documents on modern reef netting, Starks told me. I leafed through the pages. It had the handmade look of a family album yet the tone of something mystical. Brief koans peppered its pages, such as this bit of reef-net wisdom that might as well describe the fishing life in general:

> *And in my dreams I become eager,*
> *to wait again . . .*

Pictures of salmon and lyrical descriptions of their anatomy and life cycles alternated with moody landscape photographs. A hand-drawn diagram depicted the process. At its heart, the reef net is a deception. Imagine a funnel two hundred feet long, with a mouth just as wide, all of it formed by rope lines. Tied to these lines are meter-long blue or green ribbons that wave in the current, simulating shoals. Migrating salmon enter at the mouth and follow the reef as it narrows. At any time they could burst through the waving ribbons and be on their way, but they're fooled and continue forward as the reef constricts ever tighter until they are in the trap—a fifty-by-fifty-foot net strung between two small barges, each about forty feet long, that hangs out of sight below the reef's tapered exit. A spotter posted in a crow's nest above calls out to his crew when the salmon are directly over the net, which is then hoisted with electric winches in a spray of cascading water and leaping fish. All hands on deck rush to the net and bring in the catch. In a matter of seconds the salmon, maybe scores of them, are lifted from the bay's currents and guided into holding tanks, still alive.

The spotter's stand is a special place. Wearing polarized sunglasses, the spotter waits and watches from his perch twenty feet above the deck. As Woodcock writes: "The stand is a world apart." Nature's theater reveals a new act every day—every moment—in the *tidal showcase,* with perpetually shifting winds and skies, the waves "kissed with different glares and colors." But time and modernity have caught up to the reef netters. The advent of the motor changed everything. "A noisy throbbing drone blasted over waters that were once so silent. And boats moved around in pursuit of salmon rather than waiting quiet in one place." The author laments new technology, greedy fishermen, depleted fish runs. The book ends with a Hindu poem:

> *O mother earth!*
> *O wind, my father!*
> *O fire, my friend!*
> *O water, my kinsman!*
> *O sky, my noble brother!*
> *I salute you all*

"Don't lose this," Starks said to me, reluctantly handing it over. The second book, *Reef Net Technology of the Saltwater People,* was professionally printed and published by the Saanich Indian School Board. The Saanich people are part of the Coastal Salish linguistic group and now live primarily on southern Vancouver Island. Text and illustrations depicted the traditional reef-net method of catching salmon. The book begins with a myth explaining the origin of the reef net: A beautiful young Saanich woman was wooed by a handsome young man from another tribe. After rebuffing his advances, she agreed to marry him provided that he'd stay with the Saanich people for a while. In that time, he showed the people how to build a reef net from willow and they prospered with salmon. Then, as agreed, he took his wife back to his home, but instead of heading for a village on the mainland, they paddled out to sea with all their possessions loaded on the canoe. "When they reached a distance away, they simply vanished. . . ." The Saanich people realized the salmon spirit had visited them in human form and carried away one of their daughters as tribute.

I flipped through the book. The last chapter had a one-word title: "Genocide." As far as he knew, Starks told me, there were no Indian reef netters left anywhere. "People don't like to talk about it. It's a difficult topic," he said. White fishermen had appropriated the technique, using it in locations formerly occupied by indigenous reef netters, such as the choice currents off Lummi Island's Village Point. Starks was quick to point out that this transition from an Indian fishery to a white fishery had happened a long time ago, perhaps at the turn of the previous century, before even the oldest of today's reef netters was born. But it had happened nonetheless. He hoped that one day, in his lifetime, there would be Indian reef netters once again on the water. There was even a reef-net festival in the making, to be held later in the summer, and he hoped to convince tribal members to attend, though this too was controversial.

With contractions in Puget Sound's fishing industry, including state-sanctioned buyouts, the white reef-net fleet had been reduced from some fifty-odd permits to just eleven: eight on Lummi Island, and three others in the San Juan Islands. A style of fishing that had been around for perhaps thousands of years was nearly extinct. Yet there were good reasons to keep it alive. As far as Starks was concerned, reef netting was the single best way of bringing fresh salmon to market, if not the most efficient. Salmon caught in a gill net might spend hours, or maybe even an entire night, depending on the scrupulousness of the fisherman, hanging dead in the net before being pulled up. With purse seining, the fish died on deck in a smothering heap. In a reef-net operation, each fish was individually killed, bled, and iced. None of the fish died from asphyxiation, and their meat was untainted by a stressful death. They didn't get tossed around or kicked by busy fishermen trying to deal with a sudden onslaught of thousands of pounds of fish flopping on deck. A reef-net fish had every scale intact. As Starks explained it, you just pull the fish from a holding tank, cut a gill, and let it bleed out before icing it. "The fish crosses over without even knowing it," he said.

Because this is a fixed-gear form of fishing, good reef-net sites are used year after year and represent a rare instance of private property on the water, one that can be informally handed down or inherited through the years. The head-can anchors remain fixed underwater year-round; at the start of each fishing season, the cables leading from the anchors must be dredged up so that the reef can be suspended once again. Starks called it an exciting and effective way to catch salmon when the conditions are right, those necessary conditions being a flowing tide, though one not so strong that it can swamp or even flip the barges. And, as Starks pointed out, reef netting also comes with built-in advantages over other methods. The superb quality of the individually handled fish is one advantage. The other is that it's the only truly selective fishery. Rather than wasting unwanted bycatch by tossing it overboard, dead or nearly so, as is done with other fisheries, it is simply removed from the live tank and freed back into the sound. This is especially relevant for endangered or threatened stocks of salmon, which can be readily identified and released.

I leafed through the mimeographed sheaf of pages one more time and came upon sentences that might as well have been written by Starks himself:

> As a group, reef netters are moody characters. . . . The passage of time warps into a long drifting. There's an occasional bright joy and happiness which quickly absorbs back into the daily abandonment. And always there is waiting. The uncertain and unstable dream of waiting for the salmon to flicker far

down within the heart . . . And even if civilization itself were to float by and peddle its silly wares, the fishers could not comprehend; for their minds become filled with salmon and their eyes search only the wild and watery world of so many solitudes.

I closed the book and looked up at Starks. He gave a half nod of acknowledgment, as if there were passages yet to be written.

WIND GUSTS AND CHOPPY seas, typical for spring, scuttled our plan to take sea kayaks out past Village Point to see the fishing grounds. Instead, Starks drove me over to where the reef nets were dry-docked, just south of the point. Two mule deer does, docile as blushing tourists, sauntered right in front of us across the road to the beach. Starks parked in a driveway filled with old rusted fishing gear. Someone— a reef netter waiting for the fish, perhaps?—had made elaborate sculptures from the cast-off equipment. Several forty-by-twelve-foot barges, flat-bottomed and made of wood or fiberglass, formed a row on wooden cradles next to a small green house, partially obscuring its view of the bay. The arrangement suggested a seaside graveyard. Starks explained that the homeowner had been reef netting since 1942. "He wants to die reef netting. He wouldn't want his land used any other way." Head cans painted brown and bigger than medicine balls sat on the lawn like strange art installations.

After buying his first reef net in 1992, Starks spent five years learning how to fish it.

It was a do-it-yourself fishery without much of a blueprint. You couldn't just go shopping for a proper reef-net barge. "You have to one-off them," he explained, pointing to one of the older barges made of wood. "That was built by a guy in Bellingham. This one over here is fiberglass and was built by us. It's been a learning process of working together. Fishermen working together." Winch motors to hoist the net had been cannibalized from World War II bomb-bay door openers and landing gear. He pointed to a bank of solar panels mounted on one of the barges, the latest innovation in the fleet; the co-op was going green. Except to power the skiffs that run back and forth from the beach to the reef nets, no fossil fuels are burned. Solar panels mounted on the barges charge deep-cycle batteries, which in turn power the winches. "This is the most sustainable fishery in the world," said Starks. No more diesel fumes floating across the bay, no more *ka-thunk ka-thunk ka-thunk* of internal-combustion engines turning over. Now the only sound was the brief rattle of the winch's pulley grinding in the teeth of the sprocket. "That's the only noise you hear out here, and just for a few seconds. Otherwise it's silence. And the birds, of course."

Starks invited me to climb one of the spotter towers. A bell clanged somewhere down the beach, and nearby the forlorn whistle of a white-crowned sparrow reminded me that it was still spring. "Look at this piece of wood I'm standing on," he said, bending down to run his hand across its gray, weathered surface. "Look at the grain on this wood. This is holding my body up, this piece of wood. It's thin but it's strong, because it's old-growth fir. Every time I stand up here, I think, This is so wonderful." From the spotter's stand, I could look out across the entire fleet of reef-net gears. (Like everyone else in this little-known vocation, Starks calls the reef nets "gears.") There were four dry-docked here in this old-timer's yard and another four next door. A rail ran beneath the barges to the road. When it was time to fish, the barges were jacked off their cradles and lowered onto a rail car that could be towed by a steam donkey to the beach. Each reef-net owner had a designated fishing spot off Village Point.

"The quality of the fish is the main advantage," Starks said. "And it's really exciting, like a combination of sport fishing and commercial fishing. It's also sort of Zen-like. You have to pay attention. It's quiet. You're not screaming around with an engine. It takes skill." The reef net brings in fish in a matter of seconds and dumps them into live wells, where they swim around, giving the lactic-acid buildup time to dissipate, after which they're gilled and bled out in a separate tank before being transferred to totes filled with slush ice. The reef netters use a simple egg timer for each stage. Starks figured he'd honed his operation to take up to fifteen hundred fish a day, and each one of those fish was being handled individually in order to "eat well," as he put it, and also to command the highest price. These weren't salmon bound for a cannery—they were meant to be eaten within a few days of being caught, at a discriminating backyard barbecue or fine restaurant.

"When I moved here I wanted to be part of the island, and at that time there were fifty gears out there. This was what was happening on this island. This was a reef-net island. Everybody reef netted. You'd go to the store, everyone was in boots, and the opener would be posted. And after the opener, everybody would get a beer and tell war stories." In the old days, before the arrival of the white fishermen, the Lummi tribe would come here and they'd set up a camp at Village Point and they'd reef net in the summertime. They'd weave a reef from dune grass and string a net made from nettle cordage between two long canoes. The village was temporary. They'd break it down and head back to the mainland at the end of the season. Now the reef netters are all white. Starks reiterated that he'd like to see Native Americans rejoin their ranks, but his isn't a view shared by everyone. "There's a schism," he admitted. "It's political. In every schism there are two kinds of people. In this situation there's one side that's afraid of the tribe and one that isn't." The Boldt decision had put the tribes on equal footing with the nontribal fishermen, and so non-Indians had assumed a mostly defensive posture. In the first years following Boldt, there had been bad blood and lawlessness, and state officials didn't even bother trying to enforce the law. But over time a grudging acceptance had taken hold. Starks was ready for the next phase: working together to husband this extraordinary resource.

Because of the forecast size of the Fraser sockeye run, which anticipated a large return that summer, the co-op was planning to use a tender, a forty-by-fifteen-foot boat that could just as easily work up in Alaska's salmon fisheries. "We're growing up. This has to survive into the future. This is too good of a resource. It's too precious." Even so, there were pressures on the fishery, pressures that could cause it to just blink out of existence if they weren't careful. "Everyone is old, there's no new blood. No one's really making any money." Starks was trying to address this last point. He had a market for twenty thousand pounds of frozen fillets, plus his connections to fine-dining restaurants and chefs. His partner was working with Microsoft; this year their salmon would be sold in the corporate cafeteria, which made him laugh. He was reminded that his portrait was hanging at Google headquarters: "Riley the Reefnetter." It was part of a series of portraits done by a well-known photographer, Douglas Gayeton, for a project called "The Lexicon of Sustainability." Starks shrugged it off. The time to crow would be later, if and when the fishery got the recognition he thought it deserved. The big run of sockeye due in the summer would be a test. Were they ready?

STARKS MADE ME ANOTHER CUP of coffee before my ferry ride back to the mainland. His cottage was filled with the meaningful things in his life: a popcorn popper that he used to roast his coffee beans; an espresso machine; back issues of *Harper's,* just about the only reading he had time for these days; and an old guitar. Reading books was one of the casualties of his busy days. Besides preparing for the sockeye, he had plenty more work to do. Chicken farming wasn't easy for him. "It's expensive and I'm old," he said, with a sigh that suggested he might never find that perfect hybrid he was looking for. "I'm not going to ever grow a lot of chickens again. It's too hard. I can grow enough so that at least people who stay with me get to try a real bird." Fish and fowl. That was still his mantra. People loved salmon and chicken. He'd been through the ups and downs numerous times, the price swings and market shifts. He'd seen oven roasters the size of turkeys come flooding out of Arkansas and insipid farmed salmon take over the world.

"When prices started to collapse because of farmed salmon, we were told a rising tide lifts all boats. We all bought into that. Now we've pushed back and it's exactly opposite of what it was in the eighties. Farmed salmon was considered wonderful back then. Now everyone knows it's crap. They're talking two dollars a pound for sockeye in Bristol Bay this year. Last time I saw a price that good was 1989. I think we as fishermen have done a nice job. I'm proud of that." It took action. He knew a salmon fisherman who had resorted to guerrilla tactics. The guy would dress up in a full-body salmon suit—a hot, furry, claustrophobic affair that was nevertheless an essential part of his act. He'd show up uninvited to festivals and fairs, waving around a color chart with his fin, a SalmoFan—the same color chart that salmon farmers use when deciding what color to artificially dye their product. "People were shocked. They had no idea."

He handed me an espresso for the road. "My rule is, stop complaining and start doing something about it. Stand up and throw yourself in front of the fucking tank. That's really what you have to do. It doesn't always end well." He was hopeful and also wary. "I have no idea what my future is. Normally the way it works in this culture is you accumulate wealth for retirement or you get emeritus status, like in academia." What he expected or hoped for, he didn't say.

Just before I left, Starks pushed another one of his artifacts into my hands. "Just hold it for a bit," he said. "But don't drop it." It was a piece of fossilized walrus tusk from St. Lawrence Island in the Aleutians. The tusk had been carved into a sled runner. I was holding the broken tip of the runner. Little holes indicated where a primitive hunter-gatherer had repaired it with leather jesses. The thin, sepia-colored piece showed scratches on the bottom. I handed it back to him. "Ten thousand years ago it broke and was repaired. Look," Starks said. "Actual gravel marks from ten thousand years ago. I love this thing. It's such a deep connection to the past." He picked up the ancient reef-net anchor in his other hand, and for a moment he resembled the personification of balance, the weight of the past in each hand. Then he carefully replaced the tusk on a table and continued to hold the anchor, turning it in his hand. "This is a tool that some guy cared enough about to spend a lot of his life making and then passed down to his children. I knew what it was right away. I needed this. For me it has true value." I made an awkward joke about Starks being anchored to the island. "Yeah. It gets lonesome out here," he said. "I'm getting a dog. Maybe I'll train it to hunt truffles."

As I got ready to make the trip back to the mainland, Starks invited me to return when the salmon were running. He said I should spend a day on one of the gears, hauling in fish. There was nothing like it, he said. Being on the water with the salmon and seals and eagles, distant islands shimmering in a blue mist, the current moving underneath. There was the waiting and there was the sudden spasm of excitement. "Anyway, think about coming back," he said, "to see what a reef-net island is like when the salmon are here."

CHAPTER 9

THE BALLAD OF
LONESOME LARRY

OUTSIDE IT WAS A BLAST FURNACE, A HUNDRED DEGREES IN the rabbitbrush, the summer sun showing no mercy. Rene Henery and I had been driving for two days, and our car smelled like onions. Walla Walla Sweet. The bulbs came flying off tractor-trailers like wild pitches. At Sacajawea State Park, in the arid southeast corner of Washington State—where the Snake River joins its turbid flow to the Columbia, both of these immense rivers looking like mirages in an otherwise dry and dusty landscape—we washed off the road grime and floated on our backs, watching lacy cirrus clouds slip across the sky. It hadn't rained in weeks.

The confluence—flat, unremarkable, surprisingly warm—belied the badlands upstream. This was where Lewis and Clark, guided by their Shoshone interpreter—a new mother, no less—would have realized they had reached the final leg of their journey to the Pacific, on October 16, 1805. They traveled in dugout canoes carved from ponderosa pine and built upstream with the aid of Nez Perce Indians, who showed the men how to use fire, clay, and urine to hollow out and strengthen their vessels. The juncture was more menacing then, with whirlpools and tricky currents to mark the marriage of two great wild rivers. Today it was pleasant, more like a lake than a river, a playground for an armada of motorboats and Jet Skis that left undulating patterns of waves waking across the surface.

We toweled off back at the car. It was good to see Rene again. He had become a doppelgänger of sorts for me. I've always been drawn to the scientific, but the more technical aspects elude me—and, really, if I want to be honest about it, it's the natural world that holds me within its compass, not so much the hard science that takes place in a lab or in a complicated statistical regression analysis. Rene could fill in my enthusiasms with his actual knowledge and expertise. Together we looked once again at the map and decided on our route. Unlike the Corps of Discovery, we were headed against the current, shadowing the salmon as they returned home to the spawning grounds of their birth, navigating what many consider the most arduous stretch, a passage made more deadly by twentieth-century desires and technology. We drove east into the high desert, following the Columbia's largest tributary.

THE 1,078-MILE SNAKE RIVER rises near Yellowstone National Park in northwestern Wyoming and flows south along the foot of the Tetons, quickly gaining force and size from the many mountain streams surrounding Jackson Hole. It was in this country that I first learned to fly-fish, while working on a guest ranch one summer between semesters at college, pretending that I knew something about horses and wide-open spaces. In fact, I was a New England tenderfoot in full. The guests (dudes, we called them) came looking for an authentic Western experience. I led them astride gentle workhorses into the foothills above the ranch, through aspen glades and meadows, to see moose and herds of elk. In the evenings those same guests got to fish the Snake where it bordered the ranch, but the wranglers were expected to go elsewhere. We piled into a pickup and drove a half hour northeast into national forest, where the creek of my education, a lonely meander bordered by wildflower bluffs and stout conifer hummocks, came corkscrewing down from Wyoming's Gros Ventre Range. To this day it remains the template of a perfect mountain trout stream in my mind's eye. Cutthroats rose from hidden pockets to grab my pale morning duns, and it was all I could do to keep a sliver of composure and not yank the flies out of their mouths after each strike. We brought our catch back after dark to the ranch cook, a mustache-twirling Cajun who fried up trout breakfasts for us with spicy remoulades inspired by his Louisiana hometown. If you had told me then that salmon many times the size of these trout spawned in rivers not far away, I wouldn't have believed you—though it probably would have raised my pulse anyway.

When we think about this Rocky Mountain cowboy country, some of the most picturesque in the nation and commemorated by countless artists, we think of alpine climbers and white-water thrill-seekers, of nomadic Indians and grizzled fur trappers. It's not a place associated with salmon, even though these fish once populated rivers in Idaho right up to the Continental Divide. A few still do. The Snake River is the main artery through this expansive landscape. South of Jackson Hole, the river enters the Snake River Canyon (of Evel Knievel fame) and leaves Wyoming, heading west across the lava plains of southern Idaho before turning north along the Oregon border through a series of rifts and barrens, including the deepest gouge in our continental crust, Hells Canyon. A yearlong flood from prehistoric Lake Bonneville in present-day Utah carved these basalt-studded defiles 14,500 years ago. It remains some of the most remote and rugged territory in the West, with deep fissures and broad plateaus that frustrated explorers, who frequently got lost or turned around once they crossed the Divide from the east. Beguiling, yes, and also pitiless. The Snake River Basin bankrupted gold miners with dollar signs in their eyes and stymied homesteaders, who found the growing conditions marginal at best. The River of No Return Wilderness is here, as is Craters of the Moon National Monument. To this day, few roads penetrate the wilds of central Idaho. Rivers pouring off the Bitterroots and the Lemhis and the Sawtooths swell the Snake into the region's signature watercourse, an improbable torrent of water in an arid land.

Like me, Rene Henery had experienced transformative moments in this forsaken country. There was an alpine lake high in the headwaters of the Snake that had become a touchstone for him, a place to go back to every few years, to recharge and ponder changes in the interim. He'd been there in early summer, when blooming sage filled the hanging valleys of the Sawtooths with its sharp scent, and he'd returned in winter to push through ribbons of powdery snow that took flight on the wind and scattered like crystal ashes. The route was easy enough at first, just a hiking trail through the woods. Near tree line, with the hulks of whitebark pines bending over like penitents, he would leave the main path on a faint climber's spur to ascend a scree field of granite boulders the size of minivans. After a rock-hopping traverse that ended at what felt like the rim of the world, he could stand on a stone slab looking across the glassy surface of a lake nestled in a jagged bowl, its color as azure as a Caribbean lagoon. It was here, years earlier, that Rene had fallen for cutthroat trout. They cruised the shoreline and he sight-cast to them, savoring that precious moment between the rise and the take when his mark could be hooked or lost and the lull felt like infinity. They were some of the most beautiful fish he had ever seen: luminous jade flanks dotted by small black spots, a supple cream-colored belly, and those telltale orange slashes beneath the gill. The cutthroat was one of the signposts along the way that guided him into the life of a fisheries ecologist.

Rene was eager to get back into the mountains once again, maybe even return to his formative alpine lake, but first we needed to make our way through the lower reaches of the Snake in Washington State, including one of the most contested lengths of river in America: the hundred-mile stretch where four hydroelectric dams have divided citizens for decades over the prudent use of the nation's natural resources.

———

PLACE NAMES ARE AN important part of calling a region home and recognizing its attributes. The Snake River is reputedly named for a misunderstanding. The Shoshone used a hand sign to denote the river, one that depicted salmon. Early explorers interpreted the gesture to mean the slithering reptile. The confusion is telling. This was an unfamiliar landscape to the first Euro-Americans, who had no experience with wide deserts, towering rock formations, and limited water. To the settlers, it was not a home. It was a harsh landscape to be crossed to reach greener pastures and, later, a wilderness to be conquered, so that it could be remade to seem like home, or at least to yield a profit. Rene laughed at the obviousness of it all, the sort of marginalia scrawled by an undergrad in his textbook: "man vs. nature." In college he had studied colonial literature. You didn't need to know your Frantz Fanon to see what was going on here. Money and myopia—two commodities never in short supply when it came to settling the West—had conspired to impose their will on the land, typified by four fish-killing dams on the lower Snake.

"We make decisions about what should happen and then try to force the landscape to match our desired outcomes," Rene said solemnly. At a trash-strewn turnout overlooking the first of the four, Ice Harbor Dam, we watched the river churn through the dam's penstocks. There wasn't another human being in sight. A green-winged teal in otherwise perfect condition lay inexplicably dead in the middle of the tarmac, as if it had just dropped out of the sky for a nap. Nearby, the scattered remains of a red-tailed hawk littered the sagebrush. Bad omens all around. Rene collected four of the dead raptor's tail feathers for our car's growing dashboard shrine, which also included a sockeye plush toy picked up at the Bonneville Dam gift shop the day before, a droll talisman for the journey.

Lower Monumental Dam looked like something out of a *Star Wars* movie: alien, imposing, ready to do battle. Late-afternoon sun lit up the ramparts of the third, Little Goose, with an incongruous alpen-glow. High above us, a concrete fish ladder spiraled up and over the wall holding back the Snake. Ocher cliffs rose in the distance, and eroded ridgelines receded into shadow. Again, there was not another person in sight, even though the landscape in all directions invited a sense of adventure, flights of imaginative fancy. People didn't want to hang around a handcuffed river. Though visitors' hours were over, the door to the fish-ladder viewing area was ajar, so I pushed it open. "Let's not get nabbed for B&E," Rene said before following me inside. "I don't want to end up in Gitmo." The place was full of nonnative fish clogging up the algae-stained ladder: bass, bluegill, carp, assorted minnows. In the back, a lone steelhead with a seal bite near its tail ghosted in and out of the murk. We could hear the fish counter in his office, tapping away at a computer keyboard. A night janitor appeared with his push broom and told us we'd better get going before the elec-tronic gate closed.

We decided to skip the fourth, Lower Granite, the last of the dams to go online, in 1975. Anyway, the unintended consequences of that one would be apparent soon enough when we arrived in Lewiston, Idaho, 465 river miles from the Pacific, the most inland port on the West Coast. Lower Granite's reservoir, it turned out, was filling with sediment from the Clearwater River, the largest of the Snake's tribu-taries. Because of the dam, there was nowhere for the silt load to go. As a result, the city was now in danger of catastrophic flooding. Many dams are built to alleviate this problem. Lower Granite Dam was caus-ing it. Lewiston was looking at a costly retrofit to raise its levees, fur-ther walling off the river from the community—a disconnect from nature in metaphor and reality.

The lower Snake River dams embody the cultural divisions in America. They are simultaneously the most hated dams in the country and a point of pride among rural residents of the inland Northwest who don't want anyone—especially city folks from the coast—telling them what to do with their infrastructure, never mind that these dams are examples of "big government" federal projects built and managed by the U.S. Army Corps of Engineers. As with so many other cultural issues that divide Americans, both sides of the argument are easy to support with a cannonade of facts, readily downloaded from the Internet, although the strictly economic argument for the dam is becoming untenable over time as independent auditors try to weigh a complicated ledger of costs and benefits—math that doesn't add up as clearly as dam supporters would like. The fact is, these dams provide a tiny fraction of electricity to the region and little in the way of irrigation that couldn't be achieved without them; their biggest selling point—that they allow goods (mostly grain) to be barged downriver—is dependent on federal subsidies and could be replaced by road or rail. The dams represent an *idea* more than any tangible benefit—the idea that our total control of nature is a key to prosperity.

For salmon and steelhead, this control is plain lethal. Mortality comes in any number of ways. Turbines and spillways pummel migrating juveniles, at least those not already trapped and hauled around the dams, a costly process that anti-dam wags liken to flying geese south in an airplane. The young fish that manage to survive this ordeal still face a torpid river made more dangerous by slack-water predators and pathogens. A migration that once took a matter of days during the spring freshet now lasts weeks as the young fish struggle through reservoir after reservoir, dodging foes and trying to find their way downstream in a sluggish current. They get lost, diseased, and stuck in culverts. One predator of young fish is emblematic of our engineering. The Caspian tern, a handsome gull-like bird with a rakish black cap and bright orange bill, preys on the smolts in dramatic headfirst plunges into the river. So bountiful is this feast that colonies of terns have taken up residence on man-made islands (a result of dam building and dredging), feeding their nestlings with endangered salmon and steelhead. One tern colony was estimated to have eaten 22 percent of Snake River steelhead in a year. Now the Army Corps of Engineers wants to evict these federally protected birds from their rookeries.

Another predator, the northern pikeminnow, formerly called a squaw-fish, has a bounty on its head. "You can help save salmon and get paid to do it by going fishing!" a federal website trumpets. The most competent of pikeminnow paid assassins can make a full-time job of it, with the top earners grossing more than one hundred thousand dollars annually.

Returning adult salmon, though larger and stronger, aren't safe either. Sea lions have learned how to exploit the bottleneck at Bonneville Dam. Once nearly wiped out by the fur trade, the California sea lion is at an all-time population high thanks to vigorous protection, and it needs food. Salmon waiting to enter the fish ladder are easy prey for the big pinnipeds. Federal officials have plugged them with rubber bullets, detonated "seal bombs" underwater, and even deployed a fake orca in an effort to scare the predators away. When these efforts failed, they captured a few of the repeat offenders and trucked them down the coast. But the sea lions came back, sometimes swimming hundreds of miles. Now the feds and tribes want to use more deadly methods, much to the outrage of animal-rights groups, which consider the mammals scapegoats for larger, man-made quandaries. If sea lions don't get returning adults, they argue, a tepid river will. The Snake River dams in particular are blamed for raising the Columbia's summertime temperature to levels fatal to salmon.

Rene wasn't worried. The lower Snake dams were going down, he was sure of it, and likely sooner than everyone thought. Science and common sense would prevail. As the sun set over the windblown desert, he imagined an alternative future for the Snake, which involved kayakers, rafters, hikers, hunters, anglers, bird-watchers, lollygaggers, and just about anyone else who appreciates a free-flowing river in a beautifully rawboned landscape. "Let's move forward," he said, upbeat as ever. "Let's come into a new balance in which we're part of the system, not fighting it. But first we have to change our relationship to place or we're just continuing the invasive-species experience, which is essentially what colonialism is."

With darkness falling across tawny hillsides outside Lewiston, we followed a pretty branch of the Tucannon River, another tributary to the Snake. The riparian corridor here looked pretty good: tall cottonwoods shaded the creek's many braided channels with stable banks, the gravel bars giving way to willows and forest margins. "Looks fishy," Rene said with approval. And then, just like that, we popped out of this green oasis. A farmer had cultivated his fields right to the edge of the banks, eliminating all the streamside vegetation and shade. Here the creek was deeply undercut with erosion and unfit for anadromous fish. The surrounding landscape turned instantly brown and dusty. "The whole point of these high-desert creeks is that they green up with a gift from the sea," Rene said. Salmon and steelhead infuse these otherwise sterile places with ocean isotopes—nutrients from the cradle of existence—allowing life to thrive in a hard environment. The loss of these nutrients is bad for the fish and, ultimately, bad for the farmer.

Making connections between desert creeks and the wide blue ocean might seem like a stretch, but lately scientists have made another, similar connection: between the salmon of the Snake River Basin and endangered killer whales. It turns out that the decline in Puget Sound orcas can be plotted in tandem with the decline of Snake River chinook, their favorite prey. Once numbering more than three hundred whales, the Puget Sound population now hovers around eighty. Some of them are visibly malnourished. High in the watershed, Snake River tributaries, with their cool, clear flows and extensive gravel beds, historically sent millions of salmon to sea every spring. Even the Owyhee River in northern Nevada contributed a run of hardy chinook. The Snake system produced nearly half of all the chinook in the Columbia Basin before it was reengineered; many of these were the desirable springers that were so essential to both the river people and orcas because of their high fat content. Steelhead too once populated streams across the Idaho high country, until impoundments blocked much of the best habitat. Sockeye spawned in such numbers in the high mountain lakes of Oregon and Idaho that there was an inland commercial fishery for them. In the late 1800s, thousands of the long-distance migrants were caught, dressed, and salted for sale to mining camps, before dams shut them out. The Snake River sockeye's last redoubt is a chain of subalpine lakes in the Sawtooth Range near the ranching town of Stanley, Idaho, where they reach an elevation of seven thousand feet, some of the highest-elevation salmon-spawning habitat in the world. Today all these fish—Snake River spring and fall chinook, steelhead, and sockeye—are on the endangered species list. The coho weren't so fortunate. They went extinct.

People all over the world identify with species of large mammals, especially with the whales, which, like us, can communicate with one another from miles away and are doting parents. While watching orcas once at Lime Kiln State Park on San Juan Island, I met a woman who had traveled from St. Louis just to see these impressive animals. She was near tears at the sight of two calves surfacing alongside their mothers, their black dorsal fins rising and falling in synchronized succession. Like human beings, the orcas have opinions about what makes for a good salmon dinner. They want fat-laden chinook. Meanwhile, a parade of pink salmon splashed by, millions of them headed for the Fraser River. The schools of pinks jumped and cavorted near the surface of Haro Strait, and the orcas paid them no heed. When a large male with a dorsal as tall as me sounded and disappeared for minutes at a time, one of the knowledgeable whale watchers explained to the rest of us that he was probably going deep, hunting chinook.

In a warming climate, the high-country streams of central Idaho represent some of the last best spawning grounds. I was reminded of a happy-hour conversation I'd had with Joseph Bogaard, the director of Save Our Wild Salmon. He referred to this mostly undeveloped region as Noah's ark for salmon. "We don't have to do anything to the habitat," Bogaard stressed. "The habitat is there. We just need to make it accessible, and that means taking out the dams." We call biodiversity the web of life. Everything is interconnected. Whale watchers are now demanding the breaching of the lower Snake River dams to bring back the once-prolific runs of Snake River salmon. Rene Henery considers these fish the red blood cells in the landscape's vascular system.

———

IN 1992, A SINGLE sockeye salmon returned to Idaho's Redfish Lake in the Sawtooths. Just one fish, a male. He was dubbed Lonesome Larry, and his plight helped galvanize a restoration program begun the year before, when Snake River sockeye were officially listed by the Endangered Species Act. Redfish Lake sockeye swim nine hundred miles to their spawning grounds, averaging about twenty miles a day. Nine hundred miles. It can make you tired just thinking about it. And Lonesome Larry had to surmount eight hydroelectric dams along the way. For his survival against the odds, Larry was knocked over the head and relieved of all his semen (called milt), which was cryogenically preserved so that Larry's rare genes could be used over and over again until spent. Through the entire decade of the 1990s, only sixteen wild sockeye returned to Redfish Lake. Nevertheless, each one of these survivors contributed fundamental genetics to the restoration effort, so that today biologists can say that 95 percent of the historical DNA is still in the pool. Jump ahead nearly two and half decades from Lonesome Larry's requiem, and more than a thousand sockeye salmon have made it home to Redfish Lake. The story of how these fish narrowly avoided extinction turns out to be a complex tale, one that weaves together salmon biology and human intervention, and one not easily untangled, as I would soon learn.

After a quick meal in Lewiston, Rene and I got back in the car and continued our pilgrimage to Redfish Lake, the terminus of the longest salmon migration in the contiguous United States, where we hoped to meet face-to-face the descendants of Lonesome Larry. We were right on schedule. Perhaps at that very moment a small school of Snake River sockeye, driven by an innate urge we call—for lack of a better word—instinct, was making its own way up the Snake. The river was out of sight now, its upstream progress moving south toward the mostly roadless wilderness of Hells Canyon. The drive to Redfish Lake would take us away from the river and through some of the country's most dramatic territory. But first we had a slight detour to make.

TRAVIS BROWN, FAMOUS AROUND these parts as the bearded mastur-
bator of fish, didn't exactly look like a threat to polite society. For one
thing, he was clean-shaven on this day, and while I couldn't read his
mind, his intentions seemed pure, even if they involved surprising
procedures with nearby tanks full of live sockeye salmon. "Keep!"
Brown called out from his standing position behind a computer monitor, his voice echoing through the garagelike building where Idaho
Fish and Game carries out its experiments. On this command, I
marched my dip net over to tank number six, a hot tub–sized enclo-
sure directly behind Brown, and dumped a squirming five-pound
male sockeye into the "keep tank." The newest conscript darted to the
far side and quickly fell in among a group of twenty or more salmon
that moved as one, like a flock of shorebirds, circling the parameters of
their captivity. Dip net in hand, I got back in line behind Rene and the
staff, waiting for my next turn to deliver another sockeye to its fate.
Millions of years of change and adaptation had brought these Snake
River sockeye to this point in their evolution—and now I was a crucial step in the life cycle.

As co-manager of the Eagle Fish Hatchery in Boise, Idaho, Brown
probably felt he had to keep a straight face during all this, but there
was still some stifled laughter among the staff as they went about their
jobs. They had all seen their boss's sexed-up debut in a recent issue of
Men's Journal. The article described Brown jackknifing a salmon over
his thigh and running his fingers up its belly to the vent, until the fish
squirted a stream of milky sperm. It took a fair bit of creative license
to lend a shade of eroticism to the messy process of extracting milt
from a salmon. "You just give the males a good squeeze under the
belly," Brown explained a little sheepishly.

"And a kiss afterward," someone said.

With his wrestler's build and ruddy face, Travis Brown looked as if
he should be breaking horses or building a cabin. But he grew up an-

gling for steelhead in Idaho's mountain streams and would happily tell you the name of his favorite fly—the B-run Slayer—though you'd need to buy him more than one draft at the tavern to get the tying recipe. Working for Idaho's Department of Fish and Game was hardly a job. He was doing what he loved, for a paycheck. Milking salmon was just one part of it—and, anyway, the dirty business of fertilizing fish eggs wouldn't be conducted here today. Today the employees of the Eagle Fish Hatchery were busy segregating endangered Snake River sockeye, about seven hundred total, which had been collected at a weir just below Redfish Lake, a few hours away by car. These tenacious migrants had spent several weeks swimming upstream from the mouth of the Columbia River to the Snake River to Idaho's Salmon River and finally into log-choked Redfish Creek—only to be detained a few hundred yards shy of their destination at Redfish Lake and brought to this hatchery, where they were DNA-sampled and checked for disease. Some of them would be trucked back to the lake to complete their spawning run, while others would be kept at the hatchery and stripped of eggs and milt to replenish the hatchery's captive brood-stock supply—the very unsexy work that had so excited a *Men's Journal* reporter.

Sex appeal is in the eye of the beholder, of course, and there are still a few citizens in the republic turned on by the prospect of saving an endangered species. Travis Brown and his colleagues are keeping the sockeye salmon that spawn in the Snake River basin, once numbering in the many tens of thousands and now reduced to a trickle, on life support. A purist (or a penny-pincher) might say forget the Endangered Species Act; let them go extinct. After all, these fish occupy that uncomfortable niche with other charismatic fauna brought to extinction's doorstep only to hover over the threshold in a human embrace—the Sumatran rhino, California condor, and Mexican wolf, to name but a few—all of them still on the planet due to our costly ongoing intervention. Chamber of Commerce types like to trot out the numbers, talking about how many thousands of dollars each salmon costs taxpayers. Even more galling to letter-to-the-editor writers is when one of those gold-plated fish ends up in an Indian net.

What would Riley Starks make of these sockeye, I wondered. The ones he caught in his reef nets—those headed for the Fraser River in Canada—were wild and untutored in the byzantine ways of the ESA bureaucracy. Naïve, even, one might say. Most years they were fairly plentiful. Not so these American sockeye with their life cycle pestered by fish ladders, tanker trucks, hypodermics, and hatchery complexes. When it was my turn again, I approached the holding pen in my borrowed rubber Carhartt bibs and handed my net to Ken Felty, the hatchery's fish culturist. Felty stood in the middle of the pool, in brown neoprene waders with water up to his waist, as salmon swam around his feet and bunched up in the corners. He caught a female and handed the net back to me. I carried her over to a yellow arch-shaped scanner the size of a computer modem as she thrashed and threw off a spray of water. A red light blinked on, indicating that my fish's implanted chip had been successfully read. The chip, a sort of bar code sewn into the fish's abdomen, is called a passive integrated transponder, or PIT tag. There was a pause. Brown waited for the fish's ID number to appear on his laptop, then quickly searched his database. "Release," he said a moment later. I took the fish over to a different tank and freed it. All the sockeye in the holding pen were being divided into two camps: *keep* fish and *release* fish. The designations were meant to maximize genetic variation. Release fish would be trucked back to Redfish Lake and allowed to spawn in the wild. Keep fish would stay at the hatchery, ensuring a supply of brood-stock genetics in the event of calamity.

All these salmon, whether bound for the wild or not, looked small to me, certainly compared to those I'd seen hauled up by the reef netters in Puget Sound. They were just four or five pounds, and thin. You would be too, someone said, if you'd just taken a nine-hundred-mile swim upstream without a meal. Along the way, they had burned as much as 60 percent of their body mass.

Outside, the hatchery's grounds were green with irrigation and carefully tended. The complex of buildings and lawns resembled a college campus. A slow-moving creek bordered the property, with overfed rainbow trout the size of Wonderbread loaves finning languidly beneath a glassy surface. In another large building—really more of a glorified carport—additional tanks held adult Snake River sockeye salmon artificially hatched and raised on the premises using brood stock from the wild fish trapped at Redfish Lake. Many of them showed the red and green coloration of ripe salmon ready to spawn, a byproduct of hatchery life that the staff here was trying to discourage. An easy food supply and lack of predators allowed the pampered fish to mature faster than their wild kin, a trait that would not serve them well in a natural setting. Nevertheless, in an effort to diversify the population's genetics as much as possible, some of these hatchery-raised fish would win a lottery ticket to join their wild cousins at Redfish Lake. Pausing before the scanner with a handsome male sockeye in his net, Rene reflected on the schizophrenic life cycle of a fish reared in the hatchery, only to be released to the wild because a guy with a laptop says so. "What a deal. They keep you penned up most of your life in a cage, and then one day you're hauled away in a fish limo and set loose into the dating scene. You go to the club to score and then you croak."

Viewed in a certain light, the life of a salmon can seem patently unfair. Only a handful from a given redd survive to spawn, even in the best conditions. Most never reach adulthood. As fry, they nourish countless predators in the river, from other fish to birds to snapping turtles. Even a dragonfly larva is a threat to a newly hatched baby salmon. At sea they fare a little better, but not much. The original pool gets culled and culled until only a few hardy (and maybe lucky) survivors feel the pull of their home river and begin the journey back to the place of their birth. For Redfish Lake sockeye, the campaign is even more perilous: they have to contend with eight hydroelectric dams along the way. Long-term survival is a numbers game. Among the twenty-five hundred or so eggs originally deposited by a female sockeye, amazingly it takes only three or four returning adults to spawn for reproductive success. It's a heroic journey, made all the more dangerous in recent decades by the human hurdle.

IF RENE WAS SURPRISED to find himself helping out at a hatchery facility, he didn't say so. It's true that his first allegiance is to wild fish, but to work with salmon in California is to court ambiguity every day. Natural processes have been so thoroughly manipulated by human beings, from mountains to coast, that it's hard to tell where the human-engineered landscape ends and the wild—if it still exists— begins. Ditto the so-called wildlife. Herds of elk, once nearly exterminated, now roam campgrounds. Most Golden State salmon begin their lives in a temperature-controlled egg tray.

For Rene, this trip to Idaho was a mission of sorts—to learn from his colleagues and see for himself some of the most state-of-the-art techniques for recovering populations of endangered salmon. The idea of a captive brood-stock hatchery—suspect in the Pacific Northwest, where populations of wild salmon are still holding on, if barely—seemed like a luxury to Rene, certainly a much better option than relying on stray "lost fish." "In California the plan is to make new fish for the San Joaquin because the spring run is extirpated," he explained to the hatchery staff. "There aren't any wild fish. The plan is to let them loose—let them engage with nature, adapt—and hope they can survive." This sort of meddling doesn't sit right with everyone.

To be clear, the Eagle Fish Hatchery is not a mitigation hatchery, like the majority of hatcheries on the Columbia system and elsewhere. Rather than mass-producing fish to be caught in a net or on a hook, its mandate is to keep the genetics of the Redfish Lake sockeye alive, with as much variation and diversity as possible. Yet the very word *hatchery* remains blasphemous for many wild fish supporters. It stands for greed, hubris, and a misplaced trust in technology all at once. Put a new label on it—*conservation* hatchery or *captive brood-stock* hatchery—and you're still left with a hatchery, a man-made environment that can never reproduce the myriad life histories of wild salmon.

One of Rene's inspirations, retired fisheries biologist Jim Lichatowich, has expressed his own reservations about the concept in his recent memoir, *Salmon, People, and Place*. Lichatowich is known for having questioned the efficacy of hatcheries at a time when most of his colleagues were still silent on the issue. He worries that so-called conservation and brood-stock hatcheries are more of the same. When I talked to him on the phone, he softened his criticism. "In dire circumstances, putting salmon on life support is a step that can be taken—just like with humans," he said. "But the question is, for how long? The proof in the pudding will be when they stop the hatchery program and see if the run can sustain itself." The Snake River sockeye restoration is just one of many such efforts. Similar brood-stock hatcheries are up and running for Russian River coho in California, North Puget Sound chinook, and Elwha River pink salmon. Lichatowich still worries that these conservation-hatchery plans have neither end dates nor criteria for evaluating success. Furthermore, the reasons for the decline—habitat loss and so on—need to be addressed in tandem with the restoration efforts. Conservation hatcheries treat a symptom, not a cause.

"The intimate connection with the ecosystem has been lost," Lichatowich continued. "You're creating something that looks like a salmon run, that exhibits the external characteristics of a salmon run, but the intimate connection the salmon had with the habitat has eroded away. We're ending up with what look like salmon populations, but they're different." He paraphrased the philosopher and nature writer Gary Nabhan: Animals don't go extinct because we shoot them all. They go extinct because of an unraveling ecosystem. They lose *ecological companionship*. Fish hatched from brood stock, though derived from wild parents, aren't the same as those from the previous generation. "When you take a fish out of the river and put it in a hatchery, then release it, you're depriving the fish of ecological relationships."

I turned the question around for Lichatowich: Is humanity busy depriving itself of those same ecological relationships? He sighed. The world is indeed becoming a lonelier place.

"WE'RE THE OPPOSITE OF pure-breed-dog breeders," was how Christine Kozfkay put it. She's the hatchery's full-time staff geneticist. Framed degrees and watercolor paintings of salmon hang on her office walls, the sort of artwork only a fish geek could love, including one titled "The 900-Mile Journey," which depicts a male sockeye on its spawning gravels, crimson body and emerald head, its jaws twisted and toothy. Another proclaims "Sockeye Recovery" across the top and features Idaho's stunning canyon country etched into the flanks of a leaping salmon. It's Kozfkay's job to poke and prod every single sockeye that comes through the hatchery door. Her DNA samples reveal the parentage of each fish, which in turn determines whether they will spawn in the wild or remain at the hatchery. In all, nearly fifteen hundred sockeye salmon will be trapped and sorted this year. These are wild fish making the full trip upriver, and this population will be supplemented, in turn, with Redfish Lake sockeye raised in the hatchery from a parentage of previously trapped wild fish. This is what is meant by the term "captive brood stock." Kozfkay analyzes the genetics of all the fish, wild and hatchery-raised. "Then I rank them." Unlike a dog breeder, she wants as much variability in her fish as possible. "The goal is to maximize our effective population size and the retention of genetic diversity. I determine which ones they should keep and which they should release." For this she has a big spreadsheet that she continually updates with new information.

When it comes to genetics and sleuthing out the ways of salmon, the sockeye represents the pinnacle of Kozfkay's profession. Of all the Pacific salmon species, excluding steelhead, it has the most diverse life history. Though sockeye typically make use of a freshwater lake during their life cycle, spawning in tributaries above and below the lake—or sometimes in the lake itself if the substrate is gravelly and there's enough oxygenated flow—not all sockeye follow this program; some will spawn in rivers that provide a sufficient backwater-rearing habitat, known to anglers as frog water. Kozfkay has data on Redfish Lake sockeye going back about a decade. Occasionally, she said, fish that return to the lake are off the radar. These mystery sockeye, referred to as "unassigned" fish, are possibly crosses between sockeye and what the biologists call residuals. Residuals are wild sockeye that like their environment enough to skip out-migration as juveniles and stay right where they are, maturing in the lake. They never go to sea, and so they evade capture and identification. Residuals add another layer of variability to the sockeye genome. As Rene Henery would say, diversity makes the species stronger, especially in an environment prone to mishap. And there is yet one more layer: a non-anadromous form of sockeye commonly known as kokanee. Though usually landlocked and much smaller in stature, the kokanee is technically the same species as a sockeye, and given the right environmental conditions and physical access, it will sometimes head for the sea. In this way, the highly adaptive sockeye salmon has a fail-safe mechanism that has served it well through catastrophic changes in its habitat, whether natural or otherwise.

In another life, Kozfkay might have been hired to follow a cheating spouse. Teasing out the secrets of sockeye salmon isn't much different, and it too requires a dedicated financial input. Thanks to the Endangered Species Act, the funding is there, though skeptical editorial pages love to tally up the cost of each ESA-protected fish, and even many salmon advocates argue that it's a waste of money trying to keep populations of fish on life support when the funds can be used to protect more robust runs elsewhere. But these Redfish Lake sockeye, as the southernmost population in North America and with the longest, steepest migration, offer a suite of genetics that makes them special. To lose them would be a blow to the species. Rene agreed. "We used to look at genetics mainly as a predictor. Now we use genetics as a tool to help ensure we have all the material that a fish needs to fully express itself."

Kozfkay studied him for a moment. Rene was dressed in a cowboy shirt and boots, his curly black hair pulled into a ponytail, earrings flashing in the overhead lights. Still, clearly he knew a few things about fish. "Where did you say you guys have been?" she asked.

We told her about our trek.

"You don't look all that tired."

"We have a car," Rene said. "And we're eating. That would have been a nice twist—to start fasting from the get-go." As it was, we had begun our pilgrimage two days earlier with a huge plate of fish 'n' chips from the Bowpicker, a colorful take-out stand reclaimed from an old fishing boat, overlooking the windy mouth of the Columbia in Astoria, Oregon. The catch of the day wasn't salmon or Pacific cod. It was albacore tuna, an increasingly common visitor to the Northwest coast in an era of warming oceans.

We followed Kozfkay from her office to the tanks, where Travis Brown and his staff were still busy using her spreadsheets to separate keep fish from release fish. The sheer numbers of returning sockeye this year gave everyone hope. Besides preserving genetic integrity, captive brood-stock programs also boost population numbers. With more than 50 percent egg-to-adult survival—a significantly higher percentage than in the wild—such programs can multiply the overall numbers much more quickly than natural reproduction does. The question is whether these gains are temporary or not. Critics are convinced that the recent increases in Snake River sockeye have much more to do with court-mandated water spillage through the Columbia dam complex than with brood-stock hatcheries. They point to another population of Columbia Basin sockeye, those of Osoyoos Lake on the British Columbia–Washington State border, where wild sockeye have increased dramatically since 2008 due to changes in water management and better flow regimes. As a result, hatchery efforts there are being phased out. But when looked at more closely through the lens of biodiversity and overall species health, especially in an age of climate change, the high-country fish of the Sawtooths represent a unique genetic contribution that demands special attention, and Kozfkay's gumshoe perseverance gets at the root of those genetics.

"Through our pedigree work, we even know what kind of contribution Larry made," Kozfkay added, lifting her gaze. Everyone turned to look toward a far corner of the building. There, against the wall, stood an orange-and-white canister about the size of a pony keg. It was a cryogenic storage chamber, Lonesome Larry's final spawning ground. Larry was gone now, all used up. The last of his genetic material had been exhausted a couple of years earlier. Kozfkay figured Larry had sired about ten generations of Redfish Lake sockeye. But his journey isn't over. Larry's stuffed body continues to circulate around the halls of government and academia, where he brightens offices and joins exhibits, an educational trophy in red and green.

LIKE RENE'S CUTTHROAT LAKE HIGH in the mountains above us, Redfish Lake is a body of water so turquoise in color we might as well have been standing on a tropical shore. But the torn and serrated peaks of the Sawtooths surround Redfish, and come winter it ices over into the frozen domain of snowshoe hares and backcountry skiers. On this day, visitors to the lake were treated to a different sort of scenery.

With a curious crowd gathered around it, a hatchery truck backed down the boat ramp until its rear wheels were submerged to the hubs. Someone turned a valve on the truck, spilling water through a hose and into the shallows, and, one by one, fish streamed out of the hose, some of them nearly vermillion: vibrant red fish finning in teal-green water, an unlikely tone poem in Technicolor, splashed across a panoramic page. As if watching a big game from the bleachers, onlookers stood shoulder to shoulder on a nearby dock. They all seemed to know the story of these fish. Travis Brown, wearing a drysuit, floated on the surface, breathing through a snorkel and watching through his dive mask. His colleague Mike Peterson, a tall, sturdy biologist with a trim beard, stood in the lake, wearing waders, and addressed the crowd: "Not since the mid-1950s has this lake seen so much red." A cheer went up from the dock.

Soon a hundred or more fish made lazy circles as they schooled together near the outlet of the hose. Some of them rose, their emerald heads breaking the surface, before they porpoised back down through the ripples. Contrary to appearances, they weren't sipping insects the way hungry trout do; they were taking gulps of oxygen to restore the balance in their swim bladders after a long, perilous migration that included a final detour on mountain roads in the crowded confines of a mobile fish tank. Several years from now, their offspring—those few that survived—would make the same journey, and they too would come up against four dams on the lower Snake River. A brood-stock hatchery or conservation hatchery or whatever else you wanted to call it couldn't fix the problem of those dams.

Like the whale watchers I had met on San Juan Island, the people on the dock, many of them just passing through for the day, couldn't believe their good fortune at witnessing the spectacle of these rare fish. In coming weeks the females would dig redds in suitable lake-bottom gravel beds, and the males would compete to fertilize the eggs. Already some of the males displayed the elongated snouts and canine teeth they would use to nip at their competitors on the spawning grounds. They were marathoners, all of them, and their race was nearly run.

CHAPTER 10

ATTACK OF THE
KILLER BLOB

On THE THIRD HAUL OF THE DAY I FELT A WARM, TINGLING sensation spread across my left wrist. An instant later and my whole hand was throbbing as if from a million tiny pinpricks. *Jellyfish*. It was my first time grabbing web—reef-netter lingo for hauling in the net—and I was learning the hard way. I pulled my gloves back on and tried to tuck them into my cuffs. The arms of my sweatshirt were already soaked underneath my rain jacket. "The red ones really hurt," said Chef, the newest member of Lummi Island Wild. "You're pulling hard and they're all over your hands. They get mashed up in the net and there are little bits everywhere, like stinging nettles."

When Riley Starks invited me back to the island for a day on the water, I'd imagined heavy nets full of sleek salmon, not slimy invertebrates. But all sorts of flotsam drifting by gets hauled up, from seaweed and flounders to deadhead stumps and trash. The jellies were just a temporary annoyance. A flounder's stinging spine posed a more painful threat.

The reef netters didn't seem too concerned. "You can pee on jellyfish sting to make it go away," a deckhand named Sean said, and the others nodded gravely. This reminded Sean of the time one of his crewmates got stung in the eyes and was temporarily blinded. "I watched his internal turmoil until, finally, he peed into his hands and rubbed it into his eyes. Then he could work again." I peeled off my glove once more and looked at my tingling hand. Though a little red, it would survive. More urgent, I needed to iron out some issues of technique. A large sockeye, maybe eight or nine pounds, had escaped from the net because of my failure to keep a wrinkle from forming as we pulled it in, while grabbing web. This wrinkle is called a banana. With proper technique, the reef netters can haul in such a way that a single pocket of webbing siphons all the fish into the holding tank, like a slide at the playground. Bananas allow fish to wriggle out the side. No one said anything, but we'd all seen the big one escape. A few quick calculations in my head suggested a crisp twenty-dollar bill had just slipped away. Missed fish add up quickly.

On the next haul we took about thirty fish, most of them bright sockeye salmon of six or seven pounds apiece. Gorgeous fish, they flickered like diamonds, throwing all the colors of the rainbow from their glistening sides. Sockeye have a bluer complexion than other salmon, a more streamlined body shape. "Bluebacks," the Quinault Indians of the Washington Coast call them. Another reef netter, named Josh, started sorting fish as they slid into the live tank. Five of the salmon looked different from the others. Larger, with wide tails and black spots on their backs, these were chinook, and quite possibly endangered ones at that. They had noticeable adipose fins: wild fish. One after another, Josh caught each fish and gently cradled it over the side and back into the current. With a powerful flex of the tail, the chinook continued on their way, bound for rivers somewhere in Washington or British Columbia, maybe even minor tributaries nearly devoid of salmon, where their spawning might keep a population alive for another generation. Letting these big king salmon go felt just as satisfying as catching a mess of sockeye.

This is one of the things that separate the reef-net fishery from all others: It's the only truly selective fishery on the high seas.

It was late summer and the salmon were obeying their biological yearning, making journeys home to the same cobbles where they'd hatched several years ago, to spawn and die. Unlike the sockeye of Redfish Lake, these Fraser River sockeye, many from deep-interior British Columbia, don't require barging or brood-stock hatcheries or sea-lion culling. In fact, back in March, fisheries managers had predicted a banner run, calling it perhaps the biggest return to the Fraser since record keeping first began nearly a century earlier. Why this was so, in an age of general decline, was something of a mystery, and while such predictions cause excitement, they also have the adverse effect of confusing the public about the health of the region's salmon populations.

Salmon runs are naturally cyclical, ebbing and flowing due to a variety of environmental factors, from ocean productivity to river flows. A heavy winter snowpack often means high spring runoff in the rivers, which in turn helps juvenile salmon with a speedier trip to the salt and less exposure to predators. Global weather patterns can impact salmon runs for years; sudden one-off, localized events like flash floods or ice storms cause more immediate short-term impacts. The Pacific Decadal Oscillation describes a cycle of warming and cooling that alternates between the ocean's eastern and western hemispheres over the course of twenty or thirty years. Weather events like El Niño (a warming of the Pacific's surface temperature) and La Niña (a cooling) are part of that oscillation. More recently, since 1998, scientists have noticed that the pattern has shortened in duration, making for extreme fluctuations and more problematic forecasting.

While the biggest long-term threats to salmon are mostly human-caused, a favorable set of environmental conditions lining up can override man-made problems, if only briefly. This seems to be the case with the Fraser's sockeye run. True, it's less impacted by industrial development than other large river systems on the West Coast, such as the Columbia and Sacramento, and it isn't burdened with fish-killing hydroelectric dams. But the real benefactor, scientists suggest, is the North Pacific. Ocean conditions, always seesawing through periods of rich and poor, appeared to be on the upswing in recent years, at least for sockeye salmon. Upwellings of cool, nutrient-rich water from the bottom mean a bonanza of zooplankton, especially the blooms of tiny crustaceans like copepods and krill, which drift cloudlike in the currents and are a favorite of sockeye. Unfortunately, there is evidence that these fat times have already peaked and are coming to an end. Warm-water species like sunfish and mahi-mahi have started to show up on the Northwest coast—a thrilling catch for the unsuspecting angler but an ominous sign of things to come.

Riley Starks had kept tabs on the Fraser's sockeye run throughout the summer. Every now and then I'd get a text or phone message from him. "The fish are on their way," he'd say. "Better mark your calendar." I could hear the anticipation in his voice. The reef netters get two brief months to fish, maybe three if they're lucky, before fall storms make the work too dangerous and the gears are dry-docked. The rest of the year is waiting. In late June he texted me: The first pulse of returning fish was showing off the Washington coast. Scouts, he called them. The sockeye targeted by the reef netters migrate from the ocean into the Strait of Juan de Fuca before turning toward Canada in northern Puget Sound. By early July, when I heard from Starks again, the vanguard of the run had entered the Fraser, where local fishing guides were already booked up for the season. Sport anglers flooded Internet message boards with their excitement. Tribal leaders in the interior spoke of a subsistence fishery the likes of which few had experienced in their lifetimes. Like everyone else dependent on the Fraser River's salmon returns, the reef netters of Lummi Island felt a mounting buzz of anticipation. Thanks to Starks's regular reports, I was feeling the excitement too. "You've seen the forecast, right?" he asked me. "They're talking about a lot of salmon." He didn't want to quote the exact preseason numbers. It was bad luck to talk about it. But, yes, I had seen the forecast. The midrange called for twenty-three million sockeye, with a high of seventy-two million—a span that would seem to belie the very term *forecast*. *Seventy-two million*. That was even more sockeye than the best years of the famed Bristol Bay fishery in Alaska. Such numbers staggered the mind. The test fishery would reveal whether or not these ballyhooed predictions were proving accurate.

Initiated by the Pacific Salmon Commission (PSC), a body jointly formed by the governments of Canada and the United States to oversee salmon stocks, the preseason test fishery is designed to collect data for effective management and sustainable fishing. It's one of many measures to emerge from a fisheries treaty signed by the two countries in 1985, after a century of conflicts between their fishermen. Because the Fraser's mouth is right off the metropolis of Vancouver, just north of Washington State, the river's stocks are of special concern to both American and Canadian fishermen. The test fishery allows the reef netters to fish, but as the catch is technically the property of the PSC, the fishermen have to pay the commission for what they haul in, cutting into their profit margin. On the other hand, without the test fishery they wouldn't be able to fish at all until the season opened. This money helps fund the PSC's data-gathering operations, and more data mean a more accurate picture of what's happening on the spawning grounds. One of the main ways to promote sustainable fishing is to ensure that enough salmon make it to those spawning areas, and it's the PSC's job to set openings and closures to do just that.

The first reef-net test fishery of the season opened in late July. Lummi Island Wild caught nearly three hundred fish. The catch increased to nine hundred fish a few days later—and the full fleet wasn't even fishing yet, just those gears that had agreed to participate in the test fishery. I could hear the fever in Riley Starks's voice on the phone. He said I'd better get up to the island soon. It was time to fish.

ON A BLUSTERY MORNING, I woke up well before dawn and drove north through a steady rain to Ferndale, Washington. At the Lummi Indian casino, an unsightly six-story complex overlooking the Nooksack River Delta, I followed a peninsula that divides Lummi Bay from Bellingham Bay to its end and boarded the 5:00 A.M. *Whatcom Chief* ferry for Lummi Island. It was fifty-three degrees—unseasonably cold even for Puget Sound. Twenty minutes later, after a short ferry ride, I crossed the island on Legoe Bay Road and parked just south of Village Point, next to a dilapidated red shack. Across the lawn, one of the oldest living reef netters, Jerry Anderson, Lummi Island's former postmaster, was on his covered porch, hardly breaking a sweat on his StairMaster and reading the morning paper. I walked over to say hello. Jerry looked trim and fit in his gray sweatsuit, his snow-white hair crew-cut in a military style, and after a little chitchat I asked him a possibly impolite question: When did he first start reef netting? He didn't think twice about dating himself, figuring it was probably in 1943, at age ten. "Then in '47 my dad put me in charge, which was totally uncalled for," he said, thinking back over his years with the fleet, his legs moving like steady pistons on the workout machine. He punched a button on the control panel and the speed kicked up a notch. It pleased him, he said, to see a younger generation still on the water. "Good luck out there. Go get some."

Riley Starks and several of the reef netters met me at the beach with extra foul-weather gear and fleece. The rain had stopped but it was still moody out, with gusts of wind and dark skies. "Clouds on Little Bear and Big Bear," one of the crew noted, pointing west toward the San Juan Islands. We stood on the beach, looking out. This is what reef netters do when they aren't fishing—they think about fishing and the weather and what the heck an inscrutable bunch of schooled-up fish might be doing beneath the surface of pewter-stained water. "We've been dragging our heels a little bit to see what might happen," said Ian Kirouac, the crew chief of one of Lummi Island Wild's four gears. Soft-spoken and bearded, wearing a hoodie and ball cap, Ian scanned the horizon. To the south, whale-backed Lummi Mountain was shrouded in clouds, its broad peak nonexistent.

"I've got stuff to do," Starks said finally, reluctantly, after another minute or two of staring at the water and sky, both of which seemed to meld together into a seamless gray vista. I could see the yearning in his face. Wearing the marketing hat wasn't the same as grabbing web. His days of actual fishing were mostly over, except on those special occasions when he got to stand in the tower and make the call, for old times' sake. Now he had to drum up business.

With Ian at the helm, eight of us rode out to the gear in a dented aluminum skiff that might have been used by Jerry Anderson back in the day. Once aboard, the crew spent the next half hour deploying the net and fine-tuning the reef. Lines whistled through pulleys, and winches cried like overworked table saws. "Coming up on the bunt!" hollered Ian as he adjusted the back of the net. Sierra, his girlfriend, stood by herself on the opposite barge, struggling to get the net into position. "Hold on, guys, you're fighting Sierra," Ian admonished his crew. "Drop the stern line." Once the net was taut between the two barges, Sierra would spend the day inside a cramped cabin, watching a monitor with images fed from an underwater camera attached to the reef. Fish TV, they called it, one of the more recent innovations along with the solar panels. Ian continued to call out instructions while the crew scrambled around.

The test fishery is a chance to relearn the process and get the kinks out. Now there was a problem with the live well—screws were coming loose. "Tighten 'em up," someone called out. Morgan Shermer, with close-cropped ginger hair and chiseled features, waved a wrench in the air. "We've tried. They don't tighten." Morgan is a stonemason in the off-season, and sometimes he deckhands on other fishing boats. Ian told his crew in a friendly yet firm tone to find a solution. "Make new holes. Get it tight. Figure it out." This was his thirteenth year as a reef netter. Or fourteenth? Anyway, he was young by any measure. "I've always considered myself one of the new guys," he admitted. The old-timers, he said, guys like Jerry, they had more experience in their pinkies.

Josh Thomason, a tall, lean Texan with aviator sunglasses, stood up after a fruitless battle with the wrench. He was swimming in his cavernous rubber-coated Carhartt bibs. Despite the chill, he had cut the arms off his green hoodie, a simple alteration that, I would soon learn—once my own arms were soaked through after a couple of hauls—made perfect sense. Josh was second in command after Ian and conscious of modeling leadership in his own sometimes profane, down-home way. "Find me some bolts," he drawled. "I can get in there and do it, but it's gonna be shitty." Now that Josh was a new father, his fishing career looked as though it would be limited to the fairly safe arena of summertime reef netting. His winter work, crabbing, was on indefinite hold. But that was okay; he was just happy to be here. The first time he escaped the flat, arid country of West Texas and got a look at the Pacific Northwest's topography and rain-drenched evergreens, he knew he wasn't going back anytime soon.

Cara Blake, barely old enough to drive, performed her chores in a neon-orange jacket that made her the most visible person on board. A volunteer with the Lummi Island fire department, she had the quiet demeanor of someone wise beyond her years. In little more than a month she would begin her junior year in high school, and though the youngest member of the crew, she was starting her second season grabbing web and gilling fish.

Ben Siegel, a stocky, bearded deckhand with little wire-rimmed glasses that gave him the quizzical look of a professor, was the greenest. He had a paperback book with him that he pulled out whenever there was a bit of downtime: a well-worn copy of *Cod*. In his former career he was a cook in Manhattan, so everyone called him Chef. "It's about weather and visibility," Chef said to me, "and whether the fish are actually here. If they're not here, it's hard to catch them." He stood up from his seat next to the bleed tank and paced the deck. "I'm excited to pull some web."

Morgan kept his seat and continued to stare off into the distance. "It doesn't feel like a record season."

"Not yet," Chef fired back. The fishing life is all about optimism. You can see this through the centuries. You can read about hopeful fishermen in the first printed books, see fragile clay tablets under glass blanketed with cuneiform depicting the sanguine angler. Before the season starts, hope rules the day. This is something that attracted me to the fishing life from the beginning, that still attracts me today: the irresistible combination of mystery and desire. To catch a fish is to eavesdrop on one of nature's profound conversations. "It's in here," Chef said, waving his book in the air. The cod guys knew how to find fish. "Right until the end," someone said. The story of cod, everyone knew, was a cautionary tale.

Once the net was in the water, Ian climbed the ladder to his post in the bow, known as the head stand, where, peering through an oversize pair of polarized sunglasses that covered much of his face, he was usually the first to spot a school of incoming fish. Josh watched from the stern tower, or bunt stand. Sometimes Morgan stood up there with Josh, a cigarette dangling from his lip as they talked in muffled voices, their arms hanging over the railing like bait. Chef and Cara waited patiently on deck, sitting beside the live tank.

There was one other crew member today, a guest from another gear, named Sean Croke. With a mop of unruly blond hair and brilliant green eyes, he possessed the slightly unhinged look of a true believer. Sean didn't try to disguise his enthusiasm. He was pumped up for their first haul. "A bunch of winches go off," he warned me. "This area where you're standing gets busy, so look out." Sean described himself as a gardener and herbalist when he wasn't fishing. "I used to live on this weirdo commune. I lost my job and came up here."

It was hardly a surprise to learn that several of the reef netters had lived together on the same commune, near Olympia, Washington. The idealism that had brought them together in an intentional community years earlier had eventually led them north to the reef-net fishery. The job wasn't just about making money (though no one objected to a good paycheck); these fishermen were proud to be taking part in what they considered the most sustainable fishery in the world. It was almost like a secret society. Who had ever heard of reef netting? This ancient way of catching salmon numbered less than a hundred devotees in its ranks globally. Here on Lummi Island there were a total of eight gears, which made Lummi the center of the reef-net universe. Half of those eight gears were owned and operated by a single entity, Lummi Island Wild, the co-op. It was the co-op's hope that all eight gears would one day be aligned with the same mission, but as it stood, the other four gears were taking a more traditional approach to the fishery. The co-op's mantra of carefully bleeding and icing each individual fish—a time-consuming process that gave off, perhaps, the white-tablecloth whiff of overly fine dining—was not part of everyone's game plan.

Ian beckoned me up to his tower, twenty feet above the deck. The gear next to us had just hauled in some fish. A jigsaw puzzle of dark-green islands and enamel-blue water spread before us. "I haven't seen a thing," Ian said. "Except for jellyfish." The reef stretched out two hundred feet, its mouth opened to the south. The salmon would be swimming north through Rosario Strait with the current. Due west of us rose 2,400-foot Mount Constitution, the highest point on Orcas Island. We were in sixty-five feet of water. At its mouth, the reef was sixty feet deep, before shallowing out to twenty-five feet deep at the net. The whole thing is just a bit of legerdemain, a ruse. Strips of bright-blue flagging wave in the current. Salmon allow themselves to be guided by the flagging of the reef as they migrate through the channel. Instead of discerning man-made ribbons, they see shoals of land. The reef leads them into a narrower and narrower slot, all the while forcing them upward in the water column, where they can be spotted from the tower. Seals, on the other hand, see right through the artifice, and they come and go as they please, as if the reef isn't there. They also know that the salmon are fooled by it, and they use this knowledge to their advantage. Seals, sea lions, even whales, can all wreak havoc on the reef. One time a young orca got caught briefly in the net.

The head stand, with its wide-angle view across the bay, makes one prone to reflection. Ian leaned on his elbows, puzzling over fish and fishermen and what bonded the two. In some ways, the fish were the easy part of the equation. "Getting a boat full of hardheaded fishermen on the same page can be difficult," he said. "Everybody is passionate and excited about what we're able to do out here." He interrupted himself to point out a school of minnows swimming idly through the reef. Even with my polarized sunglasses, I could barely make them out after studying the water. The tide was really moving now. Flotsam coursed by, little specks of foam and plankton slipping through the mesh of the net. Half-submerged, the yellow anchor floats at the head of the reef looked as if they were plowing water. If they got too low in the rip—indicating a current that was dangerously strong—the net would need to be pulled, eliminating drag but also putting a halt to fishing. Ian was reminded of some overanxious reef netters who flipped because of a rushing tide. "Accidents are pretty rare. A couple fatalities before my time, mostly guys that fell overboard and got swept out." Once you drifted past that point, he said, gesturing north to a spit of land a few hundred yards away in turbulent water, you were swimming to Canada.

"Should we do a water haul?" Josh yelled to Ian from the other tower.

"Just for practice?"

"We have a flounder and a big ol' jellyfish."

Just then a bullet-shaped form streaked by a few feet beneath the surface, heading for the net. Normally a lone salmon wouldn't be cause for hauling—since a much larger school could be right behind it—but something about this fish suggested to Ian that it was by itself, and Josh's idea of a practice haul was a good one. "Incoming!" Ian announced. "Take it!"

Ian yanked the cord behind him, which activated a winch below us. Just like that, the barge exploded into a frantic scene of activity. The front of the net rose out of the water, scaring the salmon toward the stern. Ian pulled a second rope to raise the bridge in the middle of the net, trapping the salmon, while Josh maneuvered the bunt with his own rope-and-winch system. Morgan hurried down the tower ladder to grab web. He, Cara, Chef, and Sean pulled on the net with abandon. A single pink salmon of about four pounds—not the species they were hoping for—slid into the live tank, where it swam around by itself. Josh came down for a look.

"Now we're making money," said Sean.

"We'll have to call you a pink specialist," Ian called over to Josh, trying to make light of it. Though no one said anything, they were all thinking it: Where were all the sockeye?

Josh wondered aloud, half seriously, whether this single pink salmon would earn him a trip to the Willows Inn. Everyone knew what had happened to Morgan and Chef the previous evening. They had made a small sockeye delivery, the first of the season, to the island's destination restaurant. In appreciation, staff at the restaurant had set a table and served them the full seven-course dinner. "Wine, candlelight, and everything!" Chef confirmed. Morgan said it was a nice surprise. He looked over at Chef and batted his eyes. "But I'm just not ready to take the next step." One of the benefits of being a fisherman is taking home a fresh-caught fish, though some days there aren't enough to go around. Two days ago, Chef was the only one to get a take-home sockeye. Now he started unpacking his leftovers for an early lunch, pulling out a Tupperware filled with salmon. He had a napkin and a bottle of juice. "Who gets it?" Josh asked with mock indignation. "The guy with a family? No, the single guy!" While everyone else wolfed down sandwiches, Chef produced a fork and started in on his salmon—in soffritto, he added, with baked cauliflower. He then explained to all who cared to listen that he had slow-cooked the fillet—wrapped in plastic with sugar, salt, and butter—at 220 degrees in the oven for about twenty minutes and then unwrapped for another fifteen minutes. Tomorrow, he said, he planned to eat the rest raw as sashimi.

"You need to freeze it, dude," Josh said.

"I've never seen a worm in sockeye." Chef was revealing his greenhorn status as the newest member of the crew. To kill any parasites, salmon should be flash-frozen in an industrial freezer if it's going to be served raw. He continued his food reverie, ignoring the background chatter. Maybe he would make a ceviche—or tacos, with cabbage, cilantro, fish sauce, key lime, and finger chilies. He said he was getting good at filleting the fish. "I did it on the beach. I scaled it with my little cheese knife."

"You scaled it?"

"Sure. Why not?"

"Whatever. I never scale it. And I always eat the skin." Salmon is one type of fish that doesn't require scaling. Besides, a layer of fat is lodged between the flesh and the skin, and scaling it exposes this deep flavor to direct, withering heat. But Chef had an answer for his critics.

"You can take the scales, boil them a little bit, dry them, and deep-fry them for a snack."

"That's some Willows bullshit!" cried Josh, and even though everyone had a good laugh at the new guy's expense, the former cook pressed on, undeterred. The fact was, the crew enjoyed hearing his tales from the kitchen. They were in the artisanal-food business, after all.

"Take the collars," Chef said. "Brine and smoke them. It's like the Super Bowl. I've got this friend in Iceland—she makes kids' toys out of cod skeletons. You can make all these crazy monsters with the cheekbones."

"Cod faces are awesome. They have big ol' heads."

"Salmon-head soup," said Morgan.

"Heads are cool," Sean agreed. "At a party, eat the eyeball and they'll think you're funny. I like roasting the whole fish."

Chef had the faintest hint of a smile on his otherwise serious-looking face. He was feeling like a member of the crew. Josh leaned down from his spotting stand and gave him a high-five. "Dude, we gotta get together. Seriously, I wanna learn some salmon cooking."

Chef was all for it. "I live alone. It's driving me crazy. I like to eat."

"Do you can your fish? I've got a canner."

Sean had had enough. "We need fish!" The laughter was uneasy now. They *did* need fish. More fish than they were getting so far. The first couple of test fisheries had seemed so promising, but where were the fish now?

"Goat was the worst meat I'd ever had," Morgan said, apropos of nothing, "until I ate seal. Spanish goats pee on their own faces." And with that, thoughts of jellyfish returned to haunt us all. I checked my wrist. Though there was no visible sign of sting, it still burned. The hours ticked away. Someone questioned whether we'd see another fish before dark. "It's time to check out the squid fishery," Morgan said. "Get out here at night with our floodlight."

Josh whirled around in his tower. "Let's go! The only thing is, I'm not allowed to do anything fun. I have to stay home with the wife and baby."

IN THE LATE AFTERNOON, with skies clearing and a corner of sun showing through the clouds and the crew bantering to pass the time, Ian suddenly straightened up in the spotter's stand and made the call. We all jumped up as if a fire alarm had just gone off. Ian and Josh tripped the winches to hoist the net, and the rest of us grabbed web. The fish leaped and thrashed as they came out of the water, bouncing like a bunch of kids on a trampoline. We guided them into the live tank, a few dozen bright sockeye in all, finally. After that the schools started arriving, one after another. "Take 'em!" Ian shouted again and again. Sockeye spilled into the tank, a dozen here, three dozen there, their blue backs gleaming as they circled and circled, looking for a way out. There was no time between hauls for Chef to get any reading done. He, Morgan, and Cara spent the rest of the afternoon popping gills and moving salmon from the live tank to the bleed tank and then into totes filled with slush ice, each step of the way timed to the min- ute by the little white egg timer perched on a chopping block aboard the barge. Ian was usually the first to spot incoming fish from his posi- tion closer to the reef. Like any activity requiring keen eyesight, it's a skill that needs mastering. Even with polarized glasses, picking out fish beneath the surface is a nearly paranormal skill, based on the most infinitesimal clues and years of experience. The schools could be cryp- tic or just obscured by murkiness in the water.

"Sometimes a school looks like an overhead cloud," Ian explained, never taking his eyes off the water, "like a shadow moving across the ripples." Other times, he said, it looks like algae blooming beneath the surface or like a giant air bubble rising up. "That's one of my favorites—

fizz coming up and expanding like a diver's bubble. And sometimes it looks like fish, sure enough—unmistakably like a school of fish. You'll get them in a perfect line or a V, like a flock of geese." He relaxed at the thought, leaning into the metal brace of the spotter's stand, the memory of fish filling his imagination. "Sometimes they'll be jumping. Every group is a little bit different. Sometimes they're skittish. They see us or hear us and turn around. The spotter gives the play-by-play, sometimes for ten minutes on end. 'They're coming in! They're going out!' Finally they disappear or they come in, to a big cheer."

ALL AT ONCE, the tide changed and the current went slack. Fishing was done for the day. The reef netters had other chores to do, so I caught a ride back to the beach with Ian. Riley Starks was there, along with a tall blond woman from Atlanta, Georgia, who was packing a minivan with boxes of fish and hurrying to catch a flight back home. She ran a catering business and had joined the co-op's buying club. This trip was a little present to herself, to see the place where these incomparable fish originated and to meet the reef netters. She'd brought her daughter and stayed at Nettles Farm. The night before, Starks cooked her one of the fish they'd caught. "It was hands down the best fish I've ever had," she gushed. "I took pictures of it and everything." Starks gave a slightly embarrassed nod and made quick goodbyes, politely telling the mother and daughter they'd better get moving to catch the ferry. These visits exhausted him. He enjoyed telling the reef-net story, and he was certainly energized by what they were doing, especially the sustainability part, but dealing with the public could be draining. It was very different from taking on the elements out on the water.

He looked at me and exhaled. "How'd it go today? You need a fish too." I said no, but he insisted. We drove together back to Nettles Farm, where he had a sockeye from yesterday's catch waiting in the walk-in. We carried it through the pasture to his chicken house and washed it off on an outdoor stainless-steel cleaning table. While Starks tended to his chickens, I took a fillet knife and opened my salmon, slitting it from vent to gill. Starks reappeared and watched me warily, pronouncing my incision ugly. "Look at this," he said, holding the fish up. My knife had barely pierced the pink membrane that walls off the internal organs. "You've fucking ruined it."

"It's fine. I'm not running a restaurant."

"Yeah, but now you've opened it. See? This fish won't last nearly as long refrigerated this way."

"No problem. I'm eating it tomorrow."

Starks shook his head. It didn't matter. My knife work was a travesty. "Jeez," he muttered. "I'd better fillet it myself."

BY SUMMER'S END, WHEN I RETURNED to Lummi Island for a third time, giddy expectations for a record harvest at the co-op had been replaced by weariness. Riley Starks informed me that Trident, the seafood processor, had pulled its tender from the bay and sent it north to Alaska instead. Chef was gone, as were several of the greenest reef netters from across the fleet, let go in the absence of fish. The remaining fishermen were clocking long hours, grinding it out. Ginger-haired Morgan, even more laconic than usual, chalked it up to the fickleness of nature. "It's fish. Can't count too much on a wild animal's behavior. I just know they ain't here."

Dreams of big profits and the ascension of reef-net fish on the national market turned to a need to break even and a reality-hardened focus on the work that lay ahead. They could still make their minimum goals for the season with some more long days and maybe a stab at the coho fishery that would follow the sockeye. "We just need Morgan to smell them and Josh to feel them," Cara said. No one wanted to talk much about it. Josh tried to be upbeat, telling me that they'd been getting a couple of hundred fish a day lately, but that wasn't exactly true. Yes, the day before they'd managed to eke out two hundred sockeye, in a long slog of mostly waiting around for the fish to arrive. Many of their days before that had been goose eggs. Ian said the sockeye didn't like the warm water.

A layer of water three degrees warmer than average had formed in the Gulf of Alaska and stretched clear across the Pacific to Japan. This warm-water bubble, as some called it, forced salmon north in pursuit of colder, more nutrient-rich water. One exception to this was a band of cold water that ran along the northwest coast of British Columbia. As the Fraser-bound sockeye, driven by their need to reproduce, streamed in from the North Pacific, they ran headlong into the bubble; instead of pushing through it, they banked eastward to find cooler currents along the B.C. coastline, which then channeled them south through Johnstone Strait, between the mainland and the east side of Vancouver Island. Most years the Fraser River sockeye split their migration, with about half taking the northern route through Johnstone Strait and the other half taking the southern route through the Strait of Juan de Fuca. But this year, as far as scientists could tell, nearly all the fish were choosing the northern route. Some estimates had 99 percent of the run going through Johnstone Strait. The culprit, everyone agreed, was this warm-water bubble. A meteorologist at the University of Washington said he'd never seen anything like it. He nicknamed it "the blob."

As with any business in trouble, it's the job of the higher-ups to give the employees positive motivation, and on this particular day the reef netters had something new to be proud of. Ian met me on the beach and told me to come across the road, where the rest of the crew was waiting by an open garage. They were having a powwow. "A team meeting," one of the reef netters said. "Have we ever done this before?"

"And the good news is," someone else chimed in, *"you're all fired."*

The yard out front was filled with a haphazard array of old fishing equipment, some of it in current use, though much of it looked more like artifacts from a long-gone seaside culture: a boat trailer, assorted crab traps, buoys in red and yellow, coiled piles of thick rope, and an

ax. An angry salmon sculpture the size of a marlin, welded together
from rusted scrap metal, arched beside the driveway. Everyone shuffled over to the front lawn and sat on patchy clumps of sunburned
grass. Even here, at their first-ever team meeting, the fishermen could
gaze upon the sparkling bay where their gears waited, empty. With
his back to the water, Ian stood before the group, which included a
couple dozen reef netters from the four gears that made up the Lummi
Island Wild co-op.

"I just wanted to take a second to get everybody together so we're
all on the same page," he began. A salty breeze blew in off the water,
and I could see some of the reef netters trying to concentrate on Ian's
words even as their faces revealed the pull of distant currents. "It came
off as a little bit of a surprise to have the opportunity to bleed the entire catch yesterday." With the Trident tender out of the picture, the
four gears not associated with Lummi Island Wild suddenly had no
one to buy their fish. The co-op stepped in and offered their own services. But this offer came with the stipulation that the other gears
handle their fish in such a way that they could be sold under the
Lummi Island Wild label. This meant bleeding, icing, and delivering
quickly. "It was so cool to see the entire bay for the first time ever
cooperating to deliver a product to a unified tender," Ian continued.
He was on a roll now. "All of us got an extra thirty cents a pound.
Double thumbs-up. I'm still floored. We earned ourselves a co-op
raise." The reef netters erupted in a brief ovation. This wasn't the
speech they were expecting.

Out on the water an hour later, after lowering the net, Ian breathed
a little sigh of relief. Speaking to the whole co-op—giving them reason to be proud—was a big deal. He was wearing his usual tie-dyed
thermal sweatshirt. "My lucky sweatshirt is lucky again," he mused.

"You know it only stays lucky if you don't wash it, right?" Josh,
the Texan, yelled down from his tower.

"Is that the trick?"

"Dude, tell me you didn't wash that thing after we caught all those
fish yesterday."

"Not this year," Sierra piped in.

"Oh, okay, good. I haven't washed this underwear either since we've been catching fish." Groans all around. "Come on up, Morgan. Anyone else wanna see my tie-dyed underwear?"

Laughter was the best response to poor fishing. On cue, a little towheaded boy came rowing out past us in a miniature bright-red dinghy. It was barely sunrise and he was the first to arrive at his gear, pulling at the oars with obvious intent, biting his lower lip. Seeing the next generation of reef netters inspired awe among the fishermen. "No one knows who he is . . ." intoned Morgan theatrically.

"But he pulls web like an animal," added Ian.

I joined Ian in the tower, hoping to improve my spotting skills. From up here, looking across the bay, with eagles soaring in a blue sky and great blue herons perched like gargoyles on the head cans, it was hard to believe that the unseen depths weren't teeming with fish. Puget Sound has the same effect on all who stare out across its rippling waters. What a beautiful place—just as nature intended. But that same water masks an unpleasant stew of chemical runoff, PCBs, sewage, and all sorts of other man-made contaminants. One study has revealed traces of antidepressants and cocaine in Puget Sound salmon. And then there are the larger forces at work in the North Pacific. The blob . . . Nothing surprises the reef netters anymore. Still, Ian was feeling good about the day before.

"We tendered the whole catch. These are fish that will be marketed as reef-net caught." Ian took his eyes off the water for a rare moment and surveyed the activity below. Cara and Morgan were busy moving sockeye into the bleed tank. Josh, already in a tank top, was repairing one of the solar-powered winches. "We've spent a decade developing systems like this," he went on. "It's hard on the people to be bent over, popping gills and moving fish from well to well. We have a recipe for slushing our totes with just the right mix of ice and salt water. We have a bleed time that we use for the minimum amount of time they swim before they bleed out. When you watch those fish get cut, there's no question. You can tell instantly. Our fish, you can fillet ten, twenty, thirty, on a single piece of newspaper before changing it. If you fillet an unbled fish: one piece, covered in blood." Off in the distance an osprey circled the bay, looking for its own morning catch. "Even our processing plant tells us they love our fish. They're clean; they're easy, beautiful. You can taste the quality difference, in my view, especially out of the freezer. No fishy off-taste."

There was no question about the quality of reef-net fish. The problem was quantity. This was supposed to be the year Lummi Island Wild put reef-net salmon squarely on the culinary map from coast to coast. Instead, they were forced to look abroad for non-reef-net fish just to keep afloat. "We went up to B.C. and bought some seined fish because we thought we might not have any," Ian admitted, "and we ended up throwing out almost half. They'll be crab bait. We'll never ever put our name on something like that. Nothing we want to be a part of. That's what the seiners are bringing to the dock, what ends up at most grocery stores. They were disgusting. I was picking fish myself. They were soft, gills washed out, not iced properly, brailed up in big bags. I try not to talk bad about other fisheries because it's easy to start a holy war, but it was very apparent."

Later in the day, a pair of old-timers took over on the gear next to us. They had a couch on board. It was a sunny day at the end of summer. Shirts off. From their position on the cushions, they could reach all the winches and operate the net without even getting up from their seat. The oldest of old-timers, Jerry Anderson, visited our gear and took up his former position in the tower. Almost immediately he spied a school of fish. He studied them for a while and then fell back into casual conversation with the crew.

"What happened to the fish?" someone wanted to know.

"Oh, they went out."

"How many?"

"Ah Christ, I dunno—fifty or sixty."

Fifty or sixty fish would be a nice haul, especially in a year like this, but there was nothing to do about it. The fish entered the reef and sometimes they turned around and left the reef. Like a flock of birds wheeling through the sky, they moved in unison, in unpredictable ways. It was the spotter's job to make sure they didn't get past the net unseen. Everyone watched the octogenarian—with his specially modified sunglasses that included a homemade tweak of cardboard side panels to cut the glare—as he chatted and joked and seemingly paid no attention to his spotting duties. They all knew that if a single fish had the audacity to show itself anywhere near the surface of the reef, Anderson would spot it.

"He can see fish clear down to Lummi Rocks," said Morgan. We all looked south. In the afternoon haze, the rocks—tiny islands—appeared like little bumps on the horizon. Maybe a gigantic school of sockeye was gathering there, off in the distance, at that moment. The possibility of fish never diminished.

At the ferry that evening, I overheard a weekend couple ahead of me in line lamenting their return to the city. They hated to leave the place. The island offered so much you couldn't get on the mainland these days. Orchard trees hung low with fruit. Crab-pot buoys painted dabs of color in the bay. How many of the humble ranch houses looking out on the water would become second homes, I wondered. How many would be torn down and replaced by something bigger, more at odds with the landscape? What would happen to Jerry Anderson's house? To backyards filled with old rusty fishing gear? You couldn't really blame them, this couple. The island had changed hands in the past and it would change hands again. First it belonged to nesting seabirds, then the Lummi Indians, followed by the white fishermen. Next it would be the dominion of tech moguls or their like.

Civilization's progression has a churning finality to it that defies reproach. The city couple's Lexus SUV sported a single carefully placed bumper sticker that read LIVIN' LIFE. My own cooler in the back of my car concealed a sockeye, a beautiful bright silver one of about six pounds taken earlier that day, still uncut. I had the hale feeling of a man who has caught fish. It's an infectious feeling, one that's made Lummi Island a destination for centuries, perhaps as long as there have been people on Puget Sound.

WHEN THE SEASON WAS OVER and the fall rains had started again in earnest, I met up with Riley Starks one more time, in an unlikely location. He had business to do in Seattle and suggested we have dinner together at a chain restaurant in Northgate Mall. I got lost in the acres of parking lot and was late. After walking the mall from end to end, I finally found our destination, a California Pizza Kitchen across from Barnes & Noble. Cloying pop music filled the room, and a few disinterested couples poked at their dishes of pub food. Starks had recently returned from the Adams River, a Fraser River tributary, where he went hiking with his new dog, Stella, and filmed the spawning of the stream's famous run of large, late-returning sockeye salmon. "We went on these trails way off the beaten path and there were no people," he told me. "We got to witness the spawning drama, with big kings in there too and trout trying to steal the eggs."

The spawning drama, as he called it, is something I try to see each year as well. It's one of the great natural wonders of the world, certainly one of the few spectacles in North America that compares to the wildlife on display in a place like Africa. Each fall and into winter, I can drive a couple of hours from Seattle and see thousands of big fish rolling about with amorous resolve in a single drift—the huge chum run on the Skagit River, for instance, which attracts hundreds of bald eagles from as far away as Alaska, or even the coho that pair up all over a small stream like Pilchuck Creek, not far from the suburbs, all those colored-up fish scraping the gravel beds clean with their nest-building so that the river bottom looks as if someone has just pushed a giant vacuum cleaner across it. The pictures and documentary films that the average American is likely to encounter on the Discovery Channel or in the pages of *National Geographic*—of scarlet sockeye lolling about in a Bristol Bay drainage, or of bronzed chinook on the Kenai—are dramas that still play out in a handful of rivers throughout the populated regions of the Pacific Northwest as well, despite the odds. After nearly two centuries of intensive development and exploitation, we continue to have a few remnants of wild nature that can rival the best of what Alaska has to offer.

When my son was still a toddler, I took him to the Stillaguamish River—the Stilly, as everyone calls it—near Granite Falls, little more than an hour north of Seattle, where we watched wild pink salmon, thousands of them, use up the last of their life force in the cobbled reaches of that modest river, their humped backs sticking out of the thin water. Contorted, half-eaten bodies of salmon littered the banks. The place reeked of death and also of life. My little boy ran up and down the banks on wobbly legs, finding one twisted and desiccated carcass more grotesque than the last, until the stench was too much for both of us. I looked at him and realized the life cycle of the salmon had become part of my own annual trip around the sun. I could mark the seasons and important dates by my travels through salmon country, and one day, I hoped, when my boy was older, he would join me for the sort of backcountry fishing adventures that had become an annual highlight. In a week I would leave for British Columbia. I was heading north to go camping and fishing, as I had every fall for the last several years. People from all over the world journeyed to this region to explore the ancestral parts of their humanity. I had met Germans, Italians, Japanese, even Chinese on the banks of salmon streams, all of them drawn to wild rivers and their fish.

Starks ordered what the menu called cedar-plank salmon. This dinner was a mission of sorts, a little private-eye work. "Is it farmed or wild?" he asked the waitress, already knowing the answer. She wasn't sure and offered to check. "Don't worry about it," he said quickly. The fish was a farmed Atlantic salmon, but recently California Pizza Kitchen had been negotiating with Lummi Island Wild to buy wild pink salmon, in an effort to reinvigorate their menu. "They're trying to reinvent themselves," Starks said. "They want to be more sustainable. It's a publicly traded company. I think they're bored. They're looking at how they can change with the times. If they can't be organic, they can still offer a wild salmon." Next summer, he added, when the pinks were running, California Pizza Kitchen would buy enough to freeze and last them through the year. "It's going to have a halo effect if they embrace it."

"Halo effect?"

"Oh, that's marketing talk. My job these days," he reminded me.

I wondered whether pink salmon served at a place like California Pizza Kitchen was enough to turn the tide, to open the eyes of a public that was too busy, too harried, too uninterested in nature to care about something they saw at the supermarket's fish counter every day of the year. Sockeye, with its richer flavor and striking color, seemed like a better choice. Starks disagreed. "Take a look at how far those Fraser River pinks have to go. They average four and a half or five pounds. The fat content is huge. They're not even like a pink salmon. They're beautiful." Anyway, he said, pinks have the same flavor profile as sockeye. Both species eat the same sort of food at sea: zooplankton. The only difference is that pinks spend half the time in the ocean that sockeye do, so they never develop the deep-red color, the rich flavor. But they're still damn good. "I've shed my mantle of 'It has to be perfect,'" he went on. "I've got an open mind. I believe in pink salmon. I believe it's an amazing resource that's underutilized, and it's wrong to be underutilized. We need to get it on menus and dinner plates. It's going to be a really great thing, if people can accept it." The co-op was moving on from the disappointing sockeye season. Their new goal was to move one million pounds of pinks the next year.

And Starks had another idea: Watching his dog roll around in dead salmon carcasses on the banks of the Adams River reminded him of a new gadget he'd heard about. It was a machine that could scrape fish carcasses. The industry term is *food recovery*. After filleting, the pink salmon carcasses can be scraped, ground, and cooked into dog treats. "We're trying chum salmon too," he added, sitting up in his chair and jotting some notes in a little book. In another departure, the co-op planned to buy chums from Puget Sound seiners. "If this company is going to succeed, it needs to do more than just reef-net fish. We'll have full say over quality."

Our cedar-plank salmon arrived. Starks pronounced it dry but not bad. "It has decent texture," he said, piercing it with his fork. He took another bite and I could see him pondering the opportunity to supplant this farm-raised fish with the real thing, a wild salmon bound for an icy glacier-fed stream in British Columbia. The problem, he said, was in finding consistency. "Nature's vagaries," he added wistfully. "We were all excited about this season. It would have been wonderful if it had come off. We thought we were going to get a hell of a bump. We thought this was going to really push us." Starks took another bite. This fillet of farmed salmon that "wasn't bad" was already beginning to vex him. He pushed it around a little on the plate, studied its contours and fork-tenderness. In a way, he was besieged—with an army of farm-raised simulacra on one side and unsympathetic nature on the other—and yet, always the fisherman, he found a reason for hope. "The fact is, because we had a good line of credit we were able to buy fish, and so it played out a lot differently and it wasn't all bad. It opened doors that wouldn't have been opened otherwise. We had markets we had to fill." Hadn't Ian, the crew chief, told me that half of the seiner fish were fit only to be crab bait? "We left a few people in the lurch," Starks had to admit. "Like Metropolitan Market, for instance." He felt bad about that. He'd sent an email to the seafood buyer at Met Market recently and hadn't heard back. What was that about? Were they upset? The chain of upscale grocery stores had invested a fair piece of time and money in advertising this year's reef-net sockeye: posters, stickers, even online video. And then: no fish.

"The thing is," Starks said, "the fish came. The Canadians got them, and we got them from Canada. It's not like people didn't get fish." It was true. The blob interrupted the run, and it probably caused a level of mortality that scientists hadn't yet calculated, but it didn't crash the whole shebang. Sockeye still returned to their breeding grounds in good numbers, and many fishermen caught them along the way. The reef netters didn't get enough, and maybe this would deter markets like Metropolitan from investing similarly in next year's wild pink run—which would be a shame, Starks said, because the goal had always been to capitalize on pink salmon above all. This was the fish no one wanted at one time, at least not fresh. It was a cannery fish, pennies on the dollar. The hope was that a good sockeye run would soften up potential buyers for the next year's pink run. "This isn't the first time this kind of thing has happened, when you set your sights on something and it doesn't happen and you look like an idiot. It shows that the co-op is maturing and we were able to withstand it. We didn't sit around with our hands in our pockets. We went out and got fish." The buying clubs were still on board. There was excitement about salmon caviar—ikura and sujiko. The new tender being built by Mavrik Marine in La Conner, to the tune of $1.4 million, would be finished in December. "It looks like a big bowpicker," Starks said. At fifty-by-twenty-five feet, the tender would be able to pack fifty thousand pounds of fish at a time. There were plenty of indicators of progress.

Starks was figuring out his vision for the home front as well. "I'm recreating Nettles Farm in the form of a small Burgundy chicken farm," he said. I wasn't sure what to say to that. Was he kidding me? "No, not at all. Nettles is a good platform for marketing." Recently he had invited a few executives from California Pizza Kitchen to stay there while they negotiated the new salmon contract. "We didn't have fish for them to catch, but they got to butcher chickens," he said. "We had an intimate experience. You can't buy that kind of bond. That's how I've always marketed. It's who I am. I marketed the Willows that way, reef netting that way. 'Let's cook together. We don't even know where this is gonna go.' Get outside of your head. Get in your body, in your habitat. It's primal. And remarkably fun." He pushed his empty plate away. "One guy was a chef, he's done a lot of cooking. Never killed a chicken. He had the hardest time putting the knife in and doing a clean job of it. I forced them to go through the steps and do it. The fact is, if you go all the way through, there's a change that happens. He had to do it three times to get a good cut. Then they got to gut it and butcher it. One of them made a chicken joke and I got really serious with them. I said, 'You know what, this is food. It's an animal. I always treat these animals with reverence. This is a gift.' Everyone straightened up. It could have gone the rubber-chicken way. All three shook my hand at the end and said it was a good experience."

Starks pulled out his wallet. It was time to go. "Reverence," he said one more time, pushing out his chair and standing up. "It's the same with salmon."

CHAPTER 11

COCKTAIL HOUR ON
THE KISPIOX

A MAN LOST HIS FACE THE DAY I ARRIVED IN STEELHEAD CAMP. Everyone agreed it was a case of very bad luck—a bear with cubs. "Never knew what hit him," said an angler leaning on his fourteen-foot spey rod on the banks of the Kispiox River in central British Columbia. He said this with the resignation of someone who would walk on narrow trails through head-high willows every day for the next week to reach his favorite steelhead run—just the sort of hidden paths the bears prefer too. The sow took off the man's jaw with one swipe and left him to die beside the Morice River. Even so, he managed to crawl out to the road for help. Later, the provincial government closed the river, but after interviewing the victim at a Vancouver hospital—during which he nodded yes or no, since he couldn't speak—it was determined that the bear wouldn't be hunted down. Its behavior was entirely natural. The man just happened to be in the wrong place at the wrong time.

Our camp was several miles up the Kispiox, in a meadow next to the river, bordered by groves of firs and poplars. Even though the Morice River, where the bear attack took place, is across the Hazelton Mountains to the south, plenty of grizzlies still haunt the entire region's secluded folds and ridges. My first evening, after putting rods and reels together for the week's fishing, I took a walk before dinner. A trail led me through woods a few hundred yards downstream of camp, where it jogged down a bluff to the water's edge. Large rocks interrupted the river's flow here, creating riffles and eddies and a deep trough in the middle—just the sort of safe holding water a big steelhead prefers as it migrates upstream to its spawning grounds. An angler was working his way along the bank in last light, making long, graceful casts with his spey rod, putting his fly behind the rocks and probing the pocket water. This is a well-known stretch on the Kispiox. It's called the Bear Hole.

WHEN THE RITUALS AND TRAPPINGS of civilization become too much for me, I head for the hinterlands, the sort of places where bears and wild steelhead still lurk. My first steelhead camp was on the Hoh River in Washington State, just outside the border of Olympic National Park, in dark, mossy rainforest, about four hours by car from my home in Seattle. That was many years ago. The wild steelhead of the Hoh and just about every other river in Washington, Oregon, and California are in trouble now. When the time comes to introduce my own children to the pleasures of making camp with friends along an untamed river filled with wild steelhead, I will probably choose the eighteen-hour drive from Seattle to the Kispiox instead. For all the problems that plague even this remote watershed—logging, oil and gas development, mining—it's still a place to discover the beguiling ways of the Pacific Northwest's most legendary game fish.

The Kispiox is a tributary of the Skeena River, the lifeline of a territory that's semi-domesticated at the edges but still largely left to its own devices. In a land of big rivers, the Skeena is a giant, second in the province only to the Fraser River. It drains lonely glacier-clad peaks that give way to deeply sculpted valleys—a complicated and interconnected latticework of rivers and mountain ranges that is hardly more comprehensible on a map. The Skeena's source is the Spatsizi Plateau, sometimes called the Serengeti of British Columbia, a place of wolves, grizzlies, caribou, moose, and mountain goats. Cougars stalk the woods, and countless bald eagles stand on the sandbars, alone or in groups, like pensioners at a city park staring at a chess match. The eagles watch for a reason. All five species of Pacific salmon run up the Skeena, as do steelhead, cutthroat, bull trout, and a colorful type of char called Dolly Varden, named for a gaily-dressed character out of Dickens. The surrounding forests are also home to the spirit bear, a rare all-white black bear that owes its ghostly form to a recessive gene. Terrace, Smithers, and Houston are the largest communities along its course; combined they have fewer than thirty thousand people. Prince Rupert, just north of the river mouth on the coast, has another twelve thousand people. There are pockets of country in this watershed that still resemble North America before the first Europeans arrived, with the same merciless dynamics of predator and prey that characterize life in unbroken wilderness.

Skeena fish are all wild, and they return in enough numbers to give a fisherman hope. Of the many storied rivers in the system, including the Sustut, Babine, Bulkley, Suskwa, Morice, Zymoetz, and the mainstem Skeena itself, the Kispiox is probably the most storied, though anglers will argue the merits of their pet favorites into the wee hours. The Sustut and Babine are more remote, and the Bulkley is known for fish that are famously tempted by a dry fly, but the Kispiox is where most of the record-book fish have been caught over the years. In 1962, an angler landed a thirty-three-pound buck hooked on a fly called the Kispiox Special, a record that still stands. The fish was forty-two and a half inches long, with a girth of twenty-four inches. My friend Rocky, a champion fly-tyer (and, reportedly, a fine dentist, which requires a similar ocular skill), has twice landed steelhead nearing the thirty-pound class in this somewhat smallish river that more closely resembles a Michigan trout stream, with its colorful fall foliage and tannin-colored water. The river is too small for a typical three-person drift boat. Rocky's favorite way to fish it is to putter up and down the country by-lane that follows the river on a little red Honda minibike, ducking in and out of favored honey-holes, his rod secured in a section of PVC pipe lashed to the handlebars. The most popular way to fish it, though, is to float single-occupancy pontoon boats or one-man rafts like the Water Master. These are highly portable though somewhat flimsy vessels, and you wouldn't want to meet a bear midstream in one.

Here on the Kispiox, word travels fast about the grizzlies. Besides the news of the Morice mauling, everyone knew that a sow and her cubs had taken up residence near an oat field adjacent to the Cottonwood Hole, one of the river's most productive steelhead runs, where they'd been gorging for weeks on post-harvest leftovers and leaving their calling cards on the banks in large piles. It's common courtesy among farmers and ranchers who live along the river to let their neighbors know when a griz shows up. "I heard rustling back in the cottonwoods the other day and got out of there quick," a sturdy-looking angler from Fairbanks told me with a tight, knowing grin. When the Alaskans are being cautious, you know it's real.

Bradley Boyden, my friend and steelhead mentor, is no stranger to bears. One time, in Oregon's Rogue River Canyon, he watched a large black bear and a cougar square off over the carcass of a freshly killed mule deer. Bradley and his brother, Frank, are the owners of the wilderness homestead above the Rogue where I lived as a caretaker more than two decades earlier—where I caught my first steelhead. The brothers learned to fish there and to respect the wildlife. As children, they traveled with their parents to the remote stretch of canyon by boat, running miles of rapids to get there. A wildcat gold miner named Red Keller sometimes helped the family with chores around the cabin and took the boys hunting and fishing. Red showed them how to pan for gold in the river's crevices and how to snare a lizard with a long blade of grass tied into a slipknot. Bradley remembers watching his father fly-fish during their summers there. He had a favorite spot—Dad's Rock, as it was known—and he would stand on that rock and unfurl tremendous casts out over the river that would invariably hook a bright steelhead as long as your arm. This was before the Lost Creek Dam was built in the 1970s along with a fish hatchery. The steelhead back then were all wild. They looked and behaved differently.

These days the Rogue's fish are smaller, for some reason, and they tend to charge upriver toward the hatchery rather than hang around the lower canyon, as they used to. Still, if you time it right, you can get into some good fishing. Nearly twenty-five years ago, Bradley stood on Dad's Rock and showed me how to make a long cast out into the heavy downstream current and work a fly called a Red Ant back in among the cobbles and ledges where a steelhead was likely to hold during its upstream migration. On a river like the Rogue—gin-clear in the low flows of summer—you can sometimes see the fish material- ize off the bottom to sip in your fly. The effect is like those toy view- finders that create an image out of kaleidoscopic colors, making form out of chaos. It's startling and unforgettable. Most of my steelhead on the Rogue have been in the five-pound category, a far cry from a twenty-pound Skeena steelhead, but on a couple of occasions I've landed fish pushing ten pounds. According to Bradley, such fish were, if not the norm, much more common before the onslaught of dams and hatcheries. This is why he happily gets in his truck each Septem- ber and drives for two days to the Kispiox. To be a steelhead fisherman is to mourn for all the abused rivers and their beleaguered fish. Like the fish itself, this special breed of angler is a wanderer, forever search- ing for a lost Valhalla.

THE NEXT DAY WE LAUNCHED our pontoon boats before dawn. It was still dark when I made my first tentative casts of the trip, not expect- ing much. Near the bottom of the run, where the river turned right, a savage strike nearly pulled the rod out of my hand. All at once my reel was spinning too fast, the line knitting itself into a fright wig around the reel. A rookie mistake. I had forgotten to check the drag, and now I had a mess. As the fish ran downstream, I tried to untangle the line, but it was too late; in my confusion I allowed it to make straight for a

logjam up against the bank, where it wrapped itself around a submerged limb and vanished.

"Did you see it?" Bradley asked me as we shoved off the bar in our
pontoons.

"No, but it was a monster."

"Hmm." The trip had barely begun and already Bradley was did-
dling me over a lost fish, just the way his older brother diddled him.

Around the next corner, as we approached the Cottonwood Hole,
I was reminded again of big lumbering bugaboos. Bradley had his oars
out of the water as he drifted ahead of me in the current, scanning the
bank with purpose. The outline of the day was just starting to come
into focus as a sliver of sun peeked above the Babine Range to the east.
A line of tall cottonwood trees stretched down the left bank, their yellow leaves brittle and chattering softly in the autumn breeze. Beyond
the woods I could see the farmer's oat field, and beyond that was a
little farmhouse with a curl of smoke coming out of the chimney.
Sticker bushes surrounded stout tree trunks, obscuring the ground
with a maze of brush, and the brilliant blood-red luster of rose hips
painted the banks with color. Just then a raven flew across the river,
barking its guttural call. You have to wonder about the ravens: Do
they see things we do not? One time Bradley was floating along the
Kispiox, through a slow section that occasions the sort of peaceful
reflection that is the main draw for many anglers. He snapped out of
his reverie after a while, when it became clear that people onshore, not
ravens, were yelling at him. He looked up in time to see the bear ahead,
swimming toward him.

I beached my pontoon at the top of the Cottonwood Hole and
started working my way through the run. Halfway down, my fly got
stuck on a rock. I was about to wade out into the riffle to extract it
when line started racing off the reel, and less than a second after my
brain had begun to grasp this change in fortune, a missile-shaped fish
leaped into the air thirty yards away on the far side of the river. "Fish
on!" Bradley called from downriver, seeing my rod bent over. "Only

counts if you land it." The fish jumped again, right in front of another angler working the other side, and even from this distance I could see the shoulders of a big male, maybe eighteen pounds. The angler reeled in, as dictated by etiquette, and trudged off. Usually females are more acrobatic than males, so seeing this buck fly through the air like a football was surprising, and, amazingly, I was still attached to it. The fish tore off more line, racing up- and downriver seemingly at will, and I held on. I gained some line back, and after a tug-of-war that involved a few more hard runs, I brought the fish into the shallows, tailed it, and gently removed the barbless hook. The gill plate reflected a rosy blush, and a double maroon stripe ran down its body, betraying the fish's lineage. A steelhead, after all, is just a big, well-traveled rainbow trout.

STEELHEAD NOW CARRY THE consonant-crunching scientific name *Oncorhynchus mykiss,* thanks to a taxonomic shake-up in 1988 that caused more than a little consternation among sport fishermen, who preferred the mellifluous sound of *Salmo* and the historical linkage to two other noble game fish in that genus, the Atlantic salmon (*Salmo salar*) and brown trout (*Salmo trutta*). But it turns out that the steelhead is an anadromous form of rainbow trout and occupies a branch on the same tree as Pacific salmon, a distinction that can be seen in a big male's slightly hooked jaw during the spawn.

The rainbow evolved in the glacially carved rivers of the northern Pacific Rim. When the glaciers moved south, the rainbow waited out geologic time in the refugia of California and the upper Columbia. When the glaciers retreated, it recolonized as far north as southeast Alaska. A species with great elasticity, as biologists would say, the rainbow developed a variety of life strategies to survive in a chaotic environment severely influenced by fire and ice. There are rainbows from the coast and rainbows from the interior; there's a rainbow in the Sierras that looks nearly as gilded as a fall cottonwood and is known as a golden trout, and there's a pink-flushed rainbow called a redband trout, which evolved to survive the harsh, oscillating climate of the high desert. They're all the same species.

With access to the Pacific, rainbows learned how to leave behind their nutrient-starved rivers for the tremendous feedbag of the ocean. They grew larger in the salt than their fluvial cousins, on a diet of baitfish, squid, and amphipods, then returned to their natal rivers to spawn. Fresh from the sea, a rainbow glints bright silver, like a polished blade. Turning in the light, it can shimmer with an alabaster belly and a deep metallic black or evergreen or even indigo on top—a sheet of glistening metal right out of the forge's ice bath. A large male has visible shoulders and a high forehead. The telltale red lateral line of its youth doesn't reappear until the fish has spent some time back in the river after its saltwater sojourn. We call these sea-run rainbows "steelhead," for reasons that are both clear and shrouded in myth. Same species as a rainbow trout, different life history. Biologists, forever fielding questions about the perceived differences between rainbows and steelhead, often call them, simply, *O. mykiss*.

Meriwether Lewis described one for science in his journal at Fort Clatsop in Oregon, where the Corps of Discovery overwintered in 1806, near the mouth of the Columbia. He called it a "salmon trout," which is a pretty fair description, and he went on to note that steelhead remained good table fare long after salmon became unfit as food. This is because steelhead spawn later than salmon, usually in early spring, which made them an available food fish for Native Americans and the first white settlers in the cold dark of winter, a time of year when food could be scarce. And, unlike salmon, a small percentage of steelhead, mostly females, will survive the spawning ordeal and return to the sea. Biologists call these fish "kelts."

The taste of steelhead differs from that of a typical white-fleshed rainbow trout. A lighter shade of pink than salmon, the fillets taste like a trout that's been dining at the all-you-can-eat shrimp buffet, with a surprisingly delicate flavor that combines the nuttiness of a mountain trout with a touch of the sea. But steelhead were never as abundant as Pacific salmon, and the industrialization of their river habitat has not served them well. Wild steelhead are mostly gone from California now, and their status isn't much better in Oregon or Washington. Instead, recreational anglers depend on the manufactured steelhead pumped out of the many hatcheries throughout the region. One of the few places where an angler can keep a wild fish—all of one per year—is the remote West End of the Olympic Peninsula, a hugely controversial loophole that has conservation-minded fishermen up in arms whenever a big steelhead winds up as a wall mount, as a thirty-pounder on the Hoh River did in 2009. Such fish are essential to the dwindling genetic pool. To get that big, they're survivors, and multiple spawners at that. A fish mounted in the Smithers Airport lobby in British Columbia is estimated to have been more than forty pounds and thirteen years old when it was caught in a net, having already spawned four times. The Skeena and its tributaries probably have more of these behemoths than any other river system in the world. Anglers dream of meeting such a fish—and then releasing it back to the river to spawn again. This is the steelhead's mystique today. And if eating wild salmon is, paradoxically, good for salmon conservation, then sport fishing for wild steelhead is similarly good for those fish too, because it funnels money from license sales and river-access fees into steelhead conservation. Many anglers won't even eat a hatchery steelhead, preferring instead to release this human-engineered fish back into the river so another angler has a shot at it. I'll eat hatchery steelhead every now and again, but farmed steelhead are strictly off the menu for me. Like farmed salmon, they're a poor substitute for the real thing, and their very presence in the marketplace is bad for the wild fish. Unfortunately, when people see steelhead on the menu, they get confused and assume the fish are doing fine.

Not long ago I had dinner at a respected Seattle restaurant that tried to have it both ways. The nightly special was "ocean trout." I asked the waiter to explain the distinction. He disappeared and the chef came out, admitting they were steelhead—not wild, mind you—and spoke effusively about the wonderful character of these fish. They were farmed steelhead, probably raised in pens in a side channel of the Columbia River—or, worse, in a typically overcrowded land-based Idaho operation. When I pointed out that they had almost certainly never seen the "ocean," as the menu suggested, he walked away. I haven't been back there since.

≡≡≡

BRADLEY DROVE HIS TRUCK down a rough incline and parked beside a primitive launch where the Sweetin River empties into the Kispiox. A small grotto with just a few camping sites amid the alders, the campground was unoccupied, except for a lone tent and a note left behind on a damp picnic table. The Kispiox attracts anglers from all over the world, especially Europeans coming from places where even the most remote river valleys have long since been domesticated. The massed peaks, open spaces, and deep woods of British Columbia call out to a certain type of person who yearns for the dark and unpredictable. The author of the note was a man named Claus, and it was addressed to his friend Hans. Written in blue ink on a page torn from a spiral notebook, the missive had been smartly tucked into a Ziploc bag and weighed down with a smooth, palm-sized stone from the river. Bradley's eyes widened as he read it aloud. " 'We are out looking for the wounded bear. We will meet you here shortly.' " Bradley replaced it carefully under the rock. "Not if that old boar finds Claus first," he said with amusement. There was indeed a wounded grizzly on the prowl. Locals who had seen it described the bear as probably suffering from a calamitous fight or maybe a fall, shuffling along and contorted with what appeared to be a spinal injury, possibly even a broken back. "Not a happy bear," Bradley added. Certainly not the sort of bear you want to surprise in the willow brakes. But we understood the motivation. Opportunities to see large animals in their natural habitat don't come along often for most of us. Just then a flotilla of fishermen drifted by on pontoons. They talked loudly among themselves, as if using their voices as ad hoc bear bells. We decided to drive downstream and put in elsewhere.

At the next boat launch we hauled our pontoons off the truck and dragged them to the riverbank. Morning fog rose off the water in columns. This float would take us downstream through fifteen miles of nearly perfect habitat: braided channels, logjams, pools, riffles, runs, and tailouts. Fifteen miles of eyeballing the banks for the hunched silhouette of a wounded and pissed-off grizzly bear. And by float's end, as would be typical in most any steelhead stream, we got blanked in about 14.9 of those miles. But midway through, in a hundred-yard run with a high bluff on the opposite bank, we felt the charge of adrenaline that keeps anglers like us coming back. I tied on a fly called a Purple Peril; Bradley used a feathery Black and Blue—a time-honored color combination on the Kispiox. On my first cast, nothing. Second cast . . . *whoa*—a grab, no hookup. Third cast, *bang*. The fish exploded out of the water with my fly in the corner of its mouth and went aerial for half a dozen fits of cannonballing and somersaults across the surface. It was a large female. "A hen!" Bradley shouted. In some ways he preferred the hens to the larger males, because of their crazed gymnastics. I could see her pink complexion and watched helplessly as she executed a desperate flip and threw the hook. Game over.

I looked at Bradley, slack-jawed, and he started to laugh. He couldn't help himself. I was neither in the driver's seat nor, it would seem, in possession of a license. There's nothing really to prepare you for that accelerated moment in time when a large steelhead is on the reel—nothing but experience, of which I didn't have enough. "Get your line back out there," he said. When another fish grabbed my fly on the next cast and ran out into the middle of the river before the hook came free, we knew something special was happening. For some unknown reason, one that is unlikely ever to be divined by all the world's fisheries biologists and armchair anglers combined, they were on the bite. Next it was Bradley's turn. He hooked and fought a very large fish, quite possibly his largest fish in a lifetime of steelheading, one he figured went well in excess of twenty pounds, perhaps nearing the mythical thirty-pound mark, before it popped off near the shore. I put my camera away, unused. "Guess it doesn't count, huh?" He took a moment to compose himself. *Breathe in, breathe out.* There was nothing to do but cast again. Then the two of us hooked into fish at the same moment—a double—and fought fifteen-pound bucks side by side into the beach, not a very common occurrence on any steel-head river, anywhere. After forty-five minutes of action, the sun broke through the cloud cover and the river went cold. Forty-five minutes of nirvana. There are steelheaders who would trade in their most prized tackle for such a flurry of action.

WE PULLED INTO CAMP just before dusk. As is my habit, I looked for the pregnant shape of my tent in the meadow as we rounded the cor-ner, satisfied that it had survived another day in bear country. After hanging our waders to dry, we unpacked a celebratory bottle of Jim Beam and started walking up a muddy jeep track to the evening gath-ering. Most of the campers stay in the upper meadow, where their tents and RVs cluster around an open-air shelter. Some of them have been coming here every autumn for more than thirty years. They all know one another and enjoy socializing as much as fishing. They stay for two weeks, three weeks, even six weeks or more during the fall steelhead run, usually arriving in early September. Nonangling spouses have other pursuits during the day, like painting and bird-watching. In the evenings the shelter becomes the social hub. Beginning at around five-thirty, campers start assembling with armloads of wine, beer, crackers, cheese, olives, lox, and other goodies for cocktail hour.

Bradley and I felt good. We were steelhead anglers who had caught fish. The usual suspects sat in camp chairs on the deck. There was Got-tard from Alberta, who hunted mushrooms in the nearby woods, and

Dennis from Montreal with his wife, Diane, the painter, who made ethereal watercolors of fish and fishermen; there was a doctor from California, and some businessmen from Spokane. The Florida crew had not made the trip this year, but there were anglers from Oregon, Montana, Arizona, Texas, and a few Canadian provinces—in all, a few dozen campers, many of them retirees, who enjoyed nothing more than camping for a month along a wild British Columbia river and chasing its most celebrated and elusive denizen.

Such camping is not without its hazards. More than one defender of the wild has noted with mixed feelings that wilderness wouldn't exist without the regular presence of beasts that can eat us for dinner. Every now and again a grizzly wanders through camp, reminding everyone of their relative positions on the food chain. The day before, while we were out fishing, a young black bear visited and popped one of our spare inflatable boats. We found it fifty yards away, upside down and listing. This was not our first inflatable casualty. These boats are toys to the bears, basketballs to be bounced around at will until their clumsy moves put a hole in the thing and end the fun. Imagining such a scene brings a smile to the face, yet it was cold comfort in my dinky pup tent at night.

Our dealings with the bears so far were nothing compared to what Victor had seen today. Victor was a short, jolly-looking guy in his sixties, with apple cheeks and a puckered grin. He put down his chilled beer stein so he could use both hands. "It was at the Kindergarten Hole," he began, waving his arms around.

"That's where they teach the kids to fish!" someone razzed him.

"Yeah, yeah. So I look across the river and here comes a bear. Didn't think too much about it—it's just a bear. All of a sudden there's the damnedest thing you've ever seen in your life. Growling and howling, the water flying twenty feet in the air—and the sounds!" He took a sip of beer and nodded. "It was *two* bears."

"Bear fight!" said Bradley. He'd seen a few. One time on the Rogue he watched a yearling sitting on a ledge above the river, gnawing on a salmon carcass. All of a sudden a large male appeared. It walked out on the ledge, swatted the yearling into the river, and took its prize back into the woods.

A plate of smoked oysters made the rounds. "Well, we watched the grizzly sow and the two cubs last night at Cottonwood," an angler from Washington State said. "They were gettin' their oats." His partner noted that this sort of scene was long gone from virtually every steelhead river of the United States, where grizzlies have been hounded into oblivion. "Big sow," he said.

"She could be homecoming queen if she wants to," Victor agreed.

Bradley told them about our popped pontoon. "It's like a teething ring to bears."

"We had a wolf a couple years ago. I'm fishing and here comes this mangy German shepherd and, holy shit, it's a wolf." The conversation pivoted back, as it always does, to the fishing.

"How'd you do this afternoon?"

"Nothing."

"Nothing? How long you up here for?"

"Six weeks."

"Perfect. The river's gonna go out, you know."

Everyone nodded. It's a fact of steelheading in the upper Skeena watershed that you'll experience at some point what's known as "river out." The headwaters have been heavily logged, and all it takes is one night's rain, especially on the Kispiox, to send a brown wave of sediment and debris hurtling downriver, shutting off the fishery for a day or a week or longer and keeping all the anglers cooped up in camp, reading and playing cribbage, partaking in early cocktail hours.

Just then, Armin appeared. He was a large man, a cinematographer by profession, originally from Switzerland, with broad shoulders and a European disposition. Sometimes he wore a black beret. He walked up the path with his spey rod in one hand and a bottle of red wine in the other. He had his waders and boots on and carried his little bottomless, self-bailing inflatable boat around his waist the way a kid wears an inner tube at the pool. Only a beanie cap with propeller could have improved the look. The crowd on the deck gave him a Bronx cheer.

"Touch anything today?" someone called out as Armin came into earshot.

"Aye. Pretty little hen took me across the river and threw the hook." Armin lowered the boat, a one-man Water Master, stepped out of it, rested his rod against a porch post, and sat himself down in a plastic chair to have a drink. He'd been in camp for nearly a month now. This was his twentieth-odd year on the Kispiox. Every year, just about, there was a bear story. But the reports of rapacious logging and ornery bruins were so common and so expected that they had been reduced to story fodder, the stuff of cocktail hour. The real worry was a proposed liquefied-natural-gas pipeline, to be built right through the heart of the watershed, connecting export terminals on the coast to the fracking industry of the interior. And there was always the more immediate menace of the commercial salmon fishery. Most agreed that the gill nets were the biggest threat to the river's steelhead—at least until the gas pipeline became a reality.

DESPITE ITS WILD AND REMOTE CHARACTER, even the Skeena suffers from the usual problems that afflict salmon rivers throughout the more settled regions of the Pacific Northwest: heavy, often irresponsible timber harvest, mineral extraction, oil and gas drilling, and the ills associated with urban development along its race to the sea. What the Skeena doesn't have to contend with are dams and hatcheries, and for this reason its fish are revered for a wildness unchanged since white settlement. The river is arguably most affected by policy decisions made at Canada's Department of Fisheries and Oceans (DFO) in faraway Ottawa, especially those decisions involving commercial fishing.

Some anglers study the reports issued by DFO like Talmudic scholars analyzing dusty old parchments; they look for clues to unlock the fishing universe's secrets—or, more specifically, to foretell what their chances might be of hooking a goliath that season. The most revealing clue is the summer catch rate of sockeye salmon. Sockeye and steelhead return to the river at roughly the same time. Commercial-fishing boats set their nets in Hecate Strait just outside the Skeena's mouth to intercept the salmon before they enter the river. Large sockeye catches correlate with increased steelhead mortality, *bycatch* being the seemingly innocuous word for nontargeted fish that end up in the nets by accident. The government has concocted all sorts of regulations to limit steelhead bycatch, but the steelhead get caught anyway. Fishing boats are required to have a reviving tank on board to help release them back to the wild. This system is viewed with skepticism by recreational anglers. In a year of poor sockeye returns, the government will shut down the commercial fishery, inadvertently helping steelhead; in a year of good salmon returns, the steelhead are swept up in the nets. A big run of sockeye is now considered a death knell for steelhead.

Prince Rupert is the sort of fishing community that's hard to find these days. As the western terminus of, first, the Grand Trunk Pacific Railway and, later, the Trans-Canada Highway, Prince Rupert has never been exactly on the way to anywhere. Its founder and main booster, Charles Melville Hays, went down with the *Titanic*. Commercial fishing has been its main draw for nearly 150 years. The first cannery opened at the mouth of the Skeena in 1876, and fishing began in earnest the following year. By the turn of the century there were eleven canneries, and as many as fifteen by the peak, between 1913 and 1927. In the early years, the catch of chinook exceeded one hundred thousand fish, with coho in excess of two hundred thousand and sometimes twice that in peak years. In stark contrast to the local tribes, who over millennia had developed fishing rituals and techniques that allowed plenty of salmon to reach their spawning grounds, the white fishermen strung so many nets across the river at all hours of day and night that it's a wonder any fish made it upstream at all. Not surprisingly, the commercial catch for both species started trending down by the 1950s, with crisis levels reached in subsequent decades. By 1985 the chinook catch had fallen to twenty-five thousand, and the decline in coho was even worse, with escapement estimated at 6,333 fish in 1997, the lowest ever documented and a sharp drop from the escapement of one hundred thousand as recently as the 1960s. In 1998, DFO announced that conservation would be the new priority, and though both chinook and coho have bounced back somewhat with stricter regulations, some tributaries have yet to recover. This loss of biodiversity affects the genetic health and productivity of the entire watershed.

One of the wrinkles of salmon biology is that overfishing or otherwise depleting even a small, inconsequential stock (in economic terms) within a river system has negative genetic effects across the entire population. But gill nets, the commercial gear of choice, don't differentiate between stocks, and when one stock is extirpated from a corner of the river, the entire population throughout the system suffers a loss of genetic diversity. As the white gill-net fishery intensified in the first decades of the twentieth century, ignoring even perfunctory regulations to rein it in, one stock of salmon after another crashed. Here was a river that hadn't been subjected to the hydroelectric dams and hatcheries of the Columbia, that hadn't been sacrificed to agriculture like the Sacramento and San Joaquin, that remained relatively intact compared with other large rivers. The Skeena was brought to its knees primarily by overfishing.

The sockeye is currently the most valuable commercial species. Formerly it returned to the Skeena in numbers several million strong. By the 1950s, commercial fishing was exploiting half the sockeye population and as much as 70 percent in subsequent decades. Recent studies have shown that each stock of sockeye is genetically suited to its particular rearing lake, and genetic differences can be seen in populations even a few miles apart. Again, the nets don't distinguish between healthy populations and those on the ropes. This basic problem—that a commercial net fishery based at the river mouth can't be selective enough—is exactly what most infuriates steelhead anglers. They wonder what their beloved Skeena system would look like if this net fishery suddenly vanished. Poof! The idea of a couple hundred thousand or more wild steelhead pushing up the river each summer is the sort of thing that can make a steelheader lose sleep at night. The next question: What if the math penciled out? Is it possible that the economics of recreational fishing could possibly trump commercial fishing? For their part, steelhead anglers point to numbers supplied by DFO itself to suggest that, yes, in terms of overall monetary value from license sales and tourism, the Skeena's sport fishery is worth more than its commercial fishery and, since all steelhead must be released by nontribal anglers, is de facto more sustainable. This does not sit well with the locals in Prince Rupert. The idea of shutting down an entire industry, and a blue-collar one at that, to benefit mostly well-heeled sport fishermen is unacceptable to many.

This unfortunate set of circumstances—pitting one resource (sockeye salmon for food) against another (steelhead for sport)—was shaken up in 2011, when the government, after more than a century, recognized the Lake Babine First Nation's right to catch sockeye on its ancestral fishing grounds in the Babine River, high up in the Skeena system. This fishery, historically estimated at an annual 750,000 fish, had been banned since 1906. At the time it was convenient for the white settlers to accuse the tribes of overfishing in order to remove unwanted competition, but now most people admit that the Babine people were fishing in the most sustainable way possible: targeting one species near a river's headwaters rather than laying indiscriminate nets across a saltwater channel at the mouth. With this decision, recreational anglers hoped that more sockeye would be allowed to pass upriver—and, with them, steelhead. So far that hope has not panned out.

Riley Starks has an answer to the steelhead controversy on the Skeena: Turn the gill-net fishery into a reef-net fishery. Then the steelhead could be released immediately without incident. But that is unlikely to happen, and Bradley has no plans to boycott Canada and spend his golden years at home. When he was a younger man, he and his pals designed T-shirts to commemorate their trips. I remember seeing him outfitted in one, a black shirt with the head of a steelie covering most of the front torso and rising at an angle like a jumbo jet just after takeoff. The object of its attention: a colorful egg-sucking leech near the shirt's shoulder, a fly that's snookered more than its fair share of Kispiox steelhead over the years. These days Bradley and Rocky mostly use dry flies, waking them across the current to entice a big steelhead to strike at the surface, a low-percentage game that hardcore steelheaders consider the pinnacle of the sport.

＝＝＝

ON A GRAY OVERCAST DAY that carried a chill of impending winter, Bradley, Rocky, and I floated our pontoon boats from camp down to the bridge in town, where the Kispiox meets the Skeena. We passed venerated holes without touching a fish: the Bear Hole and the Potato Patch, Date Creek and the Gold Room. By late afternoon, we arrived fishless at the confluence, at the site of a Gitxsan community on the Kispiox Reservation. Like so many modern-day Indian villages across North America, this one was a slapdash collection of prefab houses arranged arbitrarily on a loose grid, with a few totem poles trying to dignify a city park given over to weeds. Two Kispiox men in jeans sat on concrete slabs below the bridge, dragging large treble hooks through a deep seam of the Culvert Run. They were allowed to keep the steelhead they snagged. I thought about a conversation we'd had earlier that week with the owner of a liquor store in Terrace, a man who was not a fan of the fishing regulations. "You've got the beer and the booze," he said to us cheerfully as he packed up our purchases. "Now you just need the steelhead. Make like a Native. Yank that sucker onto the bank and get it into the trunk quick, before anyone sees you. That's a proper B.C. barbecue!"

At the takeout, just a muddy ramp leading into the river, we landed our pontoons and started breaking down the rods. Normally Rocky would have found his little Honda stashed in the woods and made the ride back to camp to pick up the truck and return for the boats, but another angler, with an oversize pickup designed for hauling live-stock, offered to give us a ride. We piled the pontoons and minibike into the bed and jumped in. Driving back through town, we saw the blackened remains of a recent house fire. The driver laughed as we passed by. "Give the Indians free government housing and look what they do. Build a bonfire in the middle of the living room." An uncom-fortable silence engulfed the cab. That's when the first tentative rain-drops landed on the windshield, a fact we all took note of.

AFTER A FULL NIGHT OF RAIN, cocktail hour was commencing early at the campground, with an eye-opener for breakfast. Though the skies had cleared, a thick brown current now sluiced downstream. River out. There was nothing we could do except hope the Kispiox came back into shape in the next twenty-four hours for our final day of fishing. After that: a long drive home that would mark the end of the angling year for Bradley. Me, I had a midwinter dinner date planned for the southern reaches of salmon country, where I would meet up with Rene Henery once again for a wild salmon repast at an unlikely place.

Rocky and some of our other camp mates, clutching their rise-and-shine mugs of coffee and Bailey's, decided to spend the day tying flies. I was reminded of another steelhead campout, a few years earlier, when a bunch of us had gathered for an impromptu fly-tying class led by Harry Lemire while a muddy river surged past our camp. Nearing eighty at the time, Harry was perhaps the final living link to the his-torical origins of steelhead fly-fishing, and everyone knew this might be his last year in camp. The day before, some of his younger friends from the Skagit had helped him wade out into the Skeena's swift cur-rent above the Market Garden Hole, where he put on a clinic, nailing three bright steelhead in a row on flies that would forever be tied to his name. Later, wearing a smart-looking watch cap and bifocals, Harry guided the assembled through each step of tying his Thompson River

Caddis and Grease Liner fly patterns. When Harry generously handed me his demonstration flies at the end, Bradley whispered in my ear, "You best seal those in an airtight box and put them away in your bank vault."

With river out, Bradley and I decided to forgo a noon drink with the other campers and instead drove upriver, seeking the headwaters of the Skeena. The Babine, the largest of the upstream tributaries, is renowned as a wilderness fishery and is accessible mostly to affluent anglers who reserve spots months, sometimes years, in advance at one of a handful of lodges that operate deep within the bush. Our plan was to simply see with our own eyes where this fabled river empties into the Skeena. A logging road would get us that far.

We passed mile after mile of cutover forest. Even here, among the most celebrated wilderness fishing grounds on the continent, the lumbermen had plundered the land. On a rise, we pulled over and surveyed the country. Clear-cuts receded in all directions, many of them filled in with the regrowth of hardwoods, which blazed angry yellows and oranges in the cool autumn glare. But beyond the trimmed lines of managed, even-aged timberlands, we could see the ragged silhouette of primeval forest in the distance. Unlikely though it was, I tried to imagine that I was looking at the beginning of a swath of wilderness stretching clear up to the Arctic Circle, a place where steelhead and bears and wolves could exist beyond the greedy, fearful gaze of civilization.

In the half-light of afternoon, we arrived at a narrow bridge that spanned the Babine high above its flow. Bradley pulled over. Our map didn't show any such crossing. This was something of a disappointment. Yet another bridge, another road. I hadn't expected to traverse the Babine so easily, much less advance deeper into its watershed. We got out and walked the span to its midway point. The river moved fast and dark below, its depths impenetrable even with the aid of polarized glasses. Leaning over the railing, we studied its shifting patterns. White riffles played tricks on the eyes. The supple forms of steelhead moved steadily upriver in our imaginations. "Look at that seam,"

Bradley said. "A steelhead could be laying up behind any one of those big boulders down there." It was true. Wherever I looked, I saw the possibility of fish in the river.

After watching the shape-shifting current for a while, we back-tracked and found a spur that looked as though it might take us farther upstream. The river's pull was strong. We drove over a knoll, through an unlocked gate, and into heavy forest. The low October sun dropped behind a veil of evergreen, and cold shade enveloped the road as if we had entered a tunnel. Driving slowly with the windows down, we could smell the clean, tangy scent of conifer forest. The road angled right, and we caught a few glimpses through the trees of what looked like a gray river to our left. That's when we also saw ribbons of smoke up ahead weaving a blue haze from a dozen or more chimneys. We had arrived at a little hamlet in the woods. Small cedar-shake cabins slouched in the mud, their moss-covered roofs sagging nearly to the ground. The community looked very old, as if it had sprung from the ground itself. Maybe these were some of the people who fished for the Babine sockeye.

Bradley slowed his truck to a crawl. We didn't see a soul. It was hard to tell whether the road continued through the village or dead-ended just ahead. It didn't matter. Without a word between us, we decided to turn around. Even though there wasn't a NO TRESPASSING sign in sight, we both felt we had arrived somewhere out of bounds. As Bradley made a U-turn, an old Ford pickup truck appeared along-side us coming from the other direction and stopped. It was full of people, all men, some young and others quite elderly: four wedged into the cab and several more in back, hanging on wooden slats. The driver leaned his head out the open window, his arm casually dangling over the side, his other hand on the wheel. He was ancient, his face so wizened I could barely make out his features, and yet his calm de-meanor suggested he had all the time in the world. He took measure of us through two wrinkled slits for eyes.

"Afternoon!" said Bradley in his usual way. The driver didn't flinch, didn't move at all. His passengers remained stone-faced. Bradley glanced at me—as if to say, "What now?"—then turned back to the driver. A long beat. He started to fumble for words that wouldn't come, and the other driver lifted his chin. The man's gaze shifted from the front of Bradley's new truck to the back and then seemed to settle on a corner of the rear bumper—or perhaps on some point of interest in the background; it was hard to tell. He might have been looking at the forest beyond us or even past the forest to the tiny specks of silver that represented infinitesimal views of the river through the trees. Or past the river to sights unknown. The afternoon sighed, and then the old man did something unexpected. He whistled quietly, deliberately, through his teeth. There was another pause. I suppose everyone was pondering that whistle. Was it admiration for our truck? Recognition of the miracle of life? Or nothing at all, just a way to acknowledge our existence? The sound, barely audible yet distinct, sliced through the delicate fabric of the day. I had no idea what it meant.

"Well, have a good one," Bradley said finally. "We're on our way." He eased his foot on the gas and pulled out ever so slowly, careful not to spit a single bit of gravel. They watched us go. A hundred yards down the road and the pickup still hadn't moved an inch. We drove until it disappeared from our rearview mirror. Bradley shook his head. Meetings like this with Indians were fraught. The white man had taken most of their land and tried, nearly successfully, to eradicate them from the face of the earth. Everything else stemmed from these inescapable facts.

"That was weird," said Bradley finally.

It *was* weird. It was disconcerting and dreamlike. I could tell that Bradley was feeling the same thing I was: a sense of being unmoored from reality. I'd never had an experience with another human being quite like it. And what about that whistle? "It was like we didn't even speak the same body language." Why wouldn't they communicate? Or was it communication that we just couldn't understand? The mistakes of my ancestors, it seemed, had determined the rules of engagement generations later.

As we drove back down the road through the clear-cut forest, I thought about it some more. Perhaps the worst atrocities were a thing of the past, but less obvious threats persisted every day. Many of the tribes living along the Skeena and its tributaries had become vocal opponents of the gas pipeline, which would be buried under their ancestral lands and would terminate at a complex on the coast adjacent to one of the most critical eelgrass beds for juvenile fish as they transitioned to a life at sea. Many scientists concurred that if built, the pipeline would be a disaster for the river's salmon and steelhead. Wherever you went in the Skeena watershed, signs with a red slash through the letters LNG—liquefied natural gas—dotted the landscape. All across Indian country, indigenous peoples were rallying to put a stop to the resource plunder that had been going on for centuries as a matter of course. They were using their newly discovered power in the legal system to, as Riley Starks put it, throw themselves in front of the tanks.

We drove back to camp and the whistle stayed with me, an uncomfortable and mysterious sound in my head. Even if I couldn't understand them, I knew that I wanted those people to continue on at the mouth of the Babine. Wilderness depends on a few hardy souls living on the edge of it. That village wasn't a seasonal vacation bivouac with a daily cocktail hour. The people dwelling in those rude cabins lived among the bears and the wildcats. They were the gatekeepers. Without them, the fish of the river, including the great migratory steelhead, would one day be gone.

CHAPTER 12

MAKE WAY FOR THE
FLOODPLAIN FATTIES

RETURNING TO THE CITY AFTER A WEEK OR TWO OF CAMPING in the bush is neither depressing nor culture shock for me. I like the city. I like the same things about the city that everyone else does: the hurly-burly, the electric current in the air that suggests something big is about to happen, a feeling that can only happen in the presence of many, many human beings of all kinds brought together in a geographically limited space. Even on a Monday night.

You wouldn't know it was Monday at Casson Trenor's newest venture, Tataki Canyon, a sushi restaurant in San Francisco. Five of us squeezed into a table meant for four, as jangly music heightened the din and a clientele of mostly young professionals practiced their chopsticks skills. The waitstaff threaded their way through a tight labyrinth of unadorned wooden tables—all occupied—hurrying out platters of fish while dodging the misplaced elbow or knee-high motorcycle boot. This, the third of Trenor's sushi restaurants, is located not far from Glen Canyon Park, in a neighborhood that's changing rapidly as the country's locus of high tech continues to expand its reach beyond Silicon Valley. Whether they knew it or not, everyone in Tataki Canyon was experiencing an uncommon form of one of the fastest-growing cuisines around the developed world—sustainable sushi.

The very term strikes many as an oxymoron. It's a well-known fact that the world's seas are being strip-mined of their aquatic life, with an ever-bigger portion going to the proliferation of sushi joints. One dire prediction says the oceans will be depleted beyond repair by the middle of this century. A cynic might easily look at a sushi restaurant and see a trough for mindless consumers stuffing their faces with endangered species while congratulating themselves on their good taste. Trenor isn't a cynic. He understands the appeal of sushi, has spent time in Japan, respects the cuisine. Tall, thin, and dressed in a black chef's apron (the apron is more for show, since Trenor leaves the actual preparing of food to his knowledgeable staff), he sat down with us for a moment and then jumped back up to talk with his chef.

We'd met several times in the past and I had already tried Trenor's first sushi bar, the original Tataki, in Pacific Heights. Tonight he seemed a bit on edge, with the pent-up restlessness of someone struggling to balance work and pleasure. His friend Rolf was waiting at our table when we arrived. With round glasses and short hair parted on the side, Rolf could have been an insurance adjuster or a shoe salesman. He unbuttoned his white Oxford shirt to cool down, thought better of it, and took it off altogether, revealing a Sasquatch in midstride on his T-shirt underneath, the words NORTHERN CALIFORNIA framing the image, a battle cry for some who still believed in the Arcadian possibilities. Trenor reappeared and glanced approvingly at his friend's T-shirt. "Rolf is Greenpeace's forest-action lead," he explained. The title wasn't lost on any of us. Rolf's mild-mannered appearance was more than just politic—it was a safety issue. Better to look like an accountant than a manufacturer of pipe bombs, especially if you plan to be arrested. The last time I had encountered people like him was at an illegal encampment in the Siskiyou Mountains of southwestern Oregon, where protesters had shut down old-growth logging by literally taking to the trees. Rolf remembered that tree-sit. Greenpeace successfully scuttled the plans of the Bureau of Land Management to clear-cut a grove of cathedral firs, some of them several hundred years old, under the lame pretext of "forest thinning." "But you're more likely to find him in the jungles of Indonesia," Trenor added, "facing down guys with Kalashnikovs." That was where the real action was these days on the deforestation front. Rolf smiled thinly at this, like a character out of a Graham Greene novel.

Rene Henery, never one to shy away from dinner-table politics, raised an eyebrow at me. He ran into operators like Rolf all the time. In another life he might have been Rolf, especially if his skin had been lighter. Across from Rene was a colleague of his, Jacob Katz, who worked for California Trout. He too was used to the fray, and on that count tonight was looking up. Katz raised a miniature glass of sake to new friends, and we all drank down our rice wine.

Already the day had been a winner for Rene and Katz. They had just finished convening a small group of mostly young, like-minded advocates from multiple agencies and organizations across the salmon-restoration universe, and the buzz of an exciting new venture animated their expressions. Calling their loose affiliation the "Fish Tank," the participants were hoping to find ways to join forces to make a splash larger than the sum of their individual parts. The two had talked excitedly about the possibilities the whole drive over from Oakland, as Rene dodged and maneuvered his little car down side streets and over San Francisco's hills. After a while, as we passed one SOLD sign after another, the conversation changed from their work to the Bay Area's red-hot real estate market, a point of contention for many in the region. Rene and his wife lived in a nice little rental on the Oakland–Berkeley border, but they hoped to own a home someday. Likely it would be somewhere far away. "A boarded-up crack house just sold for over a million," he said with a fatalistic laugh. For his part, Katz was sure he had made a wise move to locate his family well beyond normal commuter range, deep in a rural part of Sonoma County, but this meant nights away from home periodically, like tonight. As Rene turned up Dolores Street in the Mission, we all looked at the cityscape. Rumor had it that the founder and CEO of Facebook was buying an entire block for himself on this palm-lined boulevard. "There goes the neighborhood," Rene said, stepping on the gas. By the time we arrived at the restaurant, Katz had to extract his lanky frame from the backseat as if crawling from a wreck, and he walked around the block a few times to shake off a sudden bout of nausea. Driving with Rene could do that to you.

The sushi dinner was my idea. Rene and Katz relied on making connections—real, in-person human connections—to allow the sometimes lonely work of science to resonate with a broader public. Casson Trenor seemed to me like a natural ally. For one thing, he wasn't just a purveyor of raw fish. Like Rolf, he worked for Greenpeace—or, at least, he *had* worked for Greenpeace until a few days ago. The previous Friday, we learned now, had been his last day with the organization's sustainable-fisheries team. He allowed this piece of information to drop like a lead fishing weight soon after we sat down. Just the week before, when he and I had spoken on the phone, Trenor had hinted that he was scrambling at work. "My latest project is in the weeds," he had said cryptically. "I've gotten into a tight spot and I'm disappointed in myself." I didn't ask for particulars. The last project he had told me about involved a blimp he and his colleagues launched over Chicken of the Sea's San Diego headquarters, with strong words painted on the side calling out the company for bad practices—a stunt that was soon grounded because it ran afoul of regulations at the municipal gliderport used as the launching pad. Risk was part of his job description, just as it was for Rolf. Tonight, the blimp sailed again as Trenor shared with us the story of its brief flight.

"A zeppelin!" chimed in Rene Henery. An apt metaphor for Trenor's final days at Greenpeace, everyone agreed.

A platter of wild king salmon sashimi came out. Plenty of people who came to a sushi restaurant that billed itself as sustainable expected to eat a farmed salmon, assuming it was more green than a wild fish, but Trenor wasn't having any. He's a Washington State native with a lifelong dedication to the region's totem fish. His restaurants use wild salmon. Now in his mid-thirties, Trenor was able to see the decline of wild salmon even within the relatively brief context of his youth in Puget Sound. This also happened to be the era of farmed salmon's ascendancy in the marketplace, with one trend masking the other. One of Tataki's first and most defining rallying cries was against industrial salmon farming. Unlike livestock, which eat grass, salmon are carnivores. To produce a pound of farmed salmon requires a minimum—even at the most efficient farms—of a pound and a half of fish down the food chain, fish that otherwise might be eaten by humans or other predators in the wild. Of course, those are smaller, less desirable fish, the sort of fish that might be on the dinner menu in third-world countries. In simple terms, you're taking a potential food source away from poorer people to produce a luxury food item, or, as Trenor put it, "You're robbing Pedro to feed Paul."

Farming is a tough issue for groups like Greenpeace, and fish farming is tough for the same reasons. There is this notion of the noble landed farmer, even though most of the work in the United States is done by a revolving immigrant workforce overseen by a corporate board. Big Ag likes to suggest that the only thing that stands between a rising population on Planet Earth and massive worldwide starvation is unfettered agriculture. Salmon farmers similarly like to say they're feeding the world. Rene wasn't buying it. "We don't have a food crisis," he said now, "we have a productivity crisis. We're so far under the productive capacity of the planet, we can barely wrap our heads around it. We say we're optimizing agriculture to feed people. That's bullshit. We're optimizing agriculture for profit. We don't have a clue what the productive capacity of the earth is. We have to totally rejigger this thing. It's like saying, 'I've got the pedal to the metal and I'm in second gear. Am I going to run out of gas before I get to the gas station?' Yes. Is that the fault of my car being fuel-inefficient? No, it's because I'm driving like a moron."

"We have an inequality crisis," Rolf shot back. Deforestation around the world, he pointed out, is due mostly to farming rather than timber harvest: slash-and-burn agriculture to grow beef; palm-oil plantations that replace native rainforest; soy production for live-stock feed. Forests, especially diverse tropical forests that yield innumerable foods as part of their natural life cycle, are being reduced to ashes in order to produce high-value meat for wealthier nations. Salmon farming is no different. I mentioned an oft-repeated mantra of doomsday adherents: seven billion humans on the planet. That number is rising, with recent estimates of eleven billion by the end of the century. Rene knew the score. At Trout Unlimited they heard such facts and figures all the time. Big Ag loves trotting out the numbers. Eleven billion. On the one hand it's a figure that we can't even conceptualize. Try to imagine eleven billion jelly beans in the cosmic jar. On the other hand, whether or not we can imagine so many digits is beside the point; it's still a number that scares people.

Trenor brought his open palm down upon the table, startling us all and rattling the sake cups. "We're living in a world that operates under a fear-based paradigm." People are afraid, he said. They're afraid of all sorts of things, especially nature. "You need to start with *this* fundamental premise: Nature is perfect." He was right. If there's a single example of perfection in the universe, it's nature. The biosphere is a marvel to begin with, and it's always recalibrating to regulate itself. Human efforts to boost productivity are localized illusions—and they come with a cost on the back end. "Just look at the massive dead zone in the Gulf of Mexico," Rene jumped in. It's caused mostly by Midwestern farms; their fertilizers are carried downstream by the Mississippi, turning seven thousand square miles of the gulf into a hypoxic graveyard. Trenor shuddered at the thought and quickly slid out of his seat to grab a platter from the counter. He brought back a hefty roll of maki cut into a dozen pieces and garnished with swirls of red sauce. He called it a ratatouille roll. It was vegetarian and a hint of things to come. Trenor was about to open his fourth sushi restaurant, one that would be entirely vegan. Vegan sushi. It sounded like the punch line to a late-night-TV joke circa 2010. Maybe change was really happening.

Speaking in almost a stream of consciousness, Trenor continued his thought as if he hadn't just left the table for a moment. Harmful fish farming comes in a variety of forms, he said. "What does it mean that we've created what is arguably the largest aquaculture facility in the world off the coast of Maine in what we call the lobster industry? Because it's basically a farm. We've killed all the cod and turned it into a farm. There's nothing else that lives there. It's a farm the size of three New England states. We've knocked off the apex predators and created all these weird animals."

With that he disappeared again, to a back room out of sight, and returned a few minutes later bearing another platter, this one with a half dozen pieces of nigiri. The slices of fish had a bluish hue that stood out against the pillows of white rice, each one topped with a little green square of seaweed. "This is my favorite dish that we serve. Saba is one of the most maligned, poorly done, absolutely dishonored fish in the fishing industry." He was talking about what the English-speaking world calls mackerel, a fish perceived by many as too oily, too fishy. "People treat it badly. If you treat it right, it's beautiful. We give it a light pickling, just a dash of rice vinegar and some other things, and add a piece of kelp candy on top, so you've got the sugar and umami of the kelp to balance the vinegar and fat of the saba. Don't use a lot of soy sauce. Take it and eat it like this, upside down." He plucked a piece from the platter with his fingers, inverted it, and dabbed a corner of the fish in a little dish of soy sauce. The rest of us followed suit. The combination of just a small sliver of pickled fish along with candied seaweed was deeply satisfying. Mackerel, he said, was a fish in good supply that people didn't want to eat, usually for the wrong reasons.

After another bite of saba, I looked around. Everyone was having a good time. Diners laughed and told stories at their crowded tables. They gestured with their hands and made eye contact and twisted their faces into complicated expressions that were at once recognizable. Some were couples, maybe on a first date. Others were groups of friends or colleagues meeting after work. Beer bottles sweated on the tables; the music blared. All these people! All of them enjoying the food and company and vitality that a night on the town could provide. It was contagious. "Anyway, we get the planet we deserve," Trenor went on—and then he too glanced around his restaurant, this meeting-and-eating spot he had dreamed up, and he must have had the same sense of sudden wonderment as me, because he laughed out loud and threw his hands in the air. "Aren't we at the heart of it?" he shouted. "If we continue to focus on saving this or protecting that, we're missing the point. It's not about protecting the oceans—it's about living in a way that promotes a healthy ocean. We can only do it as individuals. We can't do it for anyone else. And this is one of the reasons I was getting burned out at Greenpeace."

I could see Jacob Katz getting increasingly agitated. He had energy that needed an outlet. He fidgeted with his chopsticks, shifted back and forth in his seat as if he might just lift off at any moment. "I have three kids," he said finally, the pragmatist. "We're not here just for ourselves."

"All I have control over is what I put into this world, how I behave," Trenor countered. He waved his open palm, gesturing toward the four corners of his tightly packed restaurant like a magician. Not all of his customers saw any virtue in their decision to patronize Tataki. Maybe it was a neighborhood place for some; maybe they didn't even know about the restaurant's commitment to sustainability. "Or maybe they don't give a damn. It doesn't matter. I'm not focused on the problem. I'm focused on creating a solution. Regardless of the perspectives or backgrounds of the people who come into this restaurant, they are confronted with only one path forward. We control the playing field in here. I don't care why you want unagi"—he was talking about the barbecued eel that has captured the hearts of sushi lovers everywhere, the unagi that is now severely threatened throughout its range, largely because of the sushi trade—"if you order it in this restaurant, you're going to receive something we can stand by." As if to underscore his point, at that moment a server appeared with a platter of what looked like unagi, or "fauxnagi," as some call it. Instead of serving eel, Tataki substitutes a fish with a similar taste and velvety feel to it, dressed with the standard barbecue sauce that people have come to expect. The fish was black cod, also known as sablefish. It's a species with a stable population at the moment, though one increasingly in demand in Asia, causing its price to rise steadily in recent years. "You come in with your unagi issues," Trenor said. "I don't really care why. In my world, when people want that sweet, dark, sultry experience they get from unagi, this is what they're getting. In my restaurant, goddammit, that's what they're going to have." He pounded his fist on the table theatrically, the environmental impresario as mock hero.

Trenor was so sure of himself. But I found his candor bracing. Most of us suffer a form of paralysis, unsure of how anything we do can possibly make a difference. The very infrastructure of our lives hardly allows it. Every day I drive my kids somewhere: to school or soccer practice or music lessons. Our family lives in a house twice the size of what was considered normal a century ago (our hundred-year-old Craftsman having been torn down to the studs and replaced two decades ago, like so many others in Seattle). Martha and I worry about our kids' 529 college accounts and our own retirement. And yet our lives are peppered with small gestures: the weekly recycling and composting, reusing plastic bags, doing the laundry with eco-approved soap, the occasional volunteer work. Such small gestures. Trenor, on the other hand, had completely tailored his life to fit his beliefs. It was both inspiring and intimidating.

Katz couldn't contain his curiosity any longer. "Why did you work for Greenpeace anyway?"

"The better question is, why am I not anymore? The fundamental flaw with Greenpeace and many organizations like it is that at the end of the day the metric for success is the behavior of other people. I don't believe we can control or affect other people. I think the real work we have to do isn't about that. The metrics that we should use for success are about how we change *ourselves,* how we live, what we create—not by telling other people what to do."

"But what about education?" I asked him. Most American consumers probably didn't know the difference between a farmed salmon and a wild salmon, much less a hatchery salmon. How could you possibly make an informed decision if you didn't even realize there was a decision to make? Groups like Greenpeace, it seemed to me, were trying to educate the public, sometimes in provocative ways.

"Education only makes sense for people who already share the same values," Trenor replied. "When Tataki opened, we were the first sustainable sushi restaurant in the world. Now there are about twenty. Most of them came to us and asked how to do it. When I'm on my deathbed and looking back on my life, I want to know that I was on *this* side, that I did everything I could to do this the right way. I can't change other people and I can't change this industry. I don't want to define my life by what other people do. I want to define it by what I did. Maybe Tataki makes no difference, but screw it. I gave something to the world that was an example of a different way to use this cuisine that we can stand by."

Before we left, fisheries biologist Jacob Katz handed sustainable-sushi entrepreneur Casson Trenor a parting gift: a two-kilogram bag of semi-brown short-grained rice. Sushi rice. A little design of a California license plate decorated the bottom of the package: Ca Grown. The upper-right corner of the package was covered by a triangular sticker with the image of a baby salmon on it: the Nigiri Project. This was Katz's brainchild. "The world's first salmon-friendly rice," it said. Trenor, in his double-buttoned black smock, took the gift and made a slight bow in the Japanese style.

THE CONTROL TOWER WAVERED slightly in the distance, an optical illusion created by a low-lying fog, as the intense California sun evaporated what little moisture remained from the previous day's brief spate. Too little rain, too late. Despite fall weather patterns that teased drought relief, winter had not been kind to the state. We were driving across the Sacramento Valley on I-5 toward the agricultural community of Woodland, about twenty miles northwest of the state capital. After a record January that didn't see a single drop of rain, a storm had finally come in off the Pacific and dumped a couple of inches. That was all it took for the Sacramento River to turn dark and indignant. "During a typical storm, that airport over there would be under about twenty-six feet of water," Jacob Katz said. But an extensive system of levees now keeps the river mostly contained within the main channel, preventing flooding of the city and many other nearby towns. This is not what nature had in mind.

Floodplains are dynamic places, with fluctuations of dry and wet that promote a diversity of plant and animal species adapted to conditions that can change as quickly as a politician looking for votes. Modern cities, on the other hand, don't much care for the wet part. We've solved the problem by walling off our cities in flood-prone areas with levees. New Orleans, much of it below sea level and sinking, is famous for its network of levees (and its failed levees), without which it would cease to exist. Though less extreme an example, Sacramento owes its prosperity to levees too. Three major rivers converge near the city: the namesake Sacramento, the American, and the Feather. These and many others running off the Sierra Nevada and coastal mountains contributed the alluvial sediments that make the Central Valley such a rich place to farm. Fifteen miles west of Sacramento is Davis, home of UC Davis, one of the nation's top agricultural universities, where both Rene Henery and Jacob Katz got their doctoral degrees. It is farm country, no doubt about it, and it's the place where Katz was raised. His parents were part of the back-to-the-land movement in the sixties.

"My dad came here bearded, straight off the kibbutz in Israel." It was the beginning of organic farming in California. Katz remembers the many guests his parents entertained when he was a kid, the musicians and intellectuals and counterculture heroes. The Berkeley "food conspiracies"—collectives that enabled people to buy directly from farmers—gave a generation raised on TV dinners an inkling of the power of real food. In 1976, Governor Jerry Brown made Katz's father the president of the State Reclamation Board (later renamed the Central Valley Flood Protection Board), overseeing water management for the state—an inconceivable appointment a generation earlier, when conservationists were looked at like communists.

We drove past another levee, its grassy slope towering over our car like a cresting wave, and Katz explained that we were now officially within the drainage of the Yolo Bypass. "The bypass is a simple idea. The Sacramento Valley gets way too much water to just wall it in. Three storms came in a row—1903, 1907, 1911—and each one put the entire valley underwater. It became very clear that high water had to be rerouted—bypassed around cities and ag." Yolo Bypass, the lowest point in the valley, became the designated route for flooding. When it rains, the river rises up over its levee and spills into the bypass. We followed a rutted track up onto the bypass levee itself, a mound of dirt and gravel wide enough to allow for an access road, which ran in a straight line into the distance. This was the highest ground for miles around, and I suppose I expected to find a wasteland fanning out below, a place repeatedly bullied by the Sacramento River's overflow, just a lifeless gully. But it was quite the opposite. The bypass was brimming with woods and brush and grasses that made a stark contrast with the monotony of straight-edged agricultural land on the other side of the levee, where a farmer had planted a new orchard in neat rows, a water-sucking pistachio crop with an expected life span of about thirty years. Though the bypass lacked large expanses of tule—a type of giant sedge that characterized the wetlands of pre-agricultural California—a ragged collection of old walnut orchards, cottonwoods, and sycamores invited a surprising abundance of bird-life, which was now darting among the trees: bluebirds, kestrels, a pair of acorn woodpeckers in a stand of oaks. All of this land had just been wallowing in a couple of inches of floodwater a few days ago. Because of such floods, most farming in the bypass occurs in dry summer months; the rest of the year it's a de facto wildlife preserve, and come winter it becomes a pressure release valve, as Katz put it, with the ability to carry four times more water than the main-stem Sacramento. This water, like water everywhere around the globe, is a key ingredient in biodiversity, not to mention a draw for both adult and juvenile salmon, which find its current irresistible at flood stage. Attraction pulse, the biologists call it—just the sort of rushing current a salmon wants to nose into on its upstream spawning mission.

Katz has a knack for explaining complicated systems in simple terms. "It comes down to solar energy being the source of all life. Fish have to eat. Levees starve river systems by keeping them swift, deep, and with very little surface area. When you allow the river to spread out, it's a big solar cell." He was talking about a process we all learn about in school but rarely think about: photosynthesis. Plants use the sun's energy to make carbohydrates, creating the base of the food chain and at the same time releasing oxygen as a byproduct. Life on earth depends on this process. In the case of floodplains, the algae turn the sunlight into sugars that nourish zooplankton, which in turn feed salmon fry—and so on, up the food chain, which of course includes human beings too. "Almost all of our large civilizations developed along large river systems," Katz added. But rivers are messy and always changing. Every once in a while, he said, a nice warm Pineapple Express—a moisture-laden winter storm from the South Pacific— settles over California's mountain snowpack, and so much water gets liberated both from the rain and the melted snow that there's no way to keep it all within the banks of the Sacramento. "So we have this bypass system." The river pours over its banks into the bypass, and this human-engineered process was proving, counterintuitively, to be a useful conservation tool. "If you give the river a little room," Katz explained, "you allow the natural processes that are the engines of productivity to work. We can integrate that back into an intensely managed system, one that's not going to be restored—you're not going to have wall-to-wall tules—but we can have places where we have real productivity."

Neither Rene nor Katz likes the word *restoration*. They prefer *reconciliation,* with its subtext of resolving long-simmering feuds. "The idea of restoration for most people is to put something back the way it was," Rene said. "There's a growing consensus that the land will never be as it was. We live in a dynamic space; things are always changing. The future is unknown. It's not a fixed point." In other words, the landscape isn't a rusted '65 Mustang waiting under a tarp for a new owner with deep pockets. The best we can do to heal old wounds is to reconcile the land with new uses that help to bring it into some sort of balance. The Yolo Bypass, for instance. The irony is that it might prove to be better habitat than the channelized and reengineered river itself, if we let it.

"This is a process," Rene stressed. "We need to educate people to think of land as having inherent habitat value. Once we do that within the existing economic structure, hopefully my kids will just tear down the whole system and build a new one."

We parked on the levee and got out. Meadowlarks threw back their heads and sang of coming spring from perches below us in the scrub that stretched for a mile or more across the bypass. After a short hike, we stood on the concrete berm of Fremont Weir, where a small gap had been knocked out of the wall. Beyond the gap, a ditch ran a hundred yards to the Sacramento River. Katz called the gap a grudging acknowledgment by the powers that be that fish use the bypass during high flows. Right now, barring a few puddles left over from the last flood, the bypass was dry. But the next time a few inches of rain fell, the river would top its levee and spill across Fremont Weir like a waterfall. The water would inundate all sixty thousand acres of Yolo Bypass and flow down into the Sacramento–San Joaquin Delta near Rio Vista, some forty miles to the south. Meanwhile, salmon migrating up the river to spawn, including a nearly extinct winter run of chinook, take their cues from the current. Ignoring the wishes of certain bureaucrats, they enter the bypass and follow a grid of interconnected canals until, if they're lucky, they reach this small gap in the Fremont Weir. With high water, a few tail shakes is all it takes to squirm through the gap and back into the Sacramento. Once the floodwaters recede, however, the fish find just a concrete wall to bang their heads against instead. As water levels drop, the bypass remains inundated, continuing to attract salmon, steelhead, sturgeon, and other native fish, despite lacking any connection back to the river upstream.

In December 2013, a storm flooded the bypass, per design, except this time the water cleared quickly and revealed what was feared yet seldom seen: hundreds, possibly thousands, of stranded chinook salmon wallowing about in the receding water, exhausted and confused by the barriers that kept them from reaching their spawning grounds, including six hundred of the winter runs, an estimated 10 percent of the total. "For years we'd been saying there were a lot of fish up here. Now we could actually see them, and we saw that the coded wire tags in their noses showed they were endangered winter runs." Katz and others made rescue attempts, and though they managed to capture and relocate three hundred adults, it was doubtful any of them lived to spawn.

The good news, Katz said, is the state is looking into a permanent fix that will improve the small gap in the weir and give the salmon a chance to continue upstream. The bad news? The cost will be something like a billion dollars when the many ancillary line items are totaled up, an amount that seems all out of proportion to the hacked partial fix that someone had already done for next to nothing with a backhoe. Rene was hardly surprised by such numbers. "For every person who's involved, you just add the amount of money to the process that it takes to make them feel included and properly compensated. When I worked on a project in Guatemala, they complained about corruption. In the United States we've enshrined our corruption in a thing called bureaucracy and the legal system—and the price tag is a lot higher."

For a far smaller price—about $50 million—Katz was doing experiments that might in the future transform the Yolo Bypass from fish killer to fish nurturer, with consequences for a good chunk of the Sacramento floodplains. With the same sort of audacious thinking that transformed the world during the Industrial Revolution, people like Katz and Rene were dreaming up schemes to walk civilization back from the brink. "You have to get close enough to the precipice to make it real," Katz said with a chuckle. Rene agreed. Even so, there was no going back to Eden, that much was clear. As Rene put it, this new thinking was a form of survival that would impact human beings as much as salmon in the future. "Usually there are people who, when they see the cliff, they get really resourceful really quickly, and those are the early adopters," he said. "They're open to change. When you get to the precipice, the minority that are open to change become the leaders who keep their friends from going off the edge."

Salmon populations in California are certainly leaning over that precipice, but so are people in many ways. Innumerable studies appear year after year linking human health to the environment. Bird diversity, for instance, can be correlated to the health of a community. City planners across the country are busying themselves boosting tree canopy and safeguarding green spaces. This isn't wacky New Age stuff. Whether they know it or not, people need a semblance of nature around them. To this end, simple, even graceful solutions can be found—for instance, letting the Yolo Bypass provide the functionality that was lost a century ago with the diking and channelizing of the Sacramento River. Back then, when the levees were built, no one understood the biological importance of floodplains. They were something to be controlled. Now we know that such messy and inconvenient places provide ideal habitat for many species, especially baby salmon, which historically used the floodplains as nurseries where they could grow quickly and strengthen before making the dangerous trip into a hungry ocean.

As we drove south along the bypass to our next stop, Knaggs Ranch, Katz pointed out a series of rectangular fields submerged in water—the paddies responsible for a good portion of the nation's rice harvest. Such a crop requires flooding, and the lower Sacramento is ideal for this sort of farming. Traditionally, California rice farmers irrigated their fields in late winter, during the rainy season, and then drained them post harvest in the spring. Other agricultural fields in the bypass then got cultivated in the summer with warm-weather crops such as tomatoes. The Nigiri Project's idea is to hold shallow water for months at a time. After being farmed in the summer dry season, the bypass will be flooded for ducks and geese in fall, followed by a midwinter drawdown to create mudflats for migratory shore-birds; by late winter the shallow water will provide ideal habitat for young salmon and rice growers. "Then you drain the water out," Katz said, and the fish go too. In order to do this properly, some of the le-vees would need to be breached, with gates installed to control water flow in and out. The word *breach*—whether you're talking about Sac-ramento levees or Snake River dams—is not a word Big Ag likes to hear.

Knaggs Ranch, where the Nigiri Project pilot test was up and run-ning, had an experimental plot of nine rice paddies in a row. Each one was surrounded by a berm of plowed soil the width of a city sidewalk that acted as a dike, keeping water contained within the paddy. A canal ran the length of the plot. In many ways this setup was analo-gous to the relationship between the Sacramento River and the Yolo Bypass, just on a smaller scale. The canal—straight, narrow, and deep—was like the river. We parked in a muddy lot beside a utility shed and followed Katz over to the canal, where he took an aquarium net and dipped it into the murky water. The net came up empty. Next we walked over to one of the rice paddies adjacent to the canal—the Yolo Bypass in miniature, at flood stage. Again Katz dredged his aquarium net through the water. This time he came up with what looked like a thick sludge of green algae. I took a closer look. The green stuff was writhing in the fine mesh, alive with hundreds of microscopic organ-isms collectively known as zooplankton. Shallower, warmer, and spread across a much larger area, here the water combined with Katz's "solar cell" had done its work. "Fish filet mignon," Katz said, with a knowing laugh that suggested he might have tasted this smorgasbord himself out of deep scientific curiosity.

I pulled on some hip boots and waded out into the middle of one of the rice paddies, trying to keep my footing on a soft, squishy bottom. Katz unraveled what looked like a miniature beach seine, six feet long with a floating cork line on top and a lead line that dragged along the bottom. Holding either end with a wooden stake, we dragged it across ten yards of bottom to the shore. Brief flickers of lightning leaped from the net—young chinook salmon, each just a few inches in length. Judging from their ample bellies, they were well fed.

"Floodplain fatties!" cried Katz as he gathered up the fish.

Rene held a fingerling in the palm of his hand. It might as well have been a filigreed shard of porcelain from a Chinese tomb. Faint parr marks engraved its silvery flanks. A bejeweled eye rotated in its socket. The fish coiled and flopped in Rene's hand as he lowered it into the pond and let the water rise like a flood tide. The young salmon righted itself and swam back into the murk. For Rene, this was a moment that he hoped to repeat soon on his own experimental plot to the south, where he was working with both public and private landowners to a similar end. For that project, he would be taking a river—the San Joaquin—that had been even more abused and attempting to jump-start the natural engines of productivity once again. "Fins, feathers, and floods forever," he called the effort, or "F/X."

Rene's game plan was similar to Katz's: allow the river to spread out beyond its leveed walls to provide habitat for both waterfowl and fish. In the case of the San Joaquin, however, instead of rice fields, thousands of acres of restored wetland and floodplain habitat already existed near the river in the form of wildlife refuges and duck clubs—a postage stamp–sized memory of the once-vast marshes and swamps that historically characterized the San Joaquin Valley landscape, but high-quality habitat nonetheless. The only problem was that those wetlands were separated from the river channel by levees. "Unfortunately, fish don't have wings, so the levees are more of an issue for them," Rene quipped. Gates were being installed in the levees to allow water to flow in and out. One of the tricky engineering feats is the drawdown in spring, which needs to be timed perfectly to encourage the young salmon to leave such bountiful foraging grounds and continue their migration downstream. Drain too slowly and they don't get the message to leave, ending up beached; drain too quickly and they panic and seek cover in the deepest holes.

Later I would meet one of Rene's partners in the project, a Central Valley farmer named Billy Grissom, who remembers big runs of salmon on his property as recently as the eighties. "Hundreds would come through, big ones, and their backs would stick out," Grissom told me. "People would line up on the bridge to watch all the salmon." Besides being a farmer, Grissom was a duck hunter. He understood the value of habitat and kept a portion of his farmland unplowed in conservation easements, despite the cost. As we stood looking at a dried-up section of wetland that would soon get flooded for salmon habitat, he pointed to a copse of trees in the distance. "When I was a boy, I was sittin' shooting ducks by a vernal pool over there. All of a sudden a cowboy pulled up in a pickup. He got out and was like six-four." Grissom is about five-four. "The guy's name was Bert Crane. Big rancher. 'What are you doing there, boy?' I says, 'I'm shooting some ducks, sir.' He says, 'We don't allow that. This is private property. You gotta leave.' I was scared to death. I was sixteen. I got up and started through the fence and tore my shirt almost clear off me trying to get out of there." Grissom looked at me to see if I understood what he was saying. "Fifty years ago I bought that property. This is the Crane Ranch." A lot of change had happened in the past fifty years, and much more would happen in the next fifty, he was sure of it.

Rene and I followed Katz back to the shed where he kept his tools. He tromped buoyantly along in his waders and boots, looking like a big kid in a mud puddle. Sometimes he liked to don a cowboy hat— the fish wrangler—while working outside at his various project sites. "It's our job, Rene's and mine, to integrate a knowledge of biology into the operation of this system. If we can do that, we end up with a system that works better all around." Katz hung up his nets and seines and turned around to face us. "It's not a compromise. It's not fish versus farms. These solutions we're putting forth save the state billions of dollars. You don't start to see that until you see the price of mismanagement."

Mismanagement. Rene grimaced at the word. "We've created false silos in our mind that are costing us," he agreed. He listed a few of the euphemisms for *river:* flood-control channel, ag water-delivery canal, urban water-delivery canal. These are just different management terms for the same thing. "Managing all these as if they're separate has a significant cost associated with it and prevents us from capitalizing on the benefits of seeing them as integrated." Floodwaters provide seasonal habitat, fertilize soils, and allow groundwater recharge for badly depleted aquifers—the definition of a win–win. Rene took a swig from his water bottle and then held it out so that the sun's rays lit it up like a lantern. "If we put the pieces back together and begin to see the landscape and our rivers as a single thing providing multiple services, we can recover species and save ourselves a bunch of money and time in the process."

We watched the sun set over Knaggs Ranch from a nearby observation tower. Flocks of waterfowl fell out of an orange sky to feed at dusk. Canada geese, teal, pintails. A pickup pulled into the muddy parking lot below us, and out stepped a man in gumboots with a pair of large binoculars around his neck. He climbed the tower steps and sidled up to us, eyeing our waders and boots. "Looks like someone had some fun in the muck today." He was a friend of the ranch owners, a duck hunter. The season would reopen in a week, and he planned to have his blind ready to go in the most popular foraging spot. Right now, as he scanned the rice paddies with his binoculars, he was trying to decide where that spot should be.

"Look at all them specks!" he said, glassing a paddy below us. Locals call the chunky white-fronted geese "specklebellies," for the spots on their lower abdomens. Many hunters prize specks over all the other species of goose. But there was an alarming number of skinny geese this year, the hunter told us. Katz had heard the same thing. Recent conservation efforts in California and elsewhere had been so successful that there were too many birds trying to cram into too little habitat. Some were starving to death as a result. The hunter shook his head at this strange turn of events. "Could be worse," he decided aloud.

———

BEFORE I HEADED BACK north, I came across a recent article that was making the rounds in the Bay Area. It summarized many of the current tensions in the region—tensions that mimic those in my own hometown, Seattle, where schoolteachers, nurses, firefighters, and airplane machinists find themselves increasingly priced out of the city by a rising technocracy. Written by a lifelong San Franciscan and delivered as a speech at Stanford, it eulogized the city that for one hundred sixty-five years had been such a beacon to misfits, artists, and dreamers around the country, a place now reduced to a sad synecdoche: the Google bus. Provocatively titled "Don't Be a Stanford Asshole," the article lamented the moneygrubbing, materialism, and decline of basic human ethics in the region and wondered why the famous bastion of education and enlightenment nearby wasn't providing a necessary injection of humanism. What happened to the idealism? The conoclasm? The brotherly love? The city and surrounding suburbs were awash in venture capital, not to mention all that human capital, busily concocting ever more digital distractions for people everywhere. Silicon Valley was changing the world at an unprecedented pace, its programmers coding away in banks of cubicles lit by diodes and cold cathode light, dialed into infinite combinations of ones and zeroes, walled off in their own private levee system. Connected yet disconnected, from both nature and society.

I asked Rene what he thought about the speech, and he shrugged it off. "Our perception of landscape will always, collectively, mirror our perception of ourselves and our cultural divides," he said. Studies in Alaska are revealing that indigenous human populations were previously tied to salmon returns. When salmon numbers went up, so did human numbers. A severing from place, though, caused the relationship to break down, with humanity exerting ever more population pressure on the natural environment. Yes, he mourned for the city of his youth, now unavailable to most. But there's a path forward, he said, one that involves bringing people together, valuing ecosystem functions, and reimagining a sense of place within the landscape. "Binary distinctions don't hold up any longer. Nature and civilization are too complex for that sort of thinking." Programs like the Nigiri Project and F/X are using innovative approaches to reintegrate a semblance of the wild into an engineered landscape. Perhaps more significant, he added, there is an increasingly loud call across the conservation community to bridge cultural and economic gaps, an effort that can only broaden the community and make it stronger. San Francisco was struggling with this, sure, as were so many other communities across the country.

Rene's core belief—for both salmon and people—could be summed up in a few words: strength through diversity. He looked forward to a great reconciliation.

CHAPTER 13

HERDING THE PINKS

THE APPROACH TO THE HERDING GROUNDS TAKES A MERE FIFTEEN minutes during off-peak hours. From my home in Seattle's south end, I negotiate the busy intersection of Martin Luther King Jr. Way and Rainier Avenue, near the new light-rail station, then climb Beacon Hill for brief views over downtown before dropping back down into the heavy industry of Georgetown, lately a mecca for hipsters and ill-paid public servants who, increasingly in this twenty-first-century capital, can't afford to live outside the contamination zone. Lucile Street jogs me under I-5 to the city's hub of Old Economy commerce, where I turn at Harbor Freight Tools and skirt a collection of upstart businesses on Michigan Street: Orca Car Wash, Foxy Lady Latte, and I Luv Teriyaki. Here I catch my first sight of muddy green water from the 1st Avenue South Bridge.

It's a journey into Seattle's former self: the blue collar past of resource extraction, Wobblies, and Jet City, when the city was known as an industrial port rather than a high-tech campus. Once disdained for its unsightliness, Old Seattle is now taking on a patina of nostalgia as New Seattle looks increasingly unattainable. Tent cities, with their blue tarps and upended grocery carts, sprawl beneath the overpass— the built environment proving as vulnerable as the natural one. On the far side of the railroad tracks I pass more monuments to the past: SeaPort Petroleum ("Less friction"), Standard Steel, Old Dominion Freight, and geometrical stacks of shipping containers in jaunty primary colors. A new iconography emerges, almost unnoticed, in the underpass below Highway 99: a slightly creepy mural of chromatic fish and disembodied human hands. Next to Fire Station No. 26, a metal guidepost announces the mostly Hispanic neighborhood of South Park with a figurine salmon, leaping into the unknown, a seemingly incongruous touch in this hard-hat sea of industry. A few quick dodges through a residential section of duplexes leads to Duwamish Waterway Park, where my fellow anglers are gathered. Directly across the river is a long, windowless airplane factory at Boeing Field. Test flights come in low and loud to land on the adjacent runway. On our side of the river, a hydraulic excavator moves the twisted metal carcasses of junked cars as easily as a kid playing with Lego blocks. Tugboats with tires lashed to their gunwales chug upriver and down.

This stretch of the Duwamish long ago gave up any claim to the pastoral notion of "river." It's a "waterway" now—and an EPA Superfund site at that—and it would be tempting to call this a glimpse of angling's future, though none of us does. The future we imagine is of a braided, tree-lined river in the heart of a bustling metropolis, and when the pink salmon are running, it seems just a little bit more possible. At the peak of the run, around Labor Day, I make this short commute for several consecutive days in an old beater VW campervan, in which I've got my pontoon boat packed. I park on the street and carry the light aluminum frame, already assembled, over to the park's lawn, then return for two folded bladders zipped into abrasion-resistant nylon covers and a foot pump. I inflate the pontoons, each one six feet long, and attach them to the frame with handy D-ring fasteners. Oars in the oarlocks, ice chest bungee-corded to a metal shelf behind the seat. I slip into my waders and cinch a wading belt extra tight. My rod is already rigged from yesterday, in two pieces bound with twist ties. I drag the pontoon boat twenty yards across the grass—past a sign warning residents in English and Spanish not to eat the shellfish—and down a sandy embankment, a rare gap in the waterway's rocky riprap shoreline. Bank fishermen perch on boulders like gulls, turning their heads in unison to watch me ease into the dark water before turning away again.

It doesn't take long, maybe a minute, to row out into the channel and intercept the bulk of the salmon run that's splashing by, mostly out of reach of the bank casters. I decide to start directly opposite the Boeing plant, where old wooden pilings add structure that comforts the fish in their upstream migration. Two centuries ago the Duwamish would have been an obstacle course of logjams—unnavigable by boat but inviting to salmon; today, migrating up a channelized waterway, the fish will have to make do with the consolation of rotting pylons. The current here is barely perceptible to the naked eye, yet it's steady. I pull on my flippers so that I can hold my position in the water with an easy foot stroke and make minor adjustments to cast at visible fish. A few Boeing employees on break lean on the outdoor railing that runs the length of the factory above the waterway, a few hundred yards in all. Some of them will return with rods after their shifts.

It's true that this blighted reach of a long-abused river is a Superfund site, and it's true that the shellfish and ground fish are not fit for consumption. But the salmon come from the relatively clean, cold water of the North Pacific and pass through this contamination zone in the time it takes for a tidal change, heading for more clean, cold water upstream. They're fair game. Looking downriver, I can see them coming: dozens of fish jumping in the current as they make their way upstream toward me, an advertisement of surprising abundance. For each fish I can see, there are probably many more that I can't. I kick my fins and maneuver into position.

SINCE SEATTLE'S FOUNDING IN 1852, the Duwamish has served as food source, transportation artery, power generator, and dumping ground. Its headwaters historically included three color-coded tributaries to the east, rising from the steep volcanic uplift of the Cascade

Mountains: the Green, White, and Black Rivers. The White, prone to flooding, was rerouted in 1911 and now empties farther south, into Tacoma's Commencement Bay. The Black was also diverted and then rubbed out of existence with the completion of the Lake Washington Ship Canal in 1917. That left the Green as the only major tributary—a tributary of one—making for a confusing nomenclature. In all, the river flows ninety-three miles from its mountain source on Stampede Pass to Puget Sound, changing names from Green to Duwamish near the city of Tukwila, twelve miles from the mouth. The original watershed included more than a million acres; with the diversions it was cut in half. Much of the watershed was logged between 1880 and 1910. Its tidelands were filled, diked, and drained right up until World War II, and channelization would continue for another forty years, until 1980. In the postwar era, the lower river was further developed for commercial, industrial, and residential use. A final indignity, Howard Hanson Dam, near the town of Enumclaw in the Cascade foothills, came online in 1962, blocking fish from their spawning grounds upstream.

Despite all this, wild populations of salmon continue to hang on in the river, if barely. My angling preference, like most, is for a cool mountain stream without man-made affront. But I live in a city, not in the mountains, and there's something beautiful about fishing out my own back door amid the strangely compelling landscape of urban America, alive with container ships, trash compactors, cranes maneuvering overhead, tugs blowing their horns, and a silhouette of skyscrapers rising in the distance. It's not scenic in the traditional sense—it's no Montana as portrayed in *A River Runs Through It*—though it has its own appeal, which certainly has something to do with the fact that this is one of the most democratic fisheries in the world. *Everyone* is out here among the riprap, from dot-commers in their yachts to barely employed drifters. They all have a shot at the salmon passing through. Nearby there's a homeless camp, where a friend of mine delivers his catch each night to the residents, who cook the fillets on donated camp stoves.

Historians and ecologists tell us that the estuary where the Duwamish meets Elliott Bay was once one of the great tidal wetlands of
the West Coast. Extensive eelgrass beds nursed salmon fry, crabs, oysters, and countless other marine organisms. Shorebirds and waterfowl
gathered in huge flocks during migration to fatten up for their journeys. Elk and deer roamed bottomland woods. The Duwamish Indians survived on the diverse bounty, as did the first Euro-American
settlers who founded Seattle, which is named for a Duwamish chief.
Back then, with all this abundance, the pink salmon was viewed with
derision as the smallest and least valuable, in monetary terms, of the
five species of Pacific salmon that spawn in North America—a reputation that has shadowed it ever since. With a two-year life cycle, pinks
return to their natal rivers every other year. They turn olive green on
top, develop a crocodilelike snout, and, worst of all, the males grow a
hump. With this metamorphosis complete, the flesh goes soft, hardly
the stuff of a successful backyard barbecue. Anglers through the
ages—through millennia—have disdained the pink's size and silly appearance, not to mention the quality of its meat in comparison to fattier and more flavorful relatives such as chinook and sockeye. Pity the
poor pink salmon. It's sometimes called a humpback or—echoes of
Quasimodo—a hunchback. Most people call them humpies. The
hump has been an object of mirth for as long as people have been fishing for pinks. Indian boys of yore made fun of them. Salish mythology depicts the pink salmon as self-conscious and insecure: "The
Snoqualmie young people are going to laugh at me, coming up the
river," laments a pink in one tale. "They laugh at me because I have a
humpback, coming up the river."

These days, in Puget Sound, an angler who wants to know what it
was like "back in the day," who wants to know what is meant by the
public library's collection of musty archival papers that speak of rivers
"teeming" with fish, of riverbanks "lined" with people armed with
nothing more than pitchforks, of burlap bags "weighted down" by
fish—this angler must make peace with the pink, the only species of
salmon left that can even hint at what yesteryear's harvests must have

been like. Today, in the late summer of odd-numbered years, these anglers come out in force to fish the now-famous humpy run.

Beginning in the 1990s, pink salmon in Puget Sound started trending upward. This was in contrast to other salmon populations in the region, which have been crashing, especially chinook and steelhead. Even the bread-and-butter coho have struggled to hold on. The usual factors are in play: habitat destruction, hydroelectric dams, overharvest, and so on. Though token efforts are now under way to reverse the damage, with high-minded yet toothless initiatives like the Puget Sound Salmon Recovery Plan, the region has been transformed, and it will be a long time before its rivers and estuaries can support large numbers of wild salmon again. Lowly humpies are the single bright spot. In an age of decline, one might well ask: How did this happen? So I went down to the state capital to find out.

The Natural Resources Building in Olympia is a squat, bunkerlike affair in the shadow of the city's attractive capitol building, which, with its dome and steeple, resembles the U.S. Capitol in miniature. I took an elevator to the sixth floor, where I was greeted by a chatty receptionist and a glassed-in replica of a steelhead trout that might have weighed fifteen pounds. Fish in one form or another adorned every wall. This was the home of the Washington Department of Fish and Wildlife (WDFW), and I was here to talk to Aaron Dufault, one of the biologists in charge of studying the region's salmon so that future generations will still have them around. Dufault gets the usual razzing about his name, with its New Economy suggestion of business as usual, but it's actually pronounced in the French way, and his email carries the unlikely signature of "pink salmon specialist," a job description that would have been inconceivable just a few years ago. "Yeah, chinook and coho are big potatoes in comparison," he admitted. He was a young guy with close-cropped auburn hair, wearing a plaid shirt and jeans. Right away I got the impression that he was a perfect match for the humpies in his purview: humble, careful to qualify the knowns and unknowns of pink salmon biology.

Despite being the smallest species of Pacific salmon in North

America (the cherry salmon of Asia is even smaller), the humpy is also the most abundant, Dufault explained. They spawn from June to October, usually in shallow, gravel-bottomed stretches in the main stem of a river, sometimes all the way down to tidewater. Unlike other salmon, pink fry lack the camouflaging spots that are necessary for in-river survival. After hatching in the spring, they migrate quickly to salt, spending several months in estuarine habitat before heading for the open ocean. Because they have only a two-year life span, pinks return to spawn every other year. There are odd-numbered runs and even-numbered runs, from the Arctic coast of Alaska south to Washington in North America. The rivers of southern Puget Sound, notably the Nisqually, represent the practical southern boundary of the species, although strays show up as far south as California. Odd-year fish dominate the southern part of the range, including Washington and lower British Columbia, while even-year fish dominate in the north. Interestingly, Washington State has one river system, the Snohomish, with a small even-year run that has been steadily increasing in population since 1980, and scientists aren't sure how it got started.

Pinks are known to stray widely and have been observed recolonizing former spawning grounds as soon as impediments such as dams are removed. The species' historical range is somewhat unclear. Early in the previous century, a few pinks were observed spawning in rivers as far south as central California but never in large numbers, and more recently there have been only a handful of recorded sightings in rivers such as the Klamath and Sacramento. Lower Columbia tributaries like the Cowlitz see small returns as well. Population strongholds in North America include large runs in the Skeena, Fraser, and Skagit Rivers.

Because their two-year life cycle is so regular—unlike other species', which vary to some degree—the year-to-year abundance of pink salmon can fluctuate wildly. With chinook salmon, for instance, you might see adults from four different age classes spawning in a single stretch of river; their progeny will return in different years as well. With pink salmon, they're all the same age: two years old. This means a single catastrophic event can have an outsize effect on their numbers. A flood might wipe out an entire age class in one fell swoop. On the flip side, pinks are especially fecund and can rebuild their populations quickly. As a result, they're the healthiest of all salmon species and represent an important commercial and subsistence fishery. In 2010, Alaska commercially harvested 372.5 million pounds of pink salmon. Most pinks are canned, with labels that don't highlight the species. "Generally they're not a sought-after fish," Dufault said, "especially if you're a recreational fisherman." But—and here's the rub—in recent odd-numbered years Puget Sound has seen a return of several million pink salmon. Not long before that, WDFW didn't even include pinks in the forecast. "Ten years back we estimated them at 10,300 fish in the Green River." A decade later, the projection was for 1.4 million pinks in the Green, the sort of number that doesn't get tossed around much anymore with regard to Puget Sound salmon.

Dufault called such projections "remotely educated throws at a dartboard." Just the same, they're close enough to be winners in most barroom leagues. Pink salmon are among the easiest salmon to forecast, because they don't have multiple age classes on the spawning grounds at once. Since they're always two-year fish, a returning run size can be calculated simply by figuring out how many of the juveniles migrate out to sea.

After taking a seat in a conference room, I told Dufault I wanted to know how these big runs of Puget Sound pinks got started. He's a scientist, and it's a scientist's job to figure out this kind of stuff. He just shook his head. "I wish I had a good answer." The fact is, there is only speculation. Ocean conditions are one hypothesis. The Pacific's long-term cycles of heating and cooling benefit some species while hurting others. Pinks are reliant largely on zooplankton for food, in contrast to larger, baitfish-eating species like chinook and coho. High winter temperatures in the North Pacific are correlated with higher zooplankton and pink salmon survival. Temps that are too high, though, can cause a crash in the food chain.

Which leads to the elephant in the room: climate change. So far, the effects of a warming planet are more measurable on land. "More variability is what we're expecting," Dufault said. He told me that in recent years some rivers have experienced historic lows and highs within a two-month span, a volatile mix of conditions that leads to dewatering one moment (effectively shutting salmon out) and flooding the next (destroying spawning nests). The future, he said, is hard to predict.

Another young biologist, wearing a bowling shirt and goatee, sat down with us. Ryan Lathrop's title is Puget Sound Recreational Salmon Manager. He's the Saturday beach caster's go-to guy.

"Maybe pinks will benefit from climate change," Dufault continued. "There's usually a species poised to take advantage of the situation."

Lathrop frowned. No offense to his colleague, the so-called pink specialist, but given his druthers, Lathrop would take just about anything over humpies. He was nervous about the declines in coho. And chinook? Well, they're just in the tank—never mind steelhead, which are at perhaps one or two percent of their historic abundance in Puget Sound. But his lot is pink salmon these days, and fishing-license sales depend on them. Lathrop said WDFW sees a huge uptick in licenses in pink years, money that in turn goes to promoting recreational fisheries. The pink run has turned into a great tool for introducing new anglers to salmon fishing, he told me, and so, like most everyone else, he's now a grudging fan of the humpy. The central paradox of his job can be summed up in one image: a big fish toted home triumphantly by a little kid. Future stewards of our environment are created this way.

I know just how that little kid feels—as do my children. You can call it a stinky pinkie or a humpback or a humpy—it doesn't matter. Those of us who fish for them, particularly with a fly rod, know that a humpy fresh from the sea is a good biter and smokes up nicely. You don't need a boat and downriggers to fish for pinks. You don't even need to huck a heavy lure fifty yards offshore. My son caught his first pink at the age of seven on a Seattle beach. He used a Snoopy rod and tossed his two-inch Buzz-Bomb maybe thirty feet.

"It gets people outdoors fishing," Lathrop said, "and that's a good thing."

THE DUWAMISH RIVER CLEANUP Coalition envisions a future in which "residents will be able to crab in the river" and its banks will be a "welcoming and risk-free place for our children and their children to wade, fish, and play." This is a sentiment expressed by citizens' groups across the country, as they band together to restore ecological processes in urban areas and bring nature back to cities—by planting trees, daylighting creeks, cleaning up ports and bays. The narrative of the American city itself is no longer one of decay. People are returning to cities. All over the world, the trend is toward urbanization, and when people are asked why, their answers are not just about jobs. It turns out human beings actually enjoy one another's company. This would seem to contradict nearly everything I learned in American history class. *Rugged individualism. The lure of wide-open spaces. Control of nature.* These are just a few of the accepted tropes that try to explain the birth of America and the settling of the West. The reality is more complicated.

As a kid, I always assumed the city was a place of poverty and pestilence. It never occurred to me back then that I would choose to live in such a place one day, much less go fishing there. Still, cities and salmon have not been compatible for the most part. Some of the more pessimistic urban anglers I know think the pink salmon's recent upturn in Puget Sound is a cosmic joke, the beginning of the end. With other species of salmon on the ropes, here comes Mr. Humpy, an empty river all to himself. In a world ruined by the hand of man, it only makes sense that the least desirable fish is the one to inherit the earth. They call pinks the fish of the coming apocalypse. Cleaning up a river as polluted as the Duwamish is a fool's errand, they say, window dressing on Armageddon. I don't expect to drop a crab pot in sight of Boeing Field in my lifetime—but in my children's lifetimes? This is the possibility that motivates many of us. Boeing itself recently committed voluntarily to a costly restoration on its property, transforming an ugly stretch of channelized river into a tidal mudflat alive with flowering vegetation and statuesque great blue herons.

Meanwhile, some of us city folk have learned how to stock up our freezers every other year with a two-year supply of smoked salmon by fishing in our own slightly ratty yard. A humpy is an ideal candidate for the smoker. True, its thin fillet hardly leaps out at you from the cooler of a fish market the way a bright hunk of chinook does. Its flesh is less fatty than that of other species, the color a pallid pink. This is in part due to the fact that humpies spend less time in the salt than other species. Their flesh lacks bright red and orange tones, muscled firmness, and longevity on ice. As the reef netters of Lummi Island know, pinks must be bled quickly and then handled with care lest they bruise or turn rancid. For these reasons, salmon eaters have long turned their noses up at them. The problem is, most salmon eaters are now financially hard-pressed to indulge in their favorite types of wild salmon, not with fresh king fillets fetching upward of $30 per pound, never mind the price of Copper River salmon. "Once considered ugly-bumpkin cousins to glamorous sockeye and kings," reported *The Seattle Times* in 2010, "pinks are transcending their traditional $2-a-can destiny to debut as the new, eco-friendly, sustainable darlings." Many local fishermen already knew this. Perhaps the biggest believer today is Riley Starks. With a projection of more than fourteen million humpies returning to the Fraser River, he was thinking pink.

———

ACROSS SALMON COUNTRY, ANGLERS, commercial fishermen, and the tribes had prepared for a mixed year. From California to Alaska, the forecasts varied widely and proved difficult to parse. "Ocean conditions" was the common (and not so satisfactory) explanation for run sizes, whether for good or ill. In April I attended another First Salmon ceremony at the Celilo Falls longhouse, where spring chinook, most of them hatchery fish, overflowed from plastic totes. Despite ongoing drought, California managers predicted decent fall chinook returns for the Sacramento and Klamath Rivers, giving hope to coastal communities dependent on sport fishing. Washington State forecast a return of several million pinks to Puget Sound rivers even as the outlook for other species appeared bleak. By early July, tackle shops across Seattle were sold out of the most popular lures.

While our kids were off at sleepaway camp, Martha and I decided to visit San Juan Island for a few days. This was something we had agreed to do more of, at least in theory, now that our children were a little older and we could get away. We wanted to explore this beautiful place where we lived, to see its many sights, and get a little muddy in the process. The weekend before, we had gone backpacking in the Olympic Mountains. Now we embarked on a beach vacation of the sort that we had both known from our childhoods on the East Coast. Of course, a July beach trip in the Pacific Northwest might involve layering on the fleece and maybe even a down jacket, but that was okay. One morning, we got up early and drove over to the rocky shoreline along the west side of the island. Martha sat herself down on some bluffs to watch for killer whales, while I scrambled down to the wave-washed rocks below with my casting rod. It took just six casts to catch a limit of four humpies, all bright and firm, if a bit small.

Later in the month, Riley Starks called me to say that the reef-net test fishery was hauling them in as well. On a sunny afternoon in early August, I caught up with Starks at the Willows Inn on Lummi Island, his former business, lately transformed into a must-visit restaurant with a slew of laudatory reviews. Starks, wearing a sky-blue Lummi Island Wild ball cap, was in his fourth and final day of entertaining new clients. A celebratory luncheon would be the last event. His beard was a little whiter, a spray of hair on top a little more scruffy than usual when he removed the hat, but he looked contented. The Willows gathering was a victory lap. He'd landed a big fish: Patagonia.

A few years earlier, the enviro-minded clothier had launched a new food division, with smartly packaged snacks for the active person on the go, including trail bars, buffalo jerky, and smoked sockeye salmon. Now they wanted to add pink salmon to the lineup and tell the story of the reef netters on the packaging. "They're committed to a hundred thousand pounds already," Starks whispered to me before we all sat down on the restaurant's front deck, overlooking Sunset Beach and Rosario Strait. A gaggle of Patagonia reps took their seats at the table, along with a film crew they'd hired to interview chef Blaine Wetzel on the little-known charms of pink salmon. Starks leaned over again, a tumbler of sparkling water in his hand while the rest of us drank glasses of rosé. "Really, it's twice that. They'll do two hundred thousand without blinking."

Clearly, the Patagonia deal was a coup for Starks and his co-op. Lummi Island Wild is a company with a bunch of fishermen in charge—hardly a recipe for corporate success. But as the guy responsible for marketing, Starks had found a willing partner with all the right credentials. Reef-net pink salmon were about to make a coast-to-coast debut. They would be sold fresh in select fish markets too, he added. The co-op was getting fifty cents a pound. Starks hoped to sell a million pounds this year. If all went according to plan, they could wrap up by the end of September and skip the fall coho fishery. Even though the blob was still in the North Pacific, scientists didn't expect it to divert the Fraser's pink salmon run the way it had the sockeye run the year before. Still, Mother Nature has a way of throwing curveballs. So far the fish seemed smaller than average. I had noticed the same thing on San Juan Island. All four of my pinks were on the light side, two to three pounds. The reef netters were releasing fish under three pounds, because they were too small for the automated fish-cleaning machines. This was translating into a third of the catch going overboard. At least they were still alive, Starks said, unlike the bycatch in other fisheries.

Dishes started arriving at the table in twos and threes. Marinated squid with herbs and olive oil. Canning jars of duck rillettes. Salumi and cheese boards. And, finally, a trio of what the menu called "lightly smoked pink salmon." The fillets were served skin up, which seemed odd, with a few feathery green fronds of fennel on top. They were slightly crispy on the outside and tender inside, with a smoked-salmon flavor that wasn't overpowering in terms of either the smoke or the fish—the perfect sort of dish to complement a light glass of wine on a warm summer day. From my seat I saw a familiar face in the restaurant's driveway, near the smoker. I excused myself and hurried over to see Blaine Wetzel. He was in his street clothes, carrying a colander with a single Asian eggplant in it. I asked him about the pink salmon on the menu and he didn't hesitate. "I love how delicate the meat is. The skin is unlike any other salmon." He's right. Their scales are smaller and thinner than other species. Now I understood the skin-up presentation. This was a way to nudge the diner, to emphasize that the whole fillet should be enjoyed, skin and all. Jon Rowley would approve. Wetzel said he liked to smoke a pink fillet for just half an hour—long enough to take a little smoke but not so long to cook in full—and then he finished it in the pan with some butter, which gave it that crispiness we had all noted.

"They don't teach you about salmon in culinary school," he said. "I mean, you learn how to cook it some basic ways, but they don't teach you about the five different species or how they're caught." Part of his learning experience as a chef was discovering the inherent virtues of each species, as well as learning how to differentiate between the various commercial-fishing techniques. He prefers reef-net salmon to any other. There ought to be a label, he went on, explaining the method used to harvest the fish—just the way there's a label of origin, as required by law. Origin was relevant, sure, and so was the style of fishing. He treated the pinks like a big trout. Besides lightly smoking them, he liked to steam fillets in foil with herbs, or stuff whole fish and broil them in the oven. He loved the eggs, especially early in the run when they were still slightly undeveloped. He sometimes panfried the entire skein. He was even using the milt sacks of the males, poaching them in goat's milk.

"The milt?" asked one of the reps back at the table. "That's a line I don't cross." It was one I had yet to cross myself, though I'd often wondered about the opaque white liver-shaped glands.

After lunch I followed Starks back to Nettles Farm, where we went inside his cottage for a cup of coffee. He said he was tired. He had B&B guests scheduled to stay in the main house for most of the summer; the new tender was in the water, requiring his captain skills periodically; and the co-op's business continued to ramp up. But I also understood his weariness to be more of the existential variety. Keeping an age-old tradition alive was physically and mentally draining, though recently Starks was pleased to hear that members of Vancouver Island's Saanich Indian tribe had revived the practice, calling reef netting the "backbone" of society in earlier times. Using long canoes and a modern net, they hoped to catch their first reef-net salmon in a century later in the month, fishing historic grounds in the southern Gulf Islands near the U.S.–Canada border. Would there be Native American reef netters on Lummi Island ever again? Starks hoped so.

"Don't look around," he advised me after pouring us each an espresso. "Let's have it outside." We sat in cheap molded-plastic chairs in front of his cottage, more dirt driveway than patio, and sipped our coffee. Housecleaning was the last thing on Starks's long to-do list. Right now he had to feed the chickens. "But we can sit for a moment," he said, not ready to get up. At least the ravens weren't beheading his birds any longer. He'd figured that one out. His dog, Stella, curled up at his feet. He was training her to find truffles. "We found three on the property with another dog," he said optimistically.

Off to the side, a wrought-iron deck chair was in the middle of being refurbished. "I'm working on it in my spare time. It helps me relax." Starks was lining the metal frame of the seat and chair back with bamboo, which he had harvested on his property and dried himself. Each piece was individually cut to fit and lashed to the other pieces with long strips of leather. He had a few other chairs waiting in the wings. They had come from a long-defunct restaurant owned by a friend of his, a place that brewed its own beer well before the microbrew craze and served upscale pub food. "It was way ahead of its time," Starks said. When it came to business, timing could be everything. We both thought about this silently for a moment, and then Starks straightened up, admiring his work on the chairs again. They reminded him of old friends and the good times he'd had at the brewery in his younger days. Half finished, with a few strands of cracked and weathered reeds still attached to one section alongside the replacement bamboo, the chairs looked simultaneously very old and brand-new. "They'll be comfortable too," he added, smiling at himself for neglecting the most obvious benefit, as if the notion of comfort was an afterthought.

ON A CLEAR, WINDLESS MORNING just before Labor Day, the herders, as they called themselves, met at Duwamish Waterway Park for what would likely be the last time that season to commemorate their beloved urban fishery. Connected by the Internet, they came from Seattle, Portland, Yakima, Spokane, Bellingham, and elsewhere. They hauled analog-age kickboats, rafts, canoes, aluminum tubs, and other barely seaworthy vessels down to the river's roily edge. Some of them I knew only from message-board banter, by their screen names. There was Trouthole and Bubba, Blue Stimmy and Snapdad. In a semi-ironic nod to the Wild West of Zane Grey, they called this roundup "the herding of the pinks." The herders were mostly fly-fishermen. Every other year in odd-numbered years, they circled their sea-wagons in the busy commercial waterway to fish and enjoy one another's company.

Everyone had his own theory about when the bite was best. "We're too early," Foghorn worried. He had come up from Portland and preferred high tide. "Give me an incoming tide," yelled Paul over the ambient noise of a trash compactor working steadily on a diet of wrecked cars. Paul, who had been actively fishing the pink run since it first started ramping up in Puget Sound, in the early nineties, probably knew more about catching these salmon than anyone, "but I wouldn't bet my life on it," he demurred. Fish are always unpredictable. Mostly our preferences were based on past performance more than any studied triangulation of moon, tides, barometer, and whatever else might seem vaguely scientific. My own inclination was more in line with Paul's. It seemed reasonable that energy-conserving fish would nose into the river with a rising tide at their backs. As we suited up, my friend Steve rowed up on his pontoon boat, greeted by a chorus of raspberries.

"Got my limit," he said with typical angler's brevity, deflecting any questions about where or what fly he was fishing. Steve beached his craft and wrestled a cooler with six iced pink salmon off the back. "Time to tend the smoker." This is as much of a time-honored skill as the fishing itself. The fish needs to be filleted, brined overnight, rinsed off, air-dried for a few hours, and then smoked. Serious smokers tinker with their brining recipes relentlessly, trying exotic herbs and spices, adjusting the ratio of salt to sugar, adding new ingredients such as molasses or pineapple juice or cayenne pepper—and that's just for the brine, which is meant to leach out some of the water in the meat and replace it with a preserving mixture of salt and sugar. The type of wood used as the smoking agent is also critical—alder, cherry, and apple being just a few of the usual varieties—as is the style of smoker itself. Mine uses burning coals rather than an electric element and keeps the meat properly moist with a water pan placed just above the fire. Smoking salmon is an art and pastime, occasioning lawn chair, fire poker, and six-pack of beer. The finished product, if well executed, will have a salty-sweet crust and succulent interior. Pink salmon, we all agreed, are best smoked.

A photographer known as Nope snapped a shot as we all got ready to launch. "Okay, gang," he called out, twirling a fist in the air with an imaginary lariat, "head 'em up and move 'em out!" A dozen pairs of oars dug into the dirty water and we made for the middle of the channel as a flotilla, passing an anchored tug and a barge the size of a desert atoll. The barge, everyone noted with dismay, was parked right in the middle of the best fishing grounds from two years earlier. One guy, who went by the Internet handle Unfrozen Caveman, from a *Saturday Night Live* skit about a Neanderthal on the loose in modern society, puttered past us in his new wooden dory. He and his son had spent the intervening two years building it themselves in the garage. A little outboard mounted on the stern steered them into range ahead of everyone else, and he let fly with a Paleolithic cackle.

The herders formed a circle, corralling a school of pinks, and started casting. Paul hooked the first fish and paddled out of the circle with his fins to land it, while the rest of us redoubled our efforts. My rod was a nine-foot model designed for large trout, my reel hand-tooled from anodized airplane-grade aluminum to protect against the salt. I was using a clear sinking line of about fifteen feet in length that enables the fly to get down a few inches in the water column, where a fish is more apt to strike. When they're on the bite, pinks will take flies at any depth and even right on the surface, which is unusual for salmon. My fly was fuchsia-colored with dumbbell eyes, tied in the Crazy Charlie style—which is to say sparsely, with a slim crustacean look to it. Though fly choice is not crucial, hot pink is by far the favorite color, and sometimes chartreuse. What these two colors have in common is hard to know. I cast forty feet and stripped the fly back with a fishy-looking retrieve. This is probably the most contested part of the technique. Fly anglers will argue on behalf of slow retrieves, fast retrieves, and any number of speeds in the middle, as well as varying the strip with a quick jig or simply letting the fly hang suspended for a moment. All methods seem to take fish, though certain techniques will be more profitable on a day-to-day or even hour-to-hour basis, for reasons that are mostly beyond the fisherman's understanding, no matter what he may claim.

Thirty yards downstream, a dorsal fin broke the surface and the fish rose nearby. This behavior—the splashy porpoising and tail-chasing—is yet another behavior that isn't properly understood. Is the salmon acting territorial? Is it responding to a change in salinity? To its own physiological changes? Most anglers believe the strike is a form of aggression, a way for the fish to assert its seniority, or perhaps a foreshadowing of the competitiveness that kicks in once the fish are paired up on their spawning grounds. The fishing lure isn't food so much as something to be dominated. In any event, pinks spend a lot of time near the surface, where they're susceptible to flies. Sometimes the schooling fish, which are known to follow shorelines, barges, and other shadowy underwater structures as they move upstream, appear to get confused by the armada of fishermen in their pontoon boats and start slashing wantonly at any fly in front of them. Why they do this is a mystery. As with so much of fish biology—so much of nature in general—we don't know the answers. We can only hope that the objects of our study will be around long enough to one day reveal their secrets.

The fish boiled again. I aimed my fly for what trout fishermen call the "ring of the rise" and stripped it back. A swirl appeared behind my fly, and then I felt the take—an electric jolt that buzzed through my body, lighting up ancestral bulbs like a well-played pinball machine. I set the hook, and the rod doubled over. Pinks are not jumpers. They'll usually sound, taking some line off the reel, though nothing like a coho or steelhead, which might send your reel into paroxysms and leap a few times before you even register the strike. Just the same, a five-pound pink on a light fly rod is a thrill. A good fish will tow an angler on a pontoon in circles for a few minutes before it can be tired out and landed, and many fish are lost right at the boat during the frenetic, low-angle process of trying to net the thing without dumping into the drink.

Once the fish was safely in the net, I secured my rod and removed the barbless hook (required to protect endangered runs). It was a very large male, at least six pounds, still silver from the salt but showing the green upper body of a fish beginning its spawning transformation. I've caught a few pinks even larger, though most are three to five pounds. I slipped a finger through the mouth and gill for a good grip, brandished my net handle in my other hand, and performed the necessary chore. The fish quivered and its eyes stared blankly. I put down the net across my other saddlebag and used my free hand to tear the gills on both sides so it could bleed out. Pound for pound, pinks have more blood than any other species of salmon, and that blood can taint the meat if not given a careful letting. A few spurts from the still-pumping heart cascaded down the fish's body, turning it a dark crimson. I washed it off in the water before using my knife to cut a slit from the anal fin to the gill and removing all the internal organs. Now it was ready to be put in the cooler lashed behind my seat. I would fillet it later at home.

Before I could get my fly back in the water, Paul was into another fish. The horn blast of a container ship out in Elliott Bay echoed across the water, momentarily drowning out the noise of Boeing Field to our south. I spotted the Unfrozen Caveman across the river, in his homemade boat, reaching for his own net. He was fishing in the shadow of a giant barge, one of many that dock in the waterway, its hull freshly painted blue. The barge towered over him like a steep, brilliant cliff. His young son stood in the bow, wearing a bright-red life vest, trying to hold on to a spinning rod that was suddenly alive in his hands. "I've got one!" the boy declared across the river, a phrase as old as language itself. *"I've got one! I've got one! I've got one!"*

CHAPTER 14

RHYTHM OF THE RIVER

"THEY TOOK MY FISHING HOLE AWAY."

A man in a red plaid shirt and mirror sunglasses shuffled along the interpretive trail, looking dumbstruck. Newly paved, the path followed the ramparts of Glines Canyon Dam to a fenced overlook more than two hundred feet above the Elwha River in Washington State's Olympic National Park. Though the dam was gone now, demolished in 2012, fragments of its concrete tailraces hung down as a reminder, looking aged, moss-bound, and weather-beaten. The bed of the former reservoir, Lake Mills, spread out below, its dry basin cut through by the force of a free-flowing river. A blue mosaic of untouched forested hills receded into the distance on this cloudless September morning, their folds revealing the zigzag course of the river, which tumbled into view several hundred yards to the north, dodging and feinting across the floodplain to find its fastest route to the sea. Where the river ran beneath us, a respectable bungee jump below, it funneled into a choke point and disappeared around a bend into the shadowy slot of the canyon.

Glines Canyon had been an obvious choice for a dam at a time when there was little opposition to such an intrusion, at least among the white settlers, and though this dam and its counterpart eight miles downriver, Elwha Dam, had blocked the upstream migration of salmon and steelhead since 1913, the non-Native locals were accustomed to fishing for equally non-native species in the reservoirs. Now the man-made lakes were dry and the rejuvenated river was closed entirely to angling, to give remnant anadromous fish populations a chance to recover after the temporary trauma of dam removal, which had dislodged a century's worth of trapped sediments—about twenty-four million cubic yards in all, enough to fill more than two hundred thousand dump trucks.

The man took off his sunglasses in disbelief and rubbed his eyes. "Just took it all away, is what they did," he said again, to no one in particular and to everyone. He put the glasses back on and turned to face us, as if we might have an answer that was acceptable. The mended Elwha Valley reflected in miniature across his lenses, but he couldn't really see it.

"Before long you'll be able to fish for chinook salmon here," John McMillan spoke up, trying to console him. McMillan is a fisheries biologist and he's been studying the Elwha River for years, first with the National Oceanic and Atmospheric Administration and now with Trout Unlimited.

"That's all bullshit government talk."

"Actually, it's science."

"Scientists!" The man laughed outright and started to walk away.

McMillan flashed a big fake smile and cursed under his breath. For a moment I thought there might be a confrontation. Rene Henery, reading one of the interpretive signs nearby, shot me a look that said he was willing to intervene if necessary. Rene knew that his colleague—looking deceptively like a harmless vacationer today in shorts, sandals, and neatly trimmed beard—didn't put up with a lot of guff. No pencil neck, McMillan came from a "dirt poor" backwoods family by his own account and put himself through college and grad school, eventually earning a master's degree in fisheries science—not exactly a discipline guaranteed to pay off student loans. He preferred rural life, finding the people, with occasional exceptions, easier to talk to about balance and sustainability, words that got bounced around in the cities ad nauseam, with little real effect. McMillan had warned us earlier that he hadn't gotten his proper dose of morning coffee, and he wasn't one to shy away from a fight.

The plaid-shirted man took one last look over his shoulder, snorted in disgust, and shambled back toward the parking lot, secure in his belief that undoing the past was a waste of time and money. McMillan held his tongue. Watching the scene unfold, I was reminded of a story Rene had told me about meeting a retired canal supervisor during one of his community town halls on the future of the San Joaquin in California. A big, elderly, gray-bearded man, looking as if he had just pulled up on his Harley, took him aside at the end and introduced himself. "I really liked what you said about the salmon," he began. At first Rene was surprised at the compliment and wasn't sure whether the former canal supervisor was pulling his leg. He'd met a lot of veterans of the water wars, old-timers who had fought pitched battles with both nature and bureaucracy. They had played politics, taken it to the streets, and sometimes gone around the law. In many ways, California's Central Valley was theirs, its land the spoils of war. Rene nodded, keeping up his guard. "You know what," the gray-bearded man said at last. "I'm gonna tell you something. Your restoration program will succeed, and I'll tell you how I know." He looked intensely into Rene's brown eyes. "Don't take offense by this. When I was growing up, there was one black family that lived in this area. They were tolerated, but no one liked them being here. When I had kids, my daughter had a black boyfriend. I wasn't a big fan. My wife was a little better with it. Now I have grandkids, and one of them is getting married to a black guy—and my daughter is totally fine with it. When my grandparents were living here, this was a really hard place to be. They worked so that each generation could have more opportunities, so that life wouldn't be so hard. We've done the same thing for our kids. Each time, we've been successful and our kids have been getting more and more liberal. They care more. They care about other people and the environment and about people getting along and finding common ground. We do all this work to make things easier. For that reason, I'm sure that your restoration will succeed, because that's the way things are going." The old man paused, looked around the room, and lowered his voice. "But it's gonna take a little while. Because a bunch of people my age still need to die."

Rene preferred to believe that change didn't require one generation replacing the next, though after a decade in the salmon-restoration business he was still an unlikely face in the crowd. Now he gripped John McMillan by the shoulder and they exchanged a silent, collegial moment of understanding. No longer did McMillan have to convince anyone of the rightness of freeing the Elwha River—that battle was over. Even so, the euphoria surrounding the largest dam removal in U.S. history had long since worn off as well, leaving the biologist saddled with the collateral damage that came with a hard-fought victory. The truth was, McMillan heard this sort of thing all the time: jabs at pointy-headed scientists and cavils about eco-worship. There was no point in arguing. What did it matter to this guy in his blinkered mirror sunglasses that chinook salmon and steelhead were, in fact, already up here, recolonizing the seventy miles of spawning grounds that had been blocked for a hundred years? He would just complain about the temporary ban on fishing. Or the merchantable timber locked up in the park. Or the price tag for dam removal, which ended up at $325 million, nearly three times more than originally budgeted. People are set in their ways. Changing their minds is one of the great myths of politics. But sometimes, on rare occasions, it happens.

ALREADY, A THICK, UNRULY MASS of willows and alders covered the outer rim of the former reservoir, a carpet of green that would close in on the river like jungle reclaiming a long-lost temple. While the novelty of dam removal was the stuff of headline news, nothing compared to actually seeing the results firsthand. Rene absorbed the view in silence. The speed at which nature could repair itself was simultaneously hard to fathom and awe-inspiring. He had made the trip from

California to see a handful of such restoration efforts, though none of the others could compare with the Elwha in scope. To the south, on a headwater tributary of Oregon's Deschutes River, he had spent the previous day visiting upland-prairie and meadow restorations that would one day benefit wild steelhead. Though the steelhead weren't there yet, the work anticipated their arrival, as damaged watersheds were rehabilitated in advance of the sea-run trout's return.

Rene called these visits a form of cross-pollination. "It's so easy to be in your own bubble all the time," he said. Getting out of his office—getting out of California—gave him the opportunity to see new ideas at work in the field and to meet with colleagues. The meeting-with-colleagues part was especially vital. Over the years he'd made bonds with other scientists working on salmon issues who shared his sense of optimism; it was important to check in occasionally to keep the flame burning. Recently he'd seen himself quoted in a paper called "Salmon 2100," which collected the anonymous thoughts of a number of scientists across disciplines in the salmon-restoration universe; many of them were likely people that he admired and respected, perhaps even former teachers and mentors, who'd responded to the question, "Where will salmon be in the year 2100?" Rene was dismayed by the pessimism in the final printed version. "I was shocked to find that my response was the only one that said they'd be doing better," he told me. "How have we allowed ourselves to get to a place where the people working on this are so jaded that they don't believe it's possible?" For him, the Elwha was a dramatic case in point. "Look at it," he said. "Nature recovers. Give it some help and it recovers."

John McMillan understood as well as anyone that nature could recover. The Elwha was his backyard, after all. He lived just a few miles away. And his love of salmon went well beyond the professional—it was in his blood. His father, Bill, was well known to steelhead fishermen and conservationists. Back in 1974, Bill had taken his son to the very courtroom where Judge George Boldt famously awarded the treaty tribes of Washington and Oregon half the salmon catch. Some kids might remember seeing a historic concert or sporting event with their parents; McMillan was witness to the Boldt decision. Life wasn't easy growing up with a wild-salmon advocate. Besides suffering fiscal privation—conservationists being more poorly paid than even teachers—John had to learn to defend himself at school in Washougal, a tight-knit community on the Washington side of the Columbia River Gorge, where the parents of his classmates worked in the commercial or recreational salmon fishery and anyone opposed to hatcheries was at best a traitor. Using a fly to catch steelhead was considered suspicious too. One of his best friends was Native American—strike three, and another reason to learn how to use his fists. Bill and his son had come to see the massive hatchery infrastructure in the Pacific Northwest as one of the main obstacles facing salmon and steelhead. "I hate talking about the hatchery issue," he said now. "It's like peeing in the wind."

McMillan was referring to the tribal salmon hatchery on the Elwha. As part of the dam-removal deal, the Lower Elwha Klallam Tribe got a brand-new hatchery. Scientists like McMillan, who viewed the unshackling of the river as a once-in-a-lifetime opportunity—on par with the eruption of Mount St. Helens from a research perspective—would have to be satisfied with making observations that were influenced by hatchery stocks. I could remember my own reaction when I first heard this news, before the last hunk of cement had even been removed from the dams. Outrage. A grand experiment in restoring wild salmon to an environment as perfect as you'll find in the Lower 48 was about to be scuttled by short-term need. But Rene wasn't so worried. Though he would have preferred the absence of a hatchery, part of the challenge of dam removal, he argued, was selling it to the public. The hatchery made the sale easier, especially to the tribe, a key constituent that depended on salmon. As usual, he was factoring in the political dimension, something that many scientists found distasteful or even inappropriate. For Rene, coalition building, with its inherent need for compromise, had become a large part of his job description, of his success even.

"That's why we all love Rene," John conceded.

———

AT 321 SQUARE MILES in size, the Elwha drainage is not write-home-about big by Northwest terms, but it looms large in the regional consciousness. More than 80 percent of it lies within Olympic National Park, where its timbered slopes have never been cut. Even so, the great old-growth firs and cedars topple in windstorms on occasion, and those trees that are swept downstream in spring runoff create massive logjams of the sort that impressed and frustrated the first Euro-American explorers and are now mostly absent from rivers up and down the West Coast. The logjams force the river into contortionist knots that make for perilous navigation and ideal salmon habitat. Narrow canyons and fierce rapids add to the complexity. Over eons the river selected for strong fish that could make the journey, including some of the heftiest chinook salmon anywhere, with legendary hundred-pounders reported from time to time prior to damming. All five species of Pacific salmon, plus steelhead, cutthroat, and bull trout, once spawned in the Elwha.

Such storied abundance and diversity didn't safeguard the fish. Thomas Aldwell, a local pioneer, started constructing the first of the two Elwha dams in 1910, just five miles from the mouth, and after some mishaps completed the 108-foot plug three years later. Contrary to state law, the dam was built without fish passage and blocked more than 90 percent of the river's spawning habitat. To mitigate the loss (and mollify authorities), Aldwell also built a hatchery, and so began a recurring cycle of ineffectual, even harmful so-called mitigation hatcheries being used as work-arounds for illegal fish-blocking dams, a strategy that would see its apotheosis in the Columbia Basin. The power generated by the dam fueled the economic development of the frontier town of Port Angeles, specifically its lumber mill. The environmental legacy of all this was the usual unraveling of an ecosystem and the fall off of salmon runs to about one percent of their historical size.

For a long time the Elwha River seemed just out of reach for conservationists, an untouchable holy grail that powered—symbolically if not in reality—a waning logging industry in a once-prosperous and now-struggling rural community. In actuality, the dams only provided nineteen megawatts of power to a single paper mill, albeit one with well-paid jobs, and when it came time for relicensing, the cost of making necessary upgrades outweighed the benefits. Suddenly dam opponents had an opening, and in 1992 the U.S. Congress, in a surprising bit of deft politics on the part of river advocates, authorized removal. It took another two decades and plenty of maneuvering on both sides before the first chunk of concrete fell, on September 27, 2011.

When I first heard that the dams were truly coming down, I decided to take a trip into the Elwha backcountry. I wanted to see the river in its straitjacketed posture one last time, as a form of remembrance, so I drove to Whiskey Bend and backpacked fifteen miles up the Elwha Trail in Olympic National Park: through intermittent rains, down into a cool wet ravine where the Lillian River joins the Elwha, past Elkhorn Camp and the Lost River, one of the largest tributaries, and finally to the junction of the Hayes River, where I pitched my base camp in a grove of towering fir and hemlock. One of these trees had recently fallen across the trail and was subsequently notched by the park service, just enough to afford passage. I stepped through the gap and paused for a moment on the threshold. The recumbent trunk stood taller than me, its smooth red grain smelling intensely of resin. Someone had taken the time to count back the tree rings, noting in black Magic Marker the year 1492 near the center.

The next day I left camp early and hiked another dozen miles upriver, hoping to get a glimpse of the headwater glaciers where the river begins its life. Clouds moved in again and fog shrouded the Olympic peaks. Every now and then I caught a peekaboo sight of snow in the higher elevations through lofty trees and mist. Near the Low Divide, which separates the Elwha Basin from the Quinault, I veered away from the main trail on a climber's spur that followed the river. Now it was raining hard, and the muddy goat path petered out altogether somewhere past a rough shelter used by backcountry alpin-ists. It was there, off-trail in the middle of the Olympic wilderness, trying to spot the Elwha Snow Finger—the river's source, lying in a crevice between Mount Queets and Mount Barnes—that I first heard the voices.

Moments later a group of three backpackers in rain-spattered pon-chos came bursting through the brush. They were soaked and tired, and I could see them choosing their steps gingerly as they tried to avoid slick rocks and logs. When they noticed me, they all emitted audible gasps of relief. "You don't know how glad we are to see you," one of them called out. "Are we near the trail?" I led them a quarter mile back to the shelter, which they'd been searching for. They dropped their heavy packs and began peeling off wet layers. One of them lit a stove, and they all huddled around it to warm their hands before boiling water for tea.

"We've been lost for two days," the trip leader explained. They had been following the Bailey Traverse, a little-traveled high route across the Olympics. In the rain and fog, with prominent landmarks and peaks obstructed, they'd made errors in their route-finding and wound up spending a week rather than four days in the backcountry. They were still twenty-five miles from the trailhead. "If you see a ranger," a woman with an Australian accent said before I left, "please tell them we're okay. No need for a search party!"

On my way out, I took care to study the river and its ways. The Elwha up here in the park looked perfect. It had all the characteristics of a functioning river. Except that all this beautiful habitat was devoid of salmon.

IT TOOK NEARLY THREE YEARS to physically remove both dams, a process that was undertaken in stages to limit the amount of sediment flow and to give the river's remnant populations of wild fish a fighting chance. McMillan figured that about 90 percent of the young salmon in the main stem perished in the first couple of years. "My best guess is they starved to death," he told me. Some parts of the lower river saw a 95 percent reduction in macroinvertebrates—the insects, crustaceans, mollusks, and so forth that make up the primary diet of juvenile salmon. "The main stem went through hell and back." Waves of sediment locked behind the dams for a hundred years pushed through the unshackled river with each storm, smothering just about every living thing in the way. Only the tributaries provided refuge to the surviving wild fish that would be the founding population of future salmon runs. A similar scenario took place after Mount St. Helens blew its top and sent a boiling torrent of mud and debris down its flanks, with salmon runs rebounding sooner than expected. McMillan himself documented the first wild fish discovered above the lower-dam site, a thirty-five-inch male steelhead, in May 2012. The local wildlife found the new food source too. Studies revealed that in the first year after dam removal, 80 percent of the carcasses of spawned-out salmon lined the stream bank; a year later the percentage was closer to ten, the rest being carried into the woods to nourish plants and animals for the first time in a century, the way nature had intended. The same study reported a tripling of the dipper population; the small gray bird with an ebullient song is also called a water ouzel, and it spends its life along watercourses, sometimes even swimming underwater to glean insects from the rocks or steal salmon eggs from a nest.

IT WAS TIME TO put on the wetsuits. Ever since Rene and I swam with salmon in the Yuba River, I had been waiting for an opportunity to get back in the water with the big resilient fish. McMillan took us to the Gauge Hole, three miles above the lower Elwha dam site and just upstream of a U.S. Geological Survey gauge that measures the river's flow. Following a trail beaten into the brush, we scrambled down a bank covered in salal and salmonberry. Downstream at the next bend, a family played in the river, the high-pitched squeals of the children carrying across the water. "You never used to see that," McMillan said. People are attracted to a free-flowing river, especially on a hot afternoon like this one, with fall just around the corner. A group of young men sat on a rock ledge above a deep pool with their dogs, drinking tallboys and trading wild, windmilling leaps into the water. I was worried all this activity might spook the salmon. "You'd be surprised," McMillan reassured me. "These fish can put up with a lot."

Rene and I walked to the head of the riffle and plunged in. The current swept me immediately into the pool, where a chinook with a scar on its dorsal shot out from beneath me and made for darker water. I took a breath through my snorkel and went down. A sinewy lone steelhead moved snakelike along the sandy bottom. I knew it was a steelhead because McMillan had explained the different swimming strokes. Chinook use just their tails to propel them forward, while steelhead move their whole bodies. At the tailout, two rambunctious dogs paddled over to us while the boys on the rocks hooted and called them. It was a late-summer day for the ages.

Grabbing cobbles in the streambed with my gloved hands, I pulled myself back upstream through the shallows, against the current. Scores of fingerlings of some sort, two to three inches in length, darted among the rocks. They had parr marks and faint red lateral lines. I surfaced and shouted across the pool to McMillan, who sat on the rock ledge, basking in the sun. Today was his day off, and he'd been doing enough snorkel surveys as it was. "*O. mykiss*," he called back. Rainbow trout. He'd seen plenty in his surveys. Before dam removal, the upper Elwha was a favorite haunt of the backcountry angler. I too in years past had backpacked into the park to fly-fish for the river's wily rainbows, which were likely descended from steelhead that couldn't reach the sea after the first dam was built. The rainbows of the Elwha were hard to catch, rewarding the crepuscular angler who woke before dawn or fished long after the dinner bell sounded. It was hoped that these fish would seed the comeback of a once-sizable steelhead population. So far McMillan was pleased. The river was full of wild *O. mykiss* fry, and he figured many of them would head for the salt when the time came.

Farther downstream, Rene and I floated past a small school of pink salmon and a few dozen dark chinook. Maybe, during their three or four years at sea, these same kings had schooled with the Yuba chinook I had met two years earlier, somewhere out there in the deep blue pastures of the North Pacific. One species, many different stocks—or, as Rene liked to say, cultures. They followed the great Alaskan gyre, growing bigger, some of them tangling in the nets and never seen again, others struggling against the odds to make it back to their spawning gravels.

WHEN WE PICTURE A RIVER, we tend to think of glamorous white-water rapids, high in the watershed. But in many ways it is the languid estuaries in the lower riparian tidal zones that are even more crucial in the salmon life cycle. The river's mouth is where the juveniles have to be ready for the next phase of life: the ocean. They turn silver for protection and undergo the physiological changes necessary to survive in salt water. Moreover, the young salmon must find an eelgrass bed, oyster bar, or some other nook in which to hide until they can grow strong enough to make for open sea. Estuaries, if they're healthy, offer plenty of food and protection.

With the demolition of the two Elwha dams, the mouth of the river is once again taking on these characteristics. And it's proving as attractive to people as to salmon. Teenage boys with surfboards sprawled on the white-sand beach, flirting with girls in bikinis. A decent rip curl broke across the bar. Rene, the Californian, was impressed. "That's legit. Those aren't closing out; they're surfable waves." The sets were new, ever since the liberated Elwha's sediment load built the eighty acres of beach we were now standing on, but surfing here had already been going on for years, as much a reflection of youth's ingenuity as anything. McMillan said that before dam removal, kids would surf the waves made by tankers moving through the strait.

Flocks of well-fed gulls and terns stood on the mudflats. We watched salmon fry schooling near the river mouth, a rare sight these days up and down the coast, since the tidewater sections of most rivers have been developed or otherwise made inhospitable to young fish. The past winter, huge schools of eulachon—a type of smelt also called a candlefish, for its high oil content—spawned in this stretch by the millions for the first time anyone could remember, luring a feeding frenzy worthy of Animal Planet. Seals, sea lions, eagles, diving ducks, and a host of other predators gathered in droves for the feast, a sight that brought out the citizenry of Port Angeles for several straight weeks. These were the same people who, after opposing dam removal for decades, had finally come around to seeing the benefit—to their lives and their home—of supporting the once unthinkable. Change was possible.

"Look how clean this water is!" We turned to see a petite woman in sweatpants and jogging shoes, a large camera hanging from her shoulder. She was standing on a sandbar that was slowly melting into the river under her feet. Fish dimpled the surface and moved beneath the glassy water like the shadow of a cloud. "It just shows you that nature is resilient." She thought about this last statement for a moment and amended it: "We're part of nature too." The woman introduced herself. Her name was Melinda and she had just been to the dam overlook, the same place where we had started the day. Originally from California, she'd lived in Oregon for seventeen years and was now living near Olympia, Washington. "Steadily working my way northward," she added, laughing. Her trip to the Elwha today had been inspired by a piece of art.

"I bought this picture from an art gallery when I lived in Oregon," she said. "It was beautiful green and blue water. The name was 'Rhythm of the River.' I loved this picture so much and got so many comments on it. I didn't know where it was—what continent even—I just wanted to go there. I actually called the artist. I said, 'Where is this? Where did you paint it?' And he said, 'Oh, it's not a painting. It's a photograph of the Elwha River.'" The artist explained that he'd taken it in spring, when everything was fresh. "It's the light play," Melinda said. "The way the green and blue reflects on a clear day.

Blue, green, blue, green. I just love it. So here I am." She pulled the camera off her shoulder. "And now I have this. I can't take enough pictures of this beautiful river."

Rhythm of the river. A good title for a photograph that looks like a painting. Rivers have a way of doing that. They have more rhythm than we can imagine, rhythms we are only now just learning about, and rhythms yet to be discovered.

AFTER SAYING GOODBYE TO John McMillan at the mouth of the re-invigorated Elwha, Rene and I drove back toward Seattle. It was quiet in the car. We passed miles of clear-cut forest on the Olympic Peninsula, a sight that normally saddens me, but on this warm afternoon my mind was on the Rogue River in Oregon and its roadless canyon and primeval forest, where I had met my first salmon and steelhead. Like the Elwha, the Rogue had recently been the site of dam demolition, and there too the wild fish responded immediately. Rene had once caught a large chinook on the Rogue. He hoped to do the same on the San Joaquin in California someday. One of his favorite social occasions is the fishing derby on the river, a now-annual event hosted by Trout Unlimited to encourage youth angling. He called it the single most diverse event he's ever experienced, with anglers of too many different ethnic backgrounds to count, all of them living in local Central Valley farming communities and brought together by a river coming back to life. "It's a picture of California," he said. "Everybody is fishing and everybody is stoked." The fate of wild salmon, after all, rests largely in the hands of society. It's ironic that the conservation community is often slow to understand this.

"When I go to meetings, I'm almost always the only person of color," Rene went on. "What that tells me as an ecologist is that the ideosphere that's driving conservation is homogenous and not resilient. By extension, the likelihood of successfully restoring a system that's diverse and resilient is low until we diversify our own ideosphere. It's going to make for a richer understanding of how people can live with nature and how we can live with each other." He was confident that there would be a shift in this direction, eventually.

I had always called Rene an optimist, but now he corrected me. He was a scientist, he said, and as such he based his opinions on data. With salmon, as with so many other thorny issues that face humanity, there are multiple paths that can be taken. Science is just a tool to help make decisions. Rene said he was optimistic that science could work out a pathway that benefited both salmon and people. In fact, he was sure of it, because in the long run any change in our behavior that helped salmon would likely help us too. But the difficulty was not in identifying the right pathway among many possibilities. The hard part was going down it. It might take generations, he said.

I thought about a recent conversation with Riley Starks. The Lummi Indians were ready, after an absence of many decades, to begin reef netting again. He had called me with the news and left a long, excited message. The tribe had a site picked out to the north of Bellingham—Cherry Point, a site that, coincidentally, the coal industry also wanted to develop as a port for shipping American coal to China. "It will be interesting to see what happens," Starks said with his usual understatement.

A showdown at Cherry Point seemed imminent. Native Americans were flexing their political muscle throughout salmon country. They were calling for changes to Grand Coulee Dam to allow fish passage, and for the restoration of salmon runs to rivers that had been barren of anadromous fish for decades. Not far from my home in Seattle, little more than an hour's drive over a mountain pass, the Yakama tribe has been busy reintroducing sockeye to lakes in the Cascades that were cut off by irrigation dams in the early 1900s. East of the Columbia River Gorge, in a compromise with local irrigators, the Umatilla successfully reintroduced salmon to their namesake river. "We're the ones putting salmon back in the rivers," Kat Brigham told me one afternoon while pruning freshly planted petunias outside Brigham Fish Market. She invited me to a First Foods ceremony on the reservation near Pendleton, Oregon, where I met an Umatilla fisherman who said he had recently speared chinook in the traditional way for the first time in his life, how his grandfather watched from the bank with tears in his eyes. Farther south, a proposal to tear down four dams on the Klamath River near the California–Oregon border—already agreed to in theory by irrigators, tribes, and environmentalists but stalled in the do-nothing U.S. Congress—would supersede the Elwha as the largest dam removal in the country. The stakeholders were working out final details to rip out the dams with *or without* congressional approval.

The ledger is continually being rebalanced. But even as the Elwha's story of hope continues to unfold for all to see, so much uncertainty remains. In Oregon, Governor John Kitzhaber, one of the few elected officials at the higher levels of government with an honest desire to save wild salmon, was forced to resign over financial improprieties involving his fiancée. Within days, Oregon's timber industry took advantage of the power vacuum to demand an increase in harvest. Now the industry is calling for the Tillamook State Forest, owned by all Oregonians, to be opened to not 50, not 70, but 100 percent industrial timber harvest. Guido Rahr is seeing his dream of wild salmon sanctuaries pitted once again against the lumber barons. Up in Alaska, a bumper harvest of Bristol Bay sockeye has been clouded by the widely condemned Pebble Mine, which refuses to go away, as well as by a proposed dam on the Susitna River, north of Anchorage. And recent studies are beginning to reveal that all those hatchery pink salmon unleashed into the North Pacific by the state are negatively impacting wild sockeye salmon. Rahr calls these studies the smoking gun.

Most of all, the specter of climate change now looms to such a degree that even deniers are coming around. As Rene and I made our way across the Olympic Peninsula's denuded landscape, wooden signs on the roadside warned of high fire danger. After a long hot summer, the famously damp Pacific Northwest was officially in drought, with both Oregon and Washington asking for federal disaster relief. To the south, the ongoing California drought had no end in sight. The climate toll on salmon was mounting for all to see. With low snowpack resulting in little melt-off, combined with record high temperatures, the Columbia River, for one, had become a fish trap. Hundreds of thousands of sockeye salmon, some of them the long-distance marathoners bound for Idaho's Redfish Lake, had already perished, their bodies disease-ridden and covered with lesions from the abnormal water temperature. Scientists and fisheries managers feared the mortality rate for Snake River sockeye could reach 99 percent.

Though recent years have seen higher-than-average returns in the Columbia Basin, most impartial observers attribute the numbers to favorable ocean conditions as well as to the fact that the Bonneville Power Administration has been forced, by the courts, to spill water over the dams to aid downstream fish migration. Bonneville is only too ready to take credit for the boost in salmon numbers, but anyone paying attention knows that the BPA views salmon as an impediment to its mission: the generation of hydro dollars. Some see a missed opportunity. The cycle of ocean productivity, guided by the Pacific Decadal Oscillation and weather events such as El Niño, appears to be coming to an end, and yet few infrastructural changes of real consequence—such as breaching the lower Snake River dams—have come to pass during the temporary upswing. What will happen if ocean conditions deteriorate for a decade or more?

Fishing has always served me as a way to clear my head of such worldly concerns. I get lost in the elements, in the rhythm of the cast, and intrusive thoughts fade away. On our way back to the city, I suggested to Rene that we stop off at a place with one of my favorite names, Point No Point, on the northern tip of the Kitsap Peninsula, to try for a salmon. He was all for it. We had fly rods and casting rods in the back. I told him this was a great place to see marine mammals, including Dall's porpoises, which look sort of like orcas, and plenty of harbor seals, those crafty salmon-eaters that sometimes try to pilfer your catch if you aren't paying attention. It's a fishy place, with strong currents, a lighthouse at the end of the point, and year-round anglers. But, as luck would have it, we got held up on the Hood Canal Bridge, the long, low span that crosses a fjordlike finger of Puget Sound not far from a large U.S. naval base. It's rare to get stopped by the draw-bridge.

There was nothing to do about it. Everyone turned off their engines and waited. A breeze swept through our open windows, cooling us down. We got out of the car and admired an eerie sunset over the Olympic Mountains. All summer, wildfires had raged across the Pacific Northwest. The single largest forest fire in Washington State's history was burning just east of North Cascades National Park, along with dozens of other blazes around the state. There was even a months-long creeper burn in the normally wet rainforest of the Olympics near the Queets River. The wind shifted and the sky turned hazy to the point of seeming possibly unhealthy, the sun a glowing red orb that looked more like an angry moon or a stage prop. It all made for a foreboding yet pastel-beautiful sunset, and up and down the bridge, motorists got out of their vehicles to gaze and take pictures.

We had tarried at the Elwha, finding it too hard to pull ourselves away from the river, and now this unexpected delay meant we would miss out on the dusk bite at Point No Point. *"Fish are rising up like birds. . . ."* went the song on the car stereo, a wry bit of coincidence that buoyed my spirits. Maybe we would get to make a few casts before nightfall after all. From the bridge deck we watched pigeon guillemots, slightly comical seabirds tuxedoed in black and white, as they made trips back and forth between the girders and a flat gray expanse of water below us, scudding to a less-than-athletic stop on their rear ends. They dove, for who knows what—herring? salmon smolts?—and popped back up like corks.

Looking across the water was like staring at the starry sky: a view that would never get old as long as there were humans to contemplate the mysteries of life. In all directions for hundreds, even thousands of miles, it was salmon country out there. The salmon had shaped this landscape as much as the Ice Age glaciers and the foaming volcanoes had. Maybe at that very moment, under the cover of impending darkness, there was a large school of silvers coming in from the North

Pacific—"ocean hooknoses," as they're sometimes called by anglers—obeying an ancient urge to return to the river of their birth, funneling into the Strait of Juan de Fuca in a tight formation before veering south at Foulweather Bluff and gliding beneath the Hood Canal Bridge. For ten thousand years or longer, people in North America have imagined such schools of salmon on their miraculous journeys home.

We stared at the water, unable to see into its depths, the apocalyptic sun reflected on its ripples. The drawbridge was up. Would a Trident nuclear submarine surface and pass through the opening on its way to the naval base? They plied these waters too. I'd seen them here before, big tin cans with the capability to shell a coastline into submission. As the sun went down, we stood on the bridge with a crowd of people, thinking about submarines and the salmon of Point No Point, waiting to get to the other side.

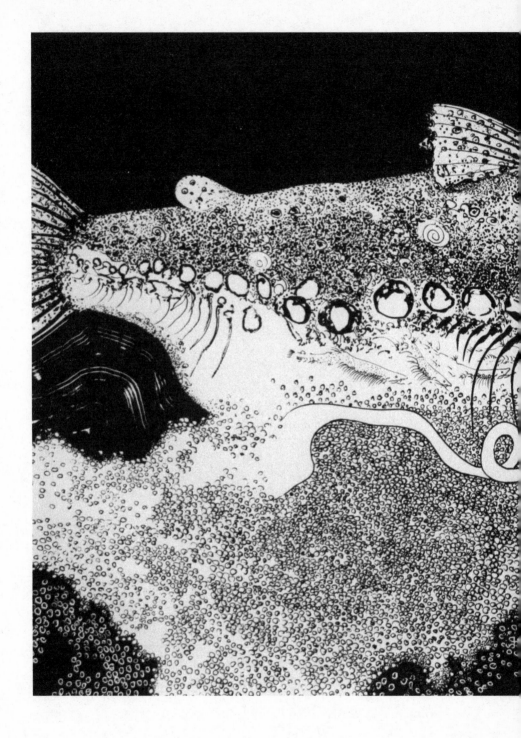

THE CLOCK OF FALL, BY FRANK BOYDEN

ACKNOWLEDGMENTS

CHASING WILD SALMON IS DEPENDENT ON THE WEATHER, the seas, the rivers—and the human element. *Upstream* would not have been possible without the enthusiasm and cooperation of a diverse cadre of salmon devotees. A heartfelt thank you, first and foremost, to fisheries ecologist Rene Henery, of Trout Unlimited in California, who took part in the initial conversations that spawned this book and then happily became my sounding board, technical adviser, and road companion along the way.

Riley Starks of Lummi Island Wild generously introduced me to life on a reef net island in Puget Sound while his crew obliged my desire to "grab web": Thank you, Ian Kirouac, Josh Thomason, Cara Blake, Morgan Shermer, Ben Siegel, Sean Croke, Sierra Montoya, and Jerry Anderson (emeritus). Blaine Wetzel, head chef at the Willows Inn, shared his intimate knowledge of reef net salmon cookery.

The community of Cordova, Alaska, graciously invited me into their homes and onto their boats. Thank you to Micah Ess and Kent "Curly" Herschleb for a crash course in gill netting on the Copper River flats, and also to Michael and Nelly Hand, Blair Hansen, Alec Herschleb, Kristin Carpenter of the Copper River Watershed Alliance, Danny Carpenter, Phil Alman, Jeremy Botz of Alaska Fish and

Game, David Reggiani of the Prince William Sound Aquaculture Corporation, Ashton Poole, Dennis Zabra, Austin Ring, George Covel, Copper River Seafoods, and the many other commercial fishermen who shared their knowledge and stories.

I am indebted to Guido Rahr, of the Wild Salmon Center in Portland, who treated me to chinook on the fly on the Oregon Coast and then helped me navigate the twists and turns of salmon conservation. Also in Oregon, the Brigham family, including Kim Brigham Campbell and Terrie Brigham, kindly opened the doors of Brigham Fish Market in the Columbia River Gorge, while matriarch Kat Brigham invited me to the Umatilla Indian Reservation in Pendleton for a memorable First Foods ceremony.

Staff at Idaho Fish and Game and the Eagle Fish Hatchery near Boise, Idaho—including Travis Brown, Dan Baker, Mike Peterson, Ken Felty, and Christine Kozfkay—took time at the height of the longest salmon run in the Lower 48 to personally introduce me to endangered Redfish Lake sockeye.

In California, Casson Trenor served up wild salmon sushi—and forthright conversation—at his San Francisco restaurant, Tataki Canyon, while biologist Jacob Katz of California Trout showed me where salmon-friendly sushi rice is grown in the Sacramento Valley.

Closer to home, I owe a debt of gratitude to Kevin Davis, chef-owner of Blueacre Seafood in Seattle, who brought me into his busy kitchen during the Copper River frenzy, and Jon Rowley, who shared culinary wisdom and memories in the dining room. My longtime fishing pal Bradley Boyden, of the Dutch Henry Institute of Technology, was a font of angling lore and all-around good action; Frank Boyden, his brother, dispensed additional good action along with his beautiful artwork, *Clock of Fall,* reprinted on pages 304–5. John McMillan of Trout Unlimited showed me the power of an undammed and reinvigorated Elwha River on the Olympic Peninsula.

Thank you to the many others who shared their passion for salmon, including David Barmon, Joseph Bogaard, Larry Collins, Aaron Dufault, Bob Van Dyk, Amy Grondin, Rocky Hammond, Sara LaBorde,

Ryan Lathrop, Jim Lichatowich, Wayne Ludvigsen, Duane Massa, Helen Neville, Don Portz, Jim Price, Joe Ray, Becky Selengut, Jon Speltz, Silas Stardance, John Sundstrom, the crew at Pacific Seafoods, including Brian Hayes, Stephen Kelly, and Kevin Hert, and the many other friends and acquaintances who spent time with me in salmon country during the research and reportage of this book.

On the other side of the continent, another group worked tirelessly to see the project into print. I offer my endless gratitude to my agent, Lisa Grubka, and her colleagues at Fletcher & Co., Melissa Chinchillo and Erin McFadden. At Ballantine, editor extraordinaire Susanna Porter offered wise counsel and necessary red ink; I salute the rest of the Penguin Random House team for their diligence: Evan Camfield, Mark Maguire, Barbara Bachman, Kathy Lord, David Stevenson, Katie Rice, Greg Kubie, Emily Hartley, and mapmakers Mapping Specialists, Ltd. My appreciation also goes out to Ryan Doherty for his early interest and Priyanka Krishnan for her feedback on the initial draft.

Finally, I can't offer enough thanks to my wife, Martha Silano, and our children, Riley and Ruby, for all their love and patience; returning to my family after faraway fishing trips is the best catch of all.

WHEN A TROUT IS A SALMON:
A NOTE ON TAXONOMY

A RAINBOW TROUT IS MORE CLOSELY RELATED TO A SOCKEYE salmon than it is to a brown trout. How can this be? Simply put, the terms *trout* and *salmon* are misleading. The former was once used to describe fish in the Salmonidae family that were thought to live strictly in fresh water, as opposed to salmon, which mature in salt water. We now know that all members of the family will sometimes seek the salt if accessible, some more than others.

For the purposes of this book, I refer to five species in North America as Pacific salmon, among a number of other species in the same genus, *Oncorhynchus*. The five are: king or chinook salmon (*Oncorhynchus tshawytscha*), silver or coho salmon (*Oncorhynchus kisutch*), red or sockeye salmon (*Oncorhynchus nerka*), chum or dog salmon (*Oncorhynchus keta*), and pink or humpback salmon (*Oncorhynchus gorbuscha*). A sixth species of Pacific salmon, the cherry or masu salmon (*Oncorhynchus masou*), spawns in Asia. Two other species that appear in the text are technically also in the Pacific salmon genus: the rainbow trout and its sea-run form known as steelhead (*Oncorhynchus mykiss*), and the cutthroat trout (*Oncorhynchus clarkii*), which also has a sea-run form.

So-called salmon and trout of the Atlantic are grouped into the

Salmo genus and offer the same confusing nomenclature: Atlantic salmon (*Salmo salar*) and brown trout (*Salmo trutta*). Finally, there is a third genus, *Salvelinus,* which includes the chars, many of which are commonly called trout: Arctic char (*Salvelinus alpinus*), bull trout (*Salvelinus confluentus*), Dolly Varden trout (*Salvelinus malma*), lake trout (*Salvelinus namaycush*), and brook trout (*Salvelinus fontinalis*), among others.

All of these fish are salmonids—enchanting creatures by any name.

SELECTED BIBLIOGRAPHY

Arax, Mark, and Rick Wartzman. *The King of California*. Public Affairs, 2003.

Barber, Katrine. *Death of Celilo Falls*. University of Washington Press, 2005.

Behnke, Robert J. *Trout and Salmon of North America*. Free Press, 2002.

Brown, Bruce. *Mountain in the Clouds: A Search for the Wild Salmon*. University of Washington Press, 1995.

Claxton, Earl, and John Elliott. *Reef Net Technology of the Saltwater People*. Saanich Indian School Board, 1994.

Cone, Joseph. *A Common Fate: Endangered Salmon and the People of the Pacific Northwest*. Henry Holt, 1995.

Cone, Joseph, and Sandy Ridlington, editors. *The Northwest Salmon Crisis: A Documentary History*. Oregon State University Press, 1996.

Deloria Jr., Vine *Indians of the Pacific Northwest: From the Coming of the White Man to the Present Day*. Fulcrum Publishing, 2012.

Dupris, Joseph C., Kathleen S. Hill, and William H. Rodgers, Jr. *The Si'lailo Way: Indians, Salmon and Law on the Columbia River*. Carolina Academic Press, 2006.

Fennelly, John F. *Steelhead Paradise*. Frank Amato Publications, 1989.

Harden, Blaine. *A River Lost*. W. W. Norton, 1996.

Hawley, Steven. *Recovering a Lost River: Removing Dams, Rewilding Salmon, Revitalizing Communities*. Beacon Press, 2011.

Hooton, Robert S. *Skeena Steelhead: Unknown Past, Uncertain Future*. Frank Amato Publications, 2011.

House, Freeman. *Totem Salmon: Life Lessons from Another Species*. Beacon Press, 2000.

Igler, David. *Industrial Cowboys: Miller & Lux and the Transformation of the Far West, 1850–1920*. University of California Press, 2005.

Layman, William D. *River of Memory: The Everlasting Columbia*. Wenatchee Valley Museum & Cultural Center in association with University of Washington Press and University of British Columbia Press, 2006.

Lethcoe, Jim and Nancy. *A History of Prince William Sound, Alaska*. Prince William Sound Books, 2001.

Lichatowich, James A. *Salmon Without Rivers: A History of the Pacific Salmon Crisis*. Island Press, 2001.

———. *Salmon, People, and Place: A Biologist's Search for Salmon Recovery*. Oregon State University Press, 2013.

Mapes, Lynda V. *Elwha: A River Reborn*. Mountaineers Books, 2013.

Martin, Irene. *Legacy and Testament: The Story of Columbia River Gillnetters*. Washington State University Press, 1994.

Montgomery, David R. *King of Fish: The Thousand-Year Run of Salmon*. Westview Press, 2003.

Taylor III, Joseph E. *Making Salmon: An Environmental History of the Northwest Fisheries Crisis*. University of Washington Press, 1999.

Ulrich, Roberta. *Empty Nets: Indians, Dams, and the Columbia River*. Oregon State University Press, 2007.

Upton, Joe. *Alaska Blues: A Fisherman's Journal*. Alaska Northwest Publishing Co., 1977.

White, Richard. *The Organic Machine: The Remaking of the Columbia River*. Hill and Wang, 1995.

Wilkinson, Charles. *Messages from Frank's Landing: A Story of Salmon, Treaties, and the Indian Way*. University of Washington Press, 2000.

Williams, Chuck. *Bridge of the Gods, Mountains of Fire: A Return to the Columbia Gorge*. Friends of the Earth/Elephant Mountain Arts, 1980.

Woodcock, American "Woody." *An Art of Reef Netting*. Washington State Library, 1978.

ABOUT THE AUTHOR

LANGDON COOK is the author of *The Mushroom Hunters: On the Trail of an Underground America*, winner of the 2014 Pacific Northwest Book Award, and *Fat of the Land: Adventures of a 21st Century Forager*. Cook's writing appears in numerous publications and has been nominated for a James Beard Award (2016) and a Pushcart Prize. He lives in Seattle with his wife and two children.

langdoncook.com
Facebook.com/langdon.cook
Twitter: @langdoncook

ABOUT THE TEXT

This book was set in Bembo, a typeface based on an old-style Roman face that was used for Cardinal Pietro Bembo's tract *De Aetna* in 1495. Bembo was cut by Francesco Griffo (1450–1518) in the early sixteenth century for Italian Renaissance printer and publisher Aldus Manutius (1449–1515). The Lanston Monotype Company of Philadelphia brought the well-proportioned letterforms of Bembo to the United States in the 1930s.